Damming the West

This book is printed on one hundred percent recycled paper.

Also Available:

ACTION FOR A CHANGE: *A Student's Manual for Public Interest Organizing,* by Ralph Nader and Donald Ross

BITTER WAGES: *Ralph Nader's Study Group Report on Disease and Injury on the Job,* by Joseph A. Page and Mary-Win O'Brien

THE CHEMICAL FEAST: *Ralph Nader's Group Report on the Food and Drug Administration,* by James S. Turner

THE CLOSED ENTERPRISE SYSTEM: *Ralph Nader's Study Group Report on Antitrust Enforcement,* by Mark J. Green, with Beverly C. Moore, Jr., and Bruce Wasserstein

THE COMPANY STATE: *Ralph Nader's Study Group Report on DuPont in Delaware,* by James Phelan and Robert Pozen

CORPORATE POWER IN AMERICA: *Ralph Nader's Conference on Corporate Accountability,* Ralph Nader and Mark J. Green, editors

THE INTERSTATE COMMERCE OMISSION: *Ralph Nader's Study Group Report on the Interstate Commerce Commission and Transportation,* by Robert C. Fellmeth

THE MONOPOLY MAKERS: *Ralph Nader's Study Group Report on Regulation and Competition,* edited by Mark J. Green

OLD AGE: THE LAST SEGREGATION: *Ralph Nader's Study Group Report on Nursing Homes,* Claire Townsend, project director

POLITICS OF LAND: *Ralph Nader's Study Group Report on Land Use in California,* Robert C. Fellmeth, project director

SMALL—ON SAFETY: *The Designed-in Dangers of the Volkswagen,* by the Center for Auto Safety

SOWING THE WIND: *A Report for Ralph Nader's Center for Study of Responsive Law on Food Safety and the Chemical Harvest,* by Harrison Wellford

UNSAFE AT ANY SPEED: *The Designed-in Dangers of the American Automobile* (expanded and updated, 1972), by Ralph Nader

VANISHING AIR: *Ralph Nader's Study Group Report on Air Pollution,* by John Esposito

THE WATER LORDS: *Ralph Nader's Study Group Report on Industry and Environmental Crisis in Savannah, Georgia,* by James M. Fallows

WATER WASTELAND: *Ralph Nader's Study Group Report on Water Pollution,* by David R. Zwick with Marcy Benstock

WHAT TO DO WITH YOUR BAD CAR: *An Action Manual for Lemon Owners,* by Ralph Nader, Lowell Dodge, and Ralf Hotchkiss

WHISTLE BLOWING: *The Report on the Conference on Professional Responsibility,* edited by Ralph Nader, Peter Petkas, and Kate Blackwell

WHO RUNS CONGRESS? by Mark J. Green, James M. Fallows, and David R. Zwick

THE WORKERS: *Portraits of Nine American Jobholders,* by Kenneth Lasson

YOU AND YOUR PENSION: *Why You May Never Get a Penny/What You Can Do About It,* by Ralph Nader and Kate Blackwell

Ralph Nader's
Study Group Report
on the Bureau
of Reclamation

Damming
the West

Richard L. Berkman
and W. Kip Viscusi

Grossman Publishers
New York   1973

All royalties from the sale of this book will be given to the Center
for Study of Responsible Law, the organization established by Ralph
Nader to conduct research into abuses of the public interest by business and governmental groups. Contributions to further this work are
tax deductible and may be sent to the Center at P.O.B. 19367, Washington, D.C. 20036.

The Study Group

Richard Lyle Berkman, Editor and Co-author
> A.B., Harvard College; Planning Review Staff, Office of Emergency Preparedness, 1970; Second Year Law Student, Harvard Law School

W. Kip Viscusi, Editor and Co-author
> A.B., Harvard College; Graduate Economics Student in Public Policy Program, John F. Kennedy School of Government, Harvard University

J. Lawrence Schultz, Project Research Director
> A.B., Yale College; J.D., Harvard Law School; Clerk for Judge Irving Kaufman, 2nd Circuit, U.S. Court of Appeals, 1970–1971

Daniel R. Barney, Assistant Editor and Writer
> Senior at Harvard College

Jamie O. Harris, Investigator and Writer
> A.B., Yale College; First Year Law Student, Yale Law School

Burt Solomon, Investigator and Writer
> A.B., Harvard College; Graduate Student in American Studies, University of Texas

Investigators:

Peter Adams
> A.B., First Year Public Administration Student, University of California at Los Angeles

Andrew Gelman
> A.B., University of Pennsylvania; J.D., University of Virginia Law School

George Locker
> A.B., Stonybrook College, State University of New York

Andra Oakes
> A.B., Bryn Mawr; J.D., University of Chicago Law School

Staff:
> Connie Jo Smith, Teddi Fine, Sherry Leibowitz, Teri Loftus, Lyn Schultz

Foreword by
Ralph Nader

To most Americans, the Bureau of Reclamation is less familiar than the moon. To others, the Bureau of Reclamation is
an agency that specializes in getting water to land near and
far. To a number of special economic interests, however, the
Bureau is a determined sugar daddy with powerful congressional allies. As this report shows in detail, the Bureau of
Reclamation has an impact on the West and on Indians,
farmers, taxpayers and recreational users that is anything but
obscure, once that impact is understood, not in terms of high-
level abstractions and slogans, but in down to earth terms of
Bureau-generated resource use and cost, direct and indirect.
As the editors and co-authors, Richard L. Berkman and W.
Kip Viscusi, analyze the Bureau's benefit-cost calculations,
its cost overruns, its tunnel-vision disregard for devastating
ecological consequences of its works, and its indifference to
the need of impoverished Indians for water, they conclude
that many of the Bureau's activities should be stopped, curtailed, or redirected. Whatever usefulness attached to the
Bureau's projects earlier in the century, before surpluses
glutted the warehouses and before the massive farm subsidies
began, in recent decades the economics and equities argue
for a serious and immediate reassessment of the Bureau's
various functions. Berkman and Viscusi conclude that
"Reclamation irrigation facilities not only cost billions of
dollars to build and operate, but also drive thousands of
other farmers out of their jobs, and increase the amount of
money that the U.S. Department of Agriculture must spend

to curtail surplus crop production and to support agricultural prices. Thus, taxpayers are hit coming and going."

The report is more than a critique of prevailing Bureau projects and policies; it strives to provide supported recommendations for changes in priorities and procedures in deciding upon what courses of action the agency is to take. As a government agency with specific and relatively finite missions, the Bureau of Reclamation looks for new waters to conquer on more and more insupportable economic grounds —and at the cost of environmental neglect. An intriguing inquiry which will not be answered until more official monitoring of Reclamation by Congress occurs is: how could the Bureau's economists and other professional employees and consultants have countenanced such specious economic rationales and such dubious projects? What kind of professional independence has been repressed by the pressures of a single-minded bureaucracy? These are critical questions because they relate to one of the principal internal checks on runaway government policies, waste, and unchallenged special interest pressure groups. Indeed, this report raises these questions in a number of contexts.

It is hoped that the graduates and students who produced this report will receive from the Bureau, not the customary self-serving responses or glib waivers, but a considered treatment of the matters discussed and the proposals put forth.

Preface

In June, 1970, a Nader Study Group study group of lawyers, graduate students, and undergraduates began an intensive study of the activities of the Bureau of Reclamation. These study group members collected volumes of raw data and interviewed hundreds of Bureau of Reclamation officials and other individuals, both inside and outside the federal government. At the end of the summer, they left Washington, taking with them the material they had gathered. During the year, some of them spent hundreds of unsalaried hours distilling their results. In the summer of 1971 two of us returned to Washington to fill in the gaps in the previous year's research and to draft a report, which was released in preliminary form in the fall.

Almost everyone we contacted was generous with his or her time and cooperative in providing what information he or she had. We would especially like to thank Professors Richard J. Zeckhauser, Robert Edelstein, and Stephen Marglin, as well as the economists at Resources for the Future, who shared their expertise with us. In the area of water law and Indian water rights, we wish to thank William Veeder of the Bureau of Indian Affairs for the special interest and help he gave us. At the Department of the Interior, several individuals helped us open up the Bureau of Reclamation and the federal bureaucracy in general, so that we could make a more informed analysis. None of these individuals, of course, bears responsibility for the contents of this report.

We also want to acknowledge the special contribution of certain individual study group members. Jamie Harris provided a draft of the Colorado River and Weather Modification

material in Chapter 3; Burt Solomon did the primary research and writing of the section on the Indians; and the
chapter on the Central Arizona Project is almost exclusively
Dan Barney's contribution. Dan Barney also provided numerous editorial suggestions. Special thanks to Judy Berkman for helping to keep our writing intelligible, and to Teri
Loftus, who was a great help typing.

In the end, however, we take full responsibility for the
information, analysis, and opinions expressed in this report.
We address it to well-intentioned civil servants and adminis-
trators, to responsive legislators and to the general American
public, with the hope that it will provide a constructive, new
perspective on the goals and operation of the Bureau of
Reclamation.

W. Kip Viscusi
Richard L. Berkman

Contents

Damming the West

1

Introduction:
Reclamation,
Past and Present

BACKGROUND OF BUREAU OF RECLAMATION ACTIVITIES

Who gives a damn about the Bureau of Reclamation? The beneficiaries of Reclamation projects give a damn—and so should the citizens who bear the cost.

Since 1902 $6 billion have been poured into Reclamation projects in the seventeen westernmost states and Hawaii.* The Federal Reclamation Act of 1902[1] was enacted by Congress to promote the economic development and settlement of the West under the homestead acts. As a part of this act, Congress created the Reclamation Service, which became the Bureau of Reclamation in 1923. During its first decade, the Bureau devoted 97 percent of its efforts to irrigation.[2] Two of the most notable projects in Reclamation history are Hoover Dam on the Colorado River between Arizona and Nevada and the Grand Coulee Dam on the Columbia River in Washington. Acclaimed by the American Society of Civil Engineers as engineering marvels, these and other early Reclamation projects have also contributed significantly to the development of the West. Bureau water has converted

* Washington, Oregon, Idaho, Montana, North Dakota, South Dakota, Wyoming, Nebraska, Kansas, Oklahoma, Texas, New Mexico, Colorado, Utah, Arizona, Nevada and California.

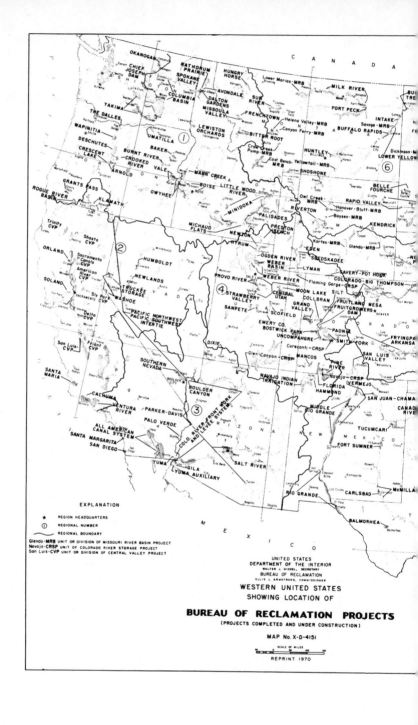

UNITED STATES
DEPARTMENT OF THE INTERIOR
WALTER J. HICKEL, SECRETARY
BUREAU OF RECLAMATION
ELLIS L. ARMSTRONG, COMMISSIONER

WESTERN UNITED STATES
SHOWING LOCATION OF

BUREAU OF RECLAMATION PROJECTS
(PROJECTS COMPLETED AND UNDER CONSTRUCTION)

MAP No. X-D-4151

SCALE OF MILES

REPRINT 1970

what was once arid wasteland into fertile fields; Bureau hydroelectric power has contributed to the growth of western cities; and Bureau dams have helped prevent many potential floods and created vast lakes for recreation. "I give them high marks," Congressman Morris K. Udall (D-Ariz.) has said. "The history of the Bureau of Reclamation for its first fifty years is tremendous, visionary."[3]

Indeed, the Bureau of Reclamation has compiled an impressive statistical record in its three score years and ten. It has spent over $6 billion of taxpayers' money, and has been authorized by Congress to spend $5.5 billion more. Congress has approved 153 projects ranging in size from a single pumping plant to the huge Missouri Basin Project, which will encompass ten states and cost over a billion dollars. Lakes and reservoirs created by dams built with funds from the Bureau have a potential storage capacity of 134,417,000 acre-feet (an acre-foot is the amount of water needed to cover one acre of land to a depth of one foot—about a third of a million gallons)—enough to flood all of New England to a depth of more than three feet. Bureau waters have irrigated over 10 million acres of land in the West, an area more than twice the size of New Jersey. In 1969, Reclamation delivered over 600 billion gallons of water to 14.5 million people for municipal and industrial use. The forty-nine hydroelectric power plants built, and in some cases operated, by the Bureau sent 48 billion kilowatt hours of electricity over 16,000 miles of transmission lines in fiscal year 1970— enough to light New York City (see Table 1-A).

These figures indicate that the Bureau of Reclamation is involved in more than merely reclaiming land. Through numerous amendatory and supplementary acts to the original Reclamation statute, Congress has expanded the responsibilities and, therefore, the porkbarrel potential of the Bureau of Reclamation.

Now, in addition to irrigating more farmland, the Bureau of Reclamation is responsible for developing adequate water supplies for municipal and industrial uses, hydroelectric power, flood control, navigation, river regulation, water quality control, recreation, and fish and wildlife. It has even extended its bureaucratic tentacles into the research and development of weather modification techniques.

The following summary of the Bureau's 1971 budget gives a good picture of the scope of current Reclamation activities. The Bureau paid the salaries of over 9,500 full-time employees. Over $319 million was appropriated and spent that year, more than the combined budgets of Phoenix, Oklahoma City, Portland, Oregon, and Seattle. More than $20 million of this was spent in an attempt to find new ways to spend more money in the future, as Reclamation undertook twenty-six reconnaissance studies, ten river basin surveys, and thirty-nine feasibility investigations. Ten times that amount was spent on construction and rehabilitation of authorized projects, and another $70 million went just to operate and maintain existing projects. Five million was loaned out under the Small Reclamation Project Loan Program. And to oversee its activities, Reclamation got $14 million for general administration. In January, 1972, President Nixon sent Congress a budget that allocated $384 million to the Bureau of Reclamation, an increase of $65 million. (see Table 1-B.)

JUSTIFYING BUREAU ACTIVITIES

While certain Bureau projects are designed to serve the public as a whole (supplying drinking water, for instance), the money doled out by the Bureau of Reclamation is frequently public money spent for private gain. For example, the investment in irrigation systems, which accounts for the greatest part of Bureau expenditures, is designed to enrich farmers in the irrigated areas. To justify spending public money for what otherwise could easily be called porkbarrel spending for special interests, the Bureau of Reclamation has devised (at Congress's insistence) an elaborate system to show that the benefits its projects provide for private interests will make their way to the public, and outweigh the public expense of the projects themselves.

When a project is requested, the Bureau may, on its own authority, launch a reconnaissance study, which takes six to eleven years and costs from $75,000 to $3 million. About 60 percent of these studies are followed by more extensive, elaborate, and expensive "feasibility" investigations. Authorized by Congress, these more detailed studies require eleven to twenty-one more years to complete and range in cost from about $275,000 to $7 million.

These feasibility reports serve as the basis for winning congressional authorization and appropriations for project construction. The Bureau submits 80–90 percent of the feasibility reports to Congress, which eventually approves almost all those submitted.[4]

One reason Reclamation projects are received so warmly on Capitol Hill is that the congressmen responsible for making the crucial decisions concerning them hail from the very states which get the projects. All but two of the sixteen members of the Senate Interior and Insular Affairs Committee of the Ninety-second Congress (1971–72) were from Reclamation states; and twenty-four of the thirty-eight members of the House Interior and Insular Affairs Committee are from Reclamation states.

Equally persuasive is the form in which the requests come. The key part of the feasibility reports, which the Bureau of Reclamation relies on to secure congressional approval, is the benefit-cost evaluation.* Long before the computer replaced the slide rule and the adding machine, and even before Robert McNamara introduced benefit-cost analysis into defense planning and decisionmaking, the Bureau of Reclamation had its own project evaluation procedures. The Bureau of Reclamation adopted the economic technique known as benefit-cost analysis in the mid-1940s as a method of justifying its projects.

Through a variety of methods, the Bureau attaches dollar values to the future benefits and costs it predicts for its projects. These values are then adjusted or "discounted" to recognize the fact that a dollar of expense today is worth more than a dollar of income some time in the distant future. If a project's total discounted benefits exceed total discounted costs, then the Bureau labels the project economically feasi-

---

* Often called cost-benefit analysis or benefit-cost analysis.

ble. Each project must pass this economic feasibility test before it is submitted to Congress. And once it is submitted, cloaked in figures that say it will provide more benefits than costs, it is almost invariably approved.

A simple shorthand has also arisen. If a project is economically feasible (benefits exceeding costs) then the ratio of discounted benefits to discounted costs—called the benefit-cost ratio—is greater than 1.0. Congressmen often rely on the benefit-cost ratio as a statistical summary of a project's relative desirability.

This congressional display of blind faith is far from commendable in view of the biases and distortions the Bureau incorporates in its benefit-cost studies. Daniel A. Dreyfus, staff member of the Senate Committee on Interior and Insular Affairs, acknowledges that the Bureau's benefit-cost analyses are "worthless and phony."[5] Even a high-ranking economist in the Bureau of Reclamation has condemned the importance attached to them: "Congressmen unfortunately take the benefit-cost ratios seriously. Really they are not too meaningful."[6] If the ratios are not to be taken seriously, one wonders why they are used at all. Since these "phony" economic feasibility figures serve as the main justification for the Bureau of Reclamation's continued existence, they merit fuller examination.*

THE THRUST OF THIS REPORT

The time has come for a thorough scrutiny of the impact of the Bureau's persistence in damming up America's waterways. Traditional critiques of Bureau activities have focused merely on specific drawbacks, such as isolated environmental damage. Since Reclamation invariably responds by pointing to its favorable benefit-cost studies, which dazzle the congressmen and effectively mute all further criticism, we decided to meet the Bureau of Reclamation on its own ground by reviewing its basic benefit-cost procedures.

---

* For a list of benefit-cost ratios of projects for which the Bureau of Reclamation requested funds for 1970, see Table 1-C. The number of projects with benefit-cost ratios that are marginal at best is quite large, as Table 1-D demonstrates.

We first looked at aspects of the Bureau's attempts to quantify project benefits and costs. Are these benefits and costs accurately calculated? Why, for example, is the irrigation of new farmland and the subsequent production of crops in the West calculated as a major benefit when the Department of Agriculture is paying billions of dollars to farmers all over the country to limit surplus crop production (Chapter 2)?

Another issue is whether the Bureau of Reclamation fully calculates the cost of their projects in terms of their impacts on our environment (Chapter 3). In particular, have they taken adequate account of water quality, recreation or fish and wildlife? Or have they fully considered the risks associated with their weather modification programs? And what other ecological impacts does—and should—the Bureau of Reclamation consider?

In Chapter 4, the report evaluates more technical distortions in the Bureau's benefit-cost procedures. What kind of data does the Bureau of Reclamation rely on in making its calculations? Why does the Bureau use one of the lowest discount rates in government and give an unjustifiable bias to its benefit-cost ratio? How does it systematically overestimate the benefits of electric power, municipal and industrial water and secondary contributions? How are the actual benefits and costs of Reclamation projects distributed in economic terms?

Since we did not confine ourselves to technical matters, this report evaluates who really benefits and who actually suffers from Bureau of Reclamation projects. In Chapter 5, we look at the Central Arizona Project and discover that bureaucrats and politicians are prime beneficiaries of the Reclamation porkbarrel. Chapter 6 reveals how Reclamation projects also give hidden subsidies to big landowners and to speculators. In particular, this chapter analyzes how the Bureau conceals subsidies in its management of repayment plans and in its lack of enforcement of the 160-acre limitation. In Chapter 7, the report exposes the federal government's unjustified violation of Indian water rights and its failure to provide Indians with the Reclamation projects they need.

Since the Bureau of Reclamation frequently defends itself by claiming it is reevaluating and updating its own goals and procedures, we felt compelled to appraise and challenge those revisions in the making. Therefore, Chapter 8 looks at how the Water Resources Council fails to address the real issues and shows how the priorities of the Bureau should be reordered.

The Bureau of Reclamation, for all its obscurity—it is not at all as well known, for example, as the Army Corps of Engineers, which performs analogous work nationwide—has had an enormous impact on the development of the West. Half the land area of the United States lies within its territory, and the Bureau has the job of watching over its water resources—which include the Missouri, Colorado, Columbia, and Snake rivers, some of the mightiest in the country. The Study Group is asking whether, after seventy years of reclamation, the Bureau of Reclamation is still serving the national interest.

Part 1 | The Analytical Deception

There are three kinds of lies: lies, damned lies, and statistics.
—Benjamin Disraeli

2 | Irrigation: Too Much of a Good Thing

When patriotic Americans recount the entities sacred to our country's traditions, agriculture rarely falls far behind motherhood and the flag. While society is presently asking challenging questions about motherhood and the flag, the study group decided to scrutinize and challenge the Bureau of Reclamation's myths about agriculture.

Congress set up the Bureau of Reclamation as an irrigation agency responsible for reclaiming—in other words, irrigating—the arid lands of the West.[1] The Bureau has performed this job well. Its water has transformed millions of acres of previously arid land into highly productive cropland. As of June 30, 1970, Bureau water served 10 million acres of land—an area larger than the combined acreage of the states of Hawaii, Rhode Island, Delaware, and Connecticut. An impressive amount of crops is produced on Bureau-irrigated lands: almost 50 million tons annually, as Table 2-A indicates.

The Bureau of Reclamation claims these crops as substantial irrigation benefits in its economic evaluations of projects. Although the specific Bureau provisions for putting dollar values on irrigation "benefits" are somewhat detailed, the basic concept involved is fairly simple. The 1959 *Reclamation Instruction* manual contains the following provision:

Direct irrigation benefits are the increase in net farm income resulting from the application of project water.[2]

The revision of the benefit evaluation procedures in 1962 by the President's Water Resources Council left this concept virtually unchanged. Irrigation benefits are still defined as "the increase in net income of agricultural production."[3] What this really means is that the Bureau claims an irrigation benefit equal to the increase in income of farmers receiving Bureau irrigation water.

While this procedure has the virtue of its simplicity, serious shortcomings arise from that simplicity. One is its geographic myopia. Several negative benefits (or "irrigation costs") must be subtracted from the Bureau's figure to get the net irrigation benefit to the entire country. One of the negative benefits, for example, is the decrease in income of farmers on lands not irrigated by water from Reclamation projects. If the Bureau were to calculate these and other negative irrigation benefits, the net benefit of irrigation would invariably be much less than the figures now used, and perhaps even negative.

DO WE NEED MORE FARM LAND?

It is difficult to find a convincing rationale for further irrigation efforts. While Reclamation has been irrigating new farm land, the Department of Agriculture has been trying to hold down excess agricultural production. These two agencies working at cross purposes waste billions of dollars of the taxpayers' money.*

---

* It should be noted that the analysis in this chapter will be based on the assumption that the Department of Agriculture will continue its price support program, as well as its various crop and acreage limitations. Ideally, such restraints on the farm economy should be eliminated—at least from the standpoint of economic efficiency. Under such circumstances, the drop in crop prices would more than offset any increase in crops sold so that the Bureau of Reclamation still would be able to claim only negligible benefits for its irrigation. In addition, there would still be the displacement effect of Reclamation irrigation as other non-Reclamation farmers are driven out of business. Finally, if we were to return to free competition for farm goods, the whole concept of a highly subsidized irrigation effort operated by the Bureau would be jeopardized.

The Department of Agriculture has undertaken several expensive programs to limit agricultural output and to take farmland out of production. The Soil Bank Program took cropland out of production; the Cropland Conversion Program, the Commodity Diversion Programs, and the Cropland Adjustment Programs are efforts to convert cropland into fields of grass and trees. In addition, various acreage allotment programs and marketing quota systems limit the amount of specified crops that can be grown.

Marion Clawson, a prominent agricultural economist and a consultant for Resources for the Future, a nonprofit natural resource research and consulting organization, recently estimated that "over 50 million acres of cropland are currently lying idle as a result of government programs."[4] Even this vast acreage is not all of the available unused farmland. The Department of Agriculture estimates that another 110 million acres of cropland are lying idle and have not been retired under government programs.[5] In short, more than one-third of the available cropland in the United States is not being used currently, and what is being used produces surpluses. Clearly, there is no present requirement for more irrigated land.

But what about future needs? Reclamation officials often cite the increased food requirements of an expanding population as justification for more irrigation. One recent Bureau publication reasoned:

> Continued and increased effort will be necessary to feed the burgeoning population of the future. . . . If supported only by presently developed resources, within a decade the West would become a deficit agricultural area—not only in terms of certain items of food, as at present, but in total production.[6]

On the surface, this argument seems sound. But one major underlying fallacy in the argument is that future crops will *not* be produced using only "presently developed resources." For example, soil banks in the East could be brought back under cultivation. Even if no more land is irrigated, existing resources will be developed more intensively through increased use of fertilizer, improved agricultural machinery, development of higher-yield crop strains, and other technological advances.

Apparently, the Bureau of Reclamation ignores these potential developments in estimating the need for irrigation. In the Mountain and Pacific regions, for example, food production increased from 16.3 million tons in 1940 to 23.4 million tons in 1960. The Bureau claimed that, in the absence of new irrigation projects, food production in this area would reach only 28 million tons by 2010.[7] However, continuation of current trends would place food output at well over 40 million tons by 2010. Although the amount of irrigated land may not increase significantly without more Reclamation projects, there is no reason to assume that food production will be adversely affected. As the National Advisory Commission on Food and Fiber argued, "Policies should be tied less closely to land, since land is becoming a less limiting factor in food and fiber production."[8]

Furthermore, it does not make sense to exacerbate current short-run surplus problems because of hypothetical long-run contingencies. The existence of substantial crop surpluses and millions of acres of retired cropland certainly give the United States enough flexibility to wait until the prospect of an agricultural shortage is more than a very shaky, long-range hypothesis. There is no need to continue to irrigate additional land as a hedge against a problem which will probably never arise.

In fact, the consensus of agricultural experts is that land shortages pose no foreseeable problem at all, even in the long run. The USDA Agricultural Stabilization and Conservation Service offered the following evaluation of agricultural production trends:

> Less and less land is being planted and harvested. Of the 460 million acres of cropland, farmers now harvest only about 300 million acres. This is the smallest harvested area since 1909. . . . Ever since 1950, after the accrued benefits of science and technology had really hit agriculture, yields almost doubled and are still climbing.
>
> Higher yields make it possible to divert more crop acres

from intensive production to grass, trees, and other conservation uses.[9]

The National Advisory Commission recently released a similar study forecasting food needs and United States agricultural output in 1980. This commission concluded that United States agricultural surpluses will be even greater in 1980 than they are now.[10]

Several individual economists also have agreed that the United States has an excess farm capacity far into the future. Roger Strobehn, the Economic Research Service economist representing the Department of Agriculture on the Water Resources Council Task Force, claimed that he "would have a hard time defending the need for more irrigated land."[11] Marion Clawson, agricultural economist for Resources for the Future, expressed similar sentiments:

> Today, there are about 3 million farms in the United States. At least two-thirds of these are unneeded in the long run.[12]

In short, leading agricultural experts tell a far different story than do Reclamation officials. There is certainly no need for more irrigated land at the present time, or in the near future. Any hypothetical need in the distant future remains hypothetical only, and experts who lack the Bureau's pro-irrigation bias doubt the need will ever materialize. We therefore conclude that there is no existing justification for sinking more money into new Reclamation irrigation efforts.

THE UNTOLD COSTS OF IRRIGATION: SURPLUS CROPS AND UNEMPLOYED FARMERS

The preceding arguments against continued irrigation focused on the Bureau's justifications for more irrigation. To determine the present overall impact of current Bureau programs, we made a crop-by-crop analysis of crops grown on Reclamation-irrigated lands. We found yet another reason why the Bureau's irrigation benefit calculations are specious.

Forage: Over 40 percent of all Reclamation-irrigated land is used to grow forage. Pasture, alfalfa, corn fodder, hay, and other such forage differ from most agricultural output in that they do not go directly into human consumption.

In fact, much of this forage is not marketable since many farmers grow their own livestock feed rather than buy it, to lower their feeding costs.

Technically speaking, the Department of Agriculture never labels forage as "surplus," since it has no price support program to buy up and store these commodities. But the effect of the increased production of forage crops due to Reclamation irrigation projects is surprisingly great. Professor Charles W. Howe,* former director of the Resources for the Future water resources program, and Professor K. William Easter,† former Bureau of the Budget economist, recently conducted an intensive study of the Bureau's impact on farm surplus problems. They found that Reclamation-irrigated forage lowered not only forage prices, but also the income of non-Reclamation farmers.[13] They reasoned that increased forage production resulted in cheaper livestock feed, which resulted in greater livestock production, which in turn resulted in decreased livestock prices and farm incomes.

Howe and Easter's study—the only detailed study of the impact of Bureau programs—points out only part of the forage surplus problem. Much of the livestock fed by this forage contributes to surplus crop problems in less direct ways. For example, every year the Department of Agriculture has to step in and boost the prices of butter, butter oil, cheese, milk, wool, and mohair. Thus, the forage supporting cows, sheep, and goats all contributes to price support costs through these livestock by-products.

Cereals: The administrative price support costs, as well as the loss in farm income for non-Reclamation farmers due to Bureau irrigation, are not limited to forage. Over 25 percent of all Reclamation-irrigated land supports the growth of cereals such as barley, corn, and wheat. Unlike forage, cereals are treated as surplus crops by the Department of Agriculture. USDA's Commodity Credit Corporation (CCC)

---

* Howe is now Professor of Economics at the University of Colorado.

† Easter is now Professor of Economics at the University of Minnesota.

pays out nearly $50 million every year in price support and surplus grain storage programs for all the major cereals produced on Reclamation-irrigated land. Howe and Easter estimate that the CCC Programs for the corn, barley, sorghum, and wheat grown using Bureau water cost the taxpayers between $19 million and $50 million every year.[14]

The administrative costs of price supports and grain storage—suffered by all the nation's taxpayers—are only part of the cost of the Bureau's efforts. Farmers all over the country—including those in the West—have been forced by excess production to sow fewer acres of corn. Meanwhile, Bureau of Reclamation irrigation projects have increased acreage for corn by 246,000 acres since 1944. Likewise, wheat production has increased by 152,000 acres on Bureau lands and declined everywhere else. Even barley acreage increased by 143,000 acres on Reclamation lands with an accompanying decrease in barley acreage in the North and South.[15]

In short, Reclamation-supported cereal crops appear to be growing at the expense of other farmers and at a direct annual cost to American taxpayers of as much as $50 million.

Field Crops: Similar drawbacks apply to field crops. The three major field crops, which use about 16 percent of all Bureau-irrigated land, are sugar beets, cotton, and beans—all of which also have an adverse effect on the national farm surplus problem.

The Department of Agriculture has attempted to cope with the cotton problem through both price supports and storage programs. Howe and Easter estimate that price supports and USDA Commodity Credit Corporation programs for cotton growth with Bureau water have cost taxpayers between $47 million and $104 million per year.[16]

Bureau-supported cotton production also hurt other cotton farmers—particularly in the South. Between 1944 and 1964, Southern cotton acreage dropped by one-third, while Reclamation cotton acreage increased by almost 300 percent—or 369,000 acres.[17] This cotton competes directly with Southern cotton. In 1961–62, for example, "45 percent of the crop produced in California, Arizona, and New Mexico was shipped directly to southeastern textile mills."[18]

The competition of Southern and Western cotton does not stem from the fact that both cottons are used in the same mills. The same mills use the cotton probably because most textile mills are in the South. What the shipping data indicate is that it is very likely that Western cotton serves as a close substitute for Southern cotton in the weaving process. Even though the strands may not be identical, an increased influx of Western cotton should lower the price that would have been paid to Southern cotton growers, thus hurting them economically.

The logic of this can be explained by an analogy to concession stands at a baseball game. Suppose originally there were only one concession stand and it sold hot dogs. If another stand is set up selling hamburgers for a price low enough to attract customers, it is highly likely that the hot dog stand will lose business as some people switch from hot dogs to hamburgers. The owners of the hot dog stand must choose between losing revenue by lowering their price or losing revenue by selling fewer hot dogs. Similarly, Southern farmers suffer a revenue loss as the purchasers of cotton substitute Western for Southern cotton. While the cotton grown in the two regions may not be perfectly interchangeable, neither are the hot dogs and hamburgers in our example.

One cannot even argue that the displacement or decreased price of cotton increases the nation's economic efficiency. The distortive effect of heavy subsidies for irrigation water, which will be discussed in later parts of this book, is great enough to discredit any argument that the Southern farmers are simply less efficient than the Westerners.

The effect of Reclamation irrigation projects on edible and dry bean production is similar. As with cotton, the Department of Agriculture has to support bean prices and buy up the bean surplus. However, the main cost of Bureau bean production is not that of the surplus crop program, but rather the cost to other farmers. As Reclamation-supported bean production has risen, bean acreage on other farms has dwindled. Bean acreage declined by 10,000 acres in the North, by 10,000 acres in the South, and by 429,000 acres in the West between 1944 and 1964. But bean acreage on Bureau irrigated land doubled—the increase being 147,000 acres—in the same period.[19] In short, Bureau of Reclamation beans appear to be competing most directly with beans grown by other Western farmers.

Finally, over 500,000 acres of Reclamation land is devoted to sugar beet production. The Department of Agriculture currently operates a sugar program designed to curtail excess sugar production. Sugar beet production on Reclamation-served land costs taxpayers $19 million annually in Sugar Act payments alone.[20] As a result, every additional sugar beet grown on United States soil hurts the taxpayer.*

Fruits, Nuts and Vegetables: The same arguments apply to what the Bureau calls "specialty" crops. Whenever we visited the Bureau of Reclamation, we heard the argument that Bureau irrigation is needed to produce "specialty crops" that cannot be grown without Reclamation water. The following statement is typical: "For the most part, Reclamation farms produce crops that can't be grown successfully in the West without irrigation water."[21] Among the speciality crops for which the Bureau claims its water is essential are fruits, nuts, and vegetables.

Only about seven percent of Reclamation land is used to grow fruits and nuts. The primary effect of this production has not been to contribute to Americans' food needs, but rather to put established fruit and nut growers out of business. Howe and Easter present the particulars concerning the Bureau's performance:

> Between 1944 and 1964 the acreage of fruits and nuts fell 50 percent in the North and dropped by 6 percent in the South. In contrast to these declines, overall acreage in the

---

* In addition, Howe and Easter estimated that curtailed domestic sugar production and increased imports could save U.S. consumers "from 3.5 cents to 4 cents a pound in the short run and 1.5 cents to 3 cents in the long run." This means that with increased imports, households would have to pay only 50 cents for a 5-pound bag of sugar instead of the 65 cents that they are now paying.

West increased by 23,000 acres while the acreage on Reclamation-served lands increased 237 percent or 270,000 acres. Hence, acreage in the non-Reclamation West must have declined by 247,000 acres, or 13 percent.[22]

To a great extent, Reclamation irrigation projects have affected vegetable production in a similar fashion. Between 1944 and 1964, vegetable acreage fell in both the North and the South by over 500,000 acres in each area. Only in the West did the vegetable acreage increase, and even there vegetable acreage declined on non-Reclamation lands. On Reclamation-irrigated lands, however, vegetable acreage (excluding potatoes) increased by 111,000 acres between 1944 and 1964 as Bureau farmers again profited at the expense of farmers elsewhere.[23]

Bureau of Reclamation potato production is equally blameworthy. Howe and Easter concluded that the Bureau's potato production has significantly reduced incomes of non-Reclamation farmers:

> Approximately $69 million of the $173-million decline in the farm value of potatoes can be attributed to increased production on lands served by Reclamation. . . . By lowering potato prices Reclamation irrigation has substantially reduced the incomes of non-Reclamation farmers.[24]

Thus, all Reclamation vegetables—including potatoes—have brought substantial harm to previously existing American farms.

Yet the Bureau persists in claiming that these "specialty crops" cannot be grown without Reclamation water. Surely, some of the 160 million acres of idle cropland elsewhere in the United States could be used to grow these so-called specialty crops. To resolve this controversy, we went to a leading United States agricultural economist, Marion Clawson, who has written or edited over nine economics books in the last fourteen years and who serves as an economic consultant for Resources for the Future. Clawson concluded:

> Land quality is somewhat better in some areas, but it's very hard to claim uniqueness. Maybe you can do this for

artichokes in California, but by and large the Bureau's claims of uniqueness are nonsense.[25]

Other Miscellaneous Crops: The final agricultural category set up by the Bureau is "other miscellaneous crops," which basically means family gardens and orchards. It is easy, and important, to cite the harmful impact of producing seeds for more alfalfa, sugar beets, and so on, but the family garden presents a problem. One could argue that family crops result in that much less food being bought in the stores, thus hurting the income of other farmers; but less than 1/400 of all Reclamation land is used for family gardens and orchards, and we may as well not begrudge a person the tomato plants in his back yard.

TOTAL OF SURPLUS CROPS AND DISPLACED FARMERS

The direct costs of Reclamation irrigation are quite substantial. In a 1959 study, agricultural economist G. S. Tolley found that the repercussions of Bureau projects were so great that "it may be that one farm worker for every twenty remaining in Southern agriculture has been displaced by federal reclamation."[26]

A more recent study by Howe and Easter concluded: "In terms of land held in retirement, reclamation has probably replaced 5–18 million acres elsewhere."[27] The pervasive impact that this has had on other American farmers cannot be overemphasized. Perhaps as many as 180,000 farm workers in other areas of the country, particularly the Southeast, have been driven from their jobs as a result of Reclamation's shortsighted policies.* In evaluating its projects, the Bureau has completely ignored these regional displacement costs and plowed ahead with its irrigation efforts, aggravating the problem even further.

Bureau of Reclamation irrigation has also placed a heavy burden on the American taxpayers. USDA programs for the cotton, wheat, feed grains, and sugar produced on Reclama-

---

* Based on a USDA estimate that there is an average of one farm worker per 100 acres of active cropland.

tion-served land cost American taxpayers between $129 million and $258 million annually.[28] And this is only part of the direct cost. Price support costs for Bureau-supported beans, mohair, wool, butter, and other crops cost taxpayers millions more annually in direct USDA outlays. In essence, every time the Bureau of Reclamation increases its "irrigation benefits," Americans actually suffer increased irrigation costs.

THE BUREAU'S REBUTTAL

Reclamation Commissioner Ellis A. Armstrong spoke for the Bureau's position in the following exchange at recent congressional hearings:

> MR. EVINS [Congressman Joe L. Evins (D-Tenn.)]: What answer could one give those who question spending money to irrigate land, at the same time the Agriculture Department is paying people to keep land out of production?
>
> MR. ARMSTRONG: As I pointed out in my slides, the major portion of the production of irrigated lands is that which doesn't contribute to agricultural surplus except for a small proportion of forage and feed grains. Where those are produced they are largely used for beef production. If they weren't produced in that area there would not be nearly as much beef production because of the location and high transportation costs.
>
> Further, one of the things I think is quite important is insurance, the stability you have with irrigated agriculture. We have been quite fortunate now for a number of years in the drought situation. We haven't had a worldwide drought for quite a number of years. When something of this nature occurs, it is good to have assured production.[29]

Mr. Armstrong's answer to the irrigation question is no answer at all. First, he sidestepped the crucial issue. Regardless of other issues, as long as over one-third of the nation's cropland (160 million acres) remains idle, with the prospect of more farmland being retired in the future, why does the nation need more irrigated land? Second, it is not true—as

Mr. Armstrong suggests—that Reclamation programs are responsible for only a small portion of crop surpluses. As demonstrated earlier, over 52 percent of Bureau crops (i.e., cereals, beans, cotton, and sugar) contribute directly to either the sugar program payments or USDA price support and surplus crop storage programs. We maintain that all Bureau-supported production of such crops should be considered surplus. Only through a bit of statistical finagling have Reclamation officials managed to come up with such low estimates of the Bureau's contribution to the surplus crop problem: wheat—2.2 percent of the surplus; corn —0.73 percent of the surplus; upland cotton—4.1 percent of the surplus; and grain sorghum—0.34 percent of the surplus. The Bureau's method of determining these figures is fallacious, however. Upland cotton, for example, is said to contribute 4.1 percent of the surplus, since 4.1 percent of the upland cotton produced in the United States depends on Reclamation water.

A more appropriate procedure would be to consider all (100 percent) of the incremental cotton production on Reclamation lands as surplus. Professor Otto Eckstein, later a member of President Johnson's Council of Economic Advisers, reached a similar conclusion in 1958:

> But the output on irrigated land should really be considered incremental for the country as a whole. If a crop is in surplus, all of the extra output caused by irrigation must be considered to add to the surplus, not just a proportionate share.[30]

For over a decade since Professor Eckstein published his analysis, Bureau officials have ignored his suggestion; continue to use surplus crop estimates that distort and understate the Bureau's contribution to the crop surplus problem. We are forced to conclude that all those Reclamation crops (utilizing 42 percent of Bureau land) that are covered by various USDA surplus crop programs should be considered surplus.

Nor is this the end of the surplus problem. As discussed

earlier, forage contributes indirectly to surpluses by providing livestock feed for animals producing wool, mohair, milk, etc.—all of which are covered by various price support programs. Finally, the remaining crops—even though not covered by USDA support programs—are in surplus in the sense that Bureau-supported production of each of these crops displaces production of these farm goods elsewhere and causes a subsequent loss of income to other farmers. Reclamation has already displaced as many as 180,000 former farmers.

Thus, virtually all Bureau of Reclamation supported crops are excess. To say, as does Commissioner Armstrong, that the "major portion" of these crops are *not* excess is a blatant distortion of the facts.

Reclamation officials often resort to defending their programs on the basis of national security; just as the oil lobbyists have argued that the trans-Alaska pipeline might be used in time of war, the Bureau has argued for irrigation as a defense in time of drought. Let us recall Commissioner Armstrong's words:

> We have been quite fortunate now for a number of years in the drought situation. We haven't had a worldwide drought for quite a number of years. When something of this nature occurs, it is good to have assured production.[31]

We were intrigued by Mr. Armstrong's fear of a worldwide drought. To determine the frequency of such phenomena, we contacted the drought experts at the Environmental Data Service (EDS) of the Department of Commerce.[32] There has never in recorded human history been what they would call a worldwide drought. In fact, meteorologists think the term "worldwide drought" is an improper description of any actual or potential scientific phenomena. When we then asked about the frequency of "nationwide" droughts, we learned that it is also misleading to refer to any drought in our history as "nationwide," although the Dustbowl of 1934 and 1936 was indeed extensive. According to EDS, even if we suffered an equally wide-ranging drought today—which is highly improbable—"the impact on our total national farm production would not be as severe as it was in the '30s."[33] Advanced farm technology can compensate for reduced rainfall by growing more crops per acre where conditions permit. In addition, we already have plenty of irrigated land to assure continued crop production. Finally, we now have millions of acres of land throughout the United States lying idle that could be brought into production if need be.

In retreat, the Bureau of Reclamation maintains that it is shifting its projects away from irrigation. While the Bureau spent 97 percent of its resources and efforts on irrigation in its first decade, it claims that now only 40 percent of its total appropriations and allotments have gone to irrigation.[34] Yet an analysis of the $5.5 billion backlog of authorized facilities the Bureau is fighting to complete indicates that irrigation is still the primary element in current and prospective Reclamation projects.* Under the 1971 budget, twenty-six projects or major project units with a total balance to complete of over $2 billion were not yet under construction (see Table 2-B). Twenty-three of these are predominantly irrigation projects; in fact, $1.2 billion, or 55 percent of the total cost of these unstarted projects is allocated to irrigation. Projects with partial construction need nearly $3.5 billion more to be completed (see Table 2-C). It is difficult to estimate with certainty how much of this balance to complete represents new irrigation costs. Nevertheless, we know from Table 2-C that among the partially completed projects are four with some construction (5 percent or less) which have yet to spend nearly $1 billion for irrigation, and another project only 11 percent constructed has over $203 million more allocated to irrigation. If all of these irrigation "benefits" were excluded as they should be, the benefit-cost ratio for most of these projects would dip below unity and our economy would be spared the burden of these costly and counterproductive undertakings.

* A similar analysis of the thirty-nine reconnaissance studies and fifty-seven feasibility investigations described in the Bureau's 1972 budget submission to Congress shows that about one-half of the reconnaissance studies and the overwhelming majority of the feasibility investigations still focus largely on irrigation.

RECOMMENDATIONS

We recommend that the billions of dollars of backlogged projects either awaiting construction funds or currently under construction be reevaluated. Until economists are able to quantify precisely the harmful external effects of irrigation, we urge that the Bureau be allowed to attribute at most a zero value for irrigation benefits. Since the bulk of the benefits claimed for these forthcoming projects are irrigation benefits, most of the projects will no longer pass the economic feasibility test. The few projects that do survive will be substantially changed as water earmarked for irrigation should become available for water quality needs as well as for municipal and industrial water supplies. This is as it should be. The original task of the Bureau of Reclamation—irrigation—has long since been completed. At least in the area of irrigation, the Bureau of Reclamation's time has passed.

3 | Salt, Silt, and Environmental Impacts

In the matter of environment, for example, I cannot believe that anyone could seriously accuse the Bureau of Reclamation of degrading the environment to the disadvantage of man in its decades of operations. This is silly.[1]

> Reclamation Commissioner
> Ellis A. Armstrong

The Bureau of Reclamation is the prime source of water pollution in the Far West. They manage their damn reservoirs as if they had blinders on. They pay absolutely no attention to hydrologic probabilities. They protect the interests of the irrigators only. They've done their job, and their time has passed.[2]

> R. L. Coughlin, of the Federal
> Water Quality Administration

The Bureau of Reclamation is less than responsive to America's need for clean water. Its disdain for water quality considerations results in increased waste in municipal water supplies, fish kills, damage to property, and hazards to public health. Nevertheless, the Bureau omits such deleterious effects from its calculations of project benefits and costs. The following case studies demonstrate the immediacy and significance of this problem.

a. The Killing of the Snake

For decades, the Snake River has been the economic and aesthetic lifeline of Northwesterners. Over a thousand miles long, it has created a fertile basin area that extends into six northwestern states. The Snake River is both an outstanding source of beauty and the leading source of anadromous fish (those that migrate up-river from the sea to breed, such as salmon and steelhead) in the entire Columbia River Basin.

In recent years, however, the Bureau of Reclamation has poured concrete where there was once a rapidly flowing river. Reclamation dams scattered along the winding reaches of the Snake River have, in effect, replaced the natural habitat with a man-made catastrophe. As of November, 1969, the Bureau listed 64 active projects and major structures on the Snake River itself, with a total of 223 in the Snake River Basin area.[3]

In constructing these facilities, the Bureau gave very low priority to their possible effects on water quality. The Federal Water Pollution Control Administration (now the Water Quality Office of the Environmental Protection Administration)* noted:

> Water quality has been largely neglected in the operating regimen of the present regulatory system. Requirements for irrigation, power production, and local flood control have generally been met without reference to possible effects on water quality.[4]

In fact, Reclamation has allocated over 97 percent of the reservoir storage space behind the four major dams on the Upper Snake River to irrigation.[5]

As might be expected, the Bureau's catering to the powerful irrigation interests has done much to harm the majority of the basin dwellers. Bureau dams have halted the Snake's majestic rushing flow to a "slim uncharacteristic

---

* The federal water pollution fighters have changed their names several times, from Federal Water Pollution Control Administration to the Federal Water Quality Administration, to the Water Quality Office of EPA. For the sake of simplicity, we shall refer to the water pollution fighters as EPA throughout, though the earlier names may, in some cases, be the correct ones.

flow" below Milner Dam.[6] Needless to say, Reclamation did not recognize these aesthetic and ecological effects in calculating the project benefits and costs that determine project design and operation.

The damage, however, is more than aesthetic. The low flow permitted to pass through Reclamation dams on the Snake has meant that the river no longer carries enough water to dilute downstream human and irrigation wastes. The consequent depletion of the water's dissolved oxygen has critically harmed the habitat for the fish. As EPA concluded:

> Fish kills have occurred in the Milner and American Falls reservoirs and in the lower Boise River because of depleted oxygen levels. The principal oxygen problems are the extreme low flows caused by the operation of storage reservoirs, by irrigation withdrawals, and by untreated or inadequately treated wastes.[7]

Between 1960 and 1968, over 1.4 million fish perished in several massive fish kills because of the drastic deterioration of water conditions on the Snake caused by the Bureau's dams.[8]

Reclamation facilities on the Snake also cause the thermal pollution, which further threatens the survival of the fish. The migration and spawning of salmon and other cold-water fish depend on water temperatures not exceeding 68° F. If the temperature is greater, they cannot continue to breed. EPA again blamed the Bureau of Reclamation for this crisis:

> The cause of temperature problems is related to the impoundment of the free flowing stream and the use of the system for irrigation. Flow depletion due to storage and diversion and the surface return of irrigation waters warmed on fields combine with solar radiation to increase temperature levels.[9]

Man, as well as fish, has suffered from the Bureau's disdain for environmental considerations. During the nonirrigation season, Reclamation dams store water principally for irrigators to use later—allowing little to pass through for other uses. Meanwhile, downstream industries are busy processing the crops and livestock raised on Bureau-irrigated land. The wastes from this processing are then dumped into the Snake River along with other municipal and industrial (M&I) wastes. Ordinarily such discharges would not pose a critical problem, for the unregulated flow of the Snake River is adequate to dilute a good deal of waste matter sufficiently to make it relatively harmless. However, the full natural flow of the Snake is not available for this dilution process because it is being stored behind Bureau dams for the next spring's irrigation.

Reclamation facilities therefore exacerbate the pollution problem both by increasing the amount of irrigated crops that have to be processed (thus increasing processing wastes) and by decreasing the available flow downstream for waste dilution. EPA reported that these problems have become so severe that "the City of Twin Falls was forced to abandon its Snake River water supply as a result of tastes and odors associated with decay of aquatic growths and other waste loads in Milner Reservoir."[10]

The human dimensions of the Snake River problem are still more complex. Traditionally the Snake has served as a major Northwest recreation area—providing unexcelled opportunities for cold-water fishing, boating, and swimming. Almost every city and town in the area has a recreational park bordering on the River. Reclamation operations pose a serious threat to this setting. As the EPA report noted, the bacterial contamination stemming from Bureau projects has made many recreational activities both unsafe and unpleasant.[11] High densities of the coliform group of bacteria have been found throughout the central basin area as well as in the Burley and Idaho Falls areas. While coliform bacteria are relatively harmless, their presence is an important indication of the likelihood that harmful contaminants (like hepatitis viruses) are present in the water.

The Bureau of Reclamation's disruption of the ecological balance has also stimulated eutrophication of the river—the prolific development of algae, and other aquatic growth. EPA claims that this process has transformed the Snake from a clear-flowing river into water with "the color and seeming consistency of pea soup."[12] Consequently, recreationists and fishermen abandoned many previously popular areas.

These negative benefits* are public externalities, which is to say that all of the people must endure the economic and health effects of polluted water if the water is not treated. If the water is treated, then treatment costs will be inflicted on the taxpayers paying for the facility and on the water users purchasing water at higher rates. Reclamation shifts the costs of polluted water from the individuals causing the pollution to the rest of society. Such an approach subsidizes the pollutor and distorts the efficient allocation of the nation's resources.

RECOMMENDATIONS

Further destruction of the Snake River and other rivers is inevitable, as long as the Bureau of Reclamation is allowed to persist in its ingrained practices. We urge that Congress or the President take action to clean up the Snake and halt all further Reclamation construction on the river until the Bureau demonstrates that such projects meet acceptable criteria for water quality. This recommendation is directed specifically at the Bureau of Reclamation's Teton Reservoir, which is in the initial stage of construction. None of the 315,000 acre-feet of storage space in the Teton Reservoir has been earmarked for water quality improvement.[13]

Evaluation of water quality benefits and costs should become an integral part of the Bureau's planning and operating policies. Currently, the Bureau does not take into account the deleterious impacts of irrigation or municipal and industrial (M&I) wastes. These negative benefits should be recognized and quantified in dollar terms when they are attributable to

* Negative benefits are very real economic costs to society. Yet they are not labeled "project costs" since "project costs" technically refers only to construction and operation costs (i.e., capital costs). This is more a question of definition than of substance. Negative benefits should lower net project benefits, decreasing the numerator of the benefit-cost ratio. All additional expenditures required of the Bureau of Reclamation should be reflected in increases in the size of the costs—in other words, in the denominator of the benefit-cost ratio.

Reclamation projects. It is intolerable for the Bureau of Reclamation to claim the benefits from irrigation, while failing to recognize the actual water quality costs resulting from that irrigation. Similarly, the Bureau should stop recognizing indirect irrigation benefits and M&I benefits unless it also recognizes the negative benefits from M&I growth and from the processing and irrigation of commodities grown on Bureau-irrigated lands.

Since EPA is the only federal agency with the ability and inclination to evaluate water quality benefits, it should be given a direct role in Bureau project planning. Future projects should be required to meet the water quality standards set by EPA (or the affected states) for the region. In the case of projects already constructed without appropriate consideration for water quality, the Bureau should construct water treatment facilities, adequate to meet the standards imposed by EPA. In short, water quality benefits and costs should be recognized in project evaluation, design, and operation.

b. Salinity on the Colorado

This same sequence, the diversion of river water into land for irrigation, followed eventually by water logging and salinity and the abandonment of land, had been repeated many times throughout history. The result was invariably the decline, and sometimes the disappearance, of the civilizations thus intervening in the hydrology cycle.[14]

The Bureau's utter disregard for water quality is nowhere more apparent than in its contribution to the growing salinity problems of the Western river basins. Belittling the adverse effect of its own irrigation projects, the Bureau has seldom determined the extent, the damages, or the causes of river pollution. The Bureau has been even more remiss in developing projects to solve water quality problems. Indeed, it has all but guaranteed the worsening of salinity problems by omitting water quality costs (or negative benefits) in its projected benefit-cost calculations.

THE PROBLEM

Salinity refers to the concentration of total dissolved solids in a given body or stream of water. Ten elements—hydrogen, sodium, magnesium, potassium, calcium, silicon, chlorine, oxygen, carbon, and sulfur—make up over 99 percent of the dissolved minerals.[15] The elements occur in solution as molecules, radicals, and ions such as calcium, chloride, and bicarbonate. Salinity is measured in the nearly equivalent units of milligrams of dissolved minerals per liter of water (mg/1) and parts per million (ppm).

Both man and nature are responsible for the increasing salinity of the Western rivers. Nature contributes dissolved minerals through diffuse and point sources. Diffuse sources include surface runoff following rain or snow and discharges of underground water. Point sources consist primarily of mineral springs and exposed mineral formations. But man-made Reclamation projects are to blame for much of the increasing pollution of Western rivers. When water is diverted from a free-flowing stream into irrigation ditches, it dissolves mineral salts in the soil it irrigates. It then carries these salts back with it to the river. As water is diverted from and returned to the river by a series of irrigation projects, it becomes more and more saline. Municipal and industrial use contributes slightly to salinity problems by adding wastes to water withdrawn and eventually returned to the river. Finally, some salt concentrating results from the reduction of water flow in the river through evaporation and transpiration (absorption by plants along the river banks).

In the arid, seven-state Colorado River Basin, salinity problems are especially severe. Basin salt levels in water and soil are naturally high and scarcity of water leads to repeated use (and increasing salinity) of available supplies. At the headwaters of the Colorado River in Wyoming, the average salinity is less than 50 mg/1. It steadily increases downstream, however, until, at Imperial Dam, between southern California and southern Arizona, it reaches 865 mg/1.[16] Over 26.1 million tons of mineral salts are added each day to the Upper Colorado River (headwaters to Lee Ferry in northern Arizona); another 3.8 million tons per day are added to the Lower Colorado River (Lee Ferry to Imperial Dam).

Net runoff from natural precipitation accounts for 48 percent of total Colorado River "salt loading" of 30 million tons per day. And natural point sources contribute another 15 percent. A significant portion of the river's salinity buildup—36 percent—comes from irrigation projects built by the Bureau of Reclamation.[17] Over thirty-five Reclamation projects, irrigating 438,780 acres of land, contribute 10.8 million tons of mineral salts to the Colorado River every day.[18] The 36-percent figure, however, seriously underrepresents the importance of irrigated agriculture in aggravating the salinity problem. If it were not for the Reclamation projects' depletion of Colorado River flow—which increases salt concentration—and the projects' highly saline return flows—which load the river with dissolved solids—the salinity of the river would pose far less severe problems for river water users.

Studies by the Bureau, the EPA, the Water Resources Council (WRC), and the Colorado River Board of California (CRBC) have shown that without control programs, salinity levels in the Colorado River will rise sharply in coming decades. Estimated levels for 1980 range from 1,000 mg/1 (Bureau of Reclamation) and 1,260 mg/1 (WRC), and for the year 2010, from 1,220 (EPA) to 1,340 mg/1 (CRBC).[19]

Salinity problems impose significant costs on water users. Increased salinity boosts the costs of M&I use by leading to added soap consumption, corrosion of metal water pipes and heaters, accelerated fabric wear, added water softening costs, and more costly treatment of water supply for drinking and industrial purposes. Salinity adversely affects agricultural uses by limiting the type of crops that can be irrigated with a given water supply and by reducing crop yields as salinity levels increase.

The effects of increased salinity on plant growth are subtle, but destructive. First, salty water tends to "waterlog" the soil; that is, little air penetrates to the root zone. Second, it harms the plants growing in the soil by causing the physical permeability of their root membranes to change, thus inhibiting water uptake even more than would be expected as a result of only the osmotic differences. In most cases, however, salinity merely reduces the size and yield of crops. As the problem becomes more severe, high salt concentration causes noticeable burning of leaves or die-back of young twigs. In extreme cases, continuing buildup of salts in soil can lead to the total destruction of the productive capacity of the land.

An extensive study released last year by the Environmental Protection Agency attached dollar values to salinity impacts. Under 1960 conditions, the report concluded, the annual economic impact of salinity in the Lower Colorado River Basin exceeded $9.5 million. Present salinity detriments have increased to $15.5 million annually. The report predicted:

> If water resources development proceeds as proposed and no salinity controls are implemented, it is estimated that average economic detriments (in 1970 dollars) would increase to $27.7 million in 1980 and $50.5 million in 2010. If future water resource development is limited to those projects now under construction the estimated annual economic detriments would increase to $21 million in 1980 and $29 million in 2010.[20]

Moreover, the study discovered that southern California, whose 20 million residents depend on the Colorado River for 75 percent of their water, will suffer three-quarters of the economic toll of increased salinity.[21]

SALINITY CONTROL ACTIVITIES

The Bureau of Reclamation has had a legal obligation to study the quality of water in the Colorado River Basin since the mid-1950s.[22] In January, 1969, the Bureau issued *Progress Report No. 4*, a volume bulging with technical information on river salinity. Like the three which preceded it, the report concluded with Candide-like optimism that all was still well and recommended doing nothing:

These studies indicate an overall increase in the concentration of total dissolved solids at the various points on the Colorado River and/or its tributaries under the conditions described, *but the quality of water will still be acceptable for present and projected uses.* [emphasis added][23]

The Bureau's *Progress Report No. 5*, issued in January, 1971, slightly amended its 1969 optimism:

These studies indicate an overall increase in the concentration of total dissolved solids at the various points on the Colorado River and its tributaries under the conditions described. The quality of water will still be acceptable for present and most projected uses although some quality control measures are desirable in order to keep the future concentrations within usable limits.[24]

The need for salinity control measures on the Colorado River was just as apparent in 1969 as it was in 1971. The Bureau's partial recognition of this need for the first time in 1971 reflects not the sudden worsening of the problem or the discovery of new information, but more likely the prodding of EPA and Colorado River Basin farmers. In its multivolume 1971 report, *The Mineral Quality Problem in the Colorado River Basin*, EPA could not have disagreed more with the Bureau's continuing optimism. EPA concluded:

Salinity concentrations in the lower river system exceed desirable levels and are approaching critical levels for some water uses. Future water resource and economic developments [i.e., more Reclamation projects] will increase streamflow depletions and add salt which in turn will result in higher salinity concentrations. . . .

Unless salinity controls are implemented, future increases in salinity concentrations will seriously affect water use patterns and will result in large economic losses.[25]

Belatedly inching toward salinity control, the Bureau of Reclamation and EPA initiated a reconnaissance study early in 1968 in the Upper Colorado Basin.[26] However, a shortage of funds resulted in its abandonment during 1970.

Also in 1968, EPA made funds available and asked the

Bureau of Reclamation to select a pilot project to test and demonstrate control methods for reducing salinity concentrations and salt loads in the Colorado River System. The Bureau took the money and plugged two flowing wells near Meeker, Colorado. When the state of Wyoming and an oil company plugged three more wells at their own expense, the salt load passing Hoover Dam was reduced by 100,000 tons —only 0.93 percent of the total. Nevertheless, the projects were easily worth it. At a cost of less than $100,000, the five well pluggings produced annual benefits equal to $400,000 in 1970 and $1 million in 2010, and with a total present value of $10 million.[27]

Despite the apparent success of this experiment, the Bureau showed little eagerness to attempt additional salinity control projects for three years. In 1971, for instance, it designated only $52,000 from its general investigations fund for salinity control studies. In 1972, the Bureau requested congressional funding for salinity control studies of $450,000.[28] Significantly, the Bureau planned to use the increased appropriations to conduct reconnaissance studies on two natural point source control projects: LaVerkin Springs in Utah and Paradox Valley in Colorado. The Bureau proposed no investigations, however, of projects to control salt contributions to the river from its own irrigation operations, although return flows from irrigation account for 37 percent of the total salt load of the river—as compared to 9 percent for natural point sources.[29]

The release of EPA's draft report in the summer of 1971 calling for an immediate "basinwide salinity control program" and the scheduling of a seventh EPA state-federal conference on Colorado River pollution prompted the Bureau to take more comprehensive action.[30] In February, 1972, it published a ninety-page proposal entitled *Colorado River Water Quality Improvement Program*.[31] The program would involve measures to control salinity from irrigation projects by repairing the linings of irrigation canals and improving the management techniques of the irrigators.

The Bureau also anticipates various construction projects to reduce salt loading from diffuse and point sources. And, in a section of the report entitled "Allied Programs," the Bureau outlines proposals for ambitious, expensive, and as yet not fully researched programs for desalination, weather modification,* interbasin transfers of river water, and development of geothermal resources.[32] Ironically, the Bureau's program includes no moratorium on Reclamation project development on the Colorado River, even though existing projects are mainly to blame for the river's excessive salinity.

The Bureau's salinity control program would take ten years and $400 to $500 million to accomplish.[33] The key question of who is to provide the financing remains in some doubt. Will the irrigators, who are almost exclusively responsible for the spiraling salinity damages, pay the great majority of the control program costs? That would appear to be just, if only because the proposed control program would not significantly reduce the current level of salinity (865 mg/1 at Imperial Dam). Instead it would obtain levels of 880 mg/1 in 1980 and 845 mg/1 in 2010[34] that in effect would merely neutralize expected increases due to continued development of irrigation projects.

But the Bureau of Reclamation seems to have a different repayment scheme in mind:

> The investigation program would be financed by the federal government under the authority of laws previously cited herein. As feasibility of specific control projects is demonstrated, *beneficiaries* will be identified and cost-sharing and repayment formulas will be developed. [emphasis added][35]

"Beneficiaries" could easily imply the 20 million municipal and industrial water users of southern California. Already they are bearing the costs of purifying the Colorado River water made increasingly saline by Bureau of Reclamation projects. Now, apparently, they are to help pay for remedying a problem which they had nothing to do with creating. And as the Bureau continues building new Colorado River irrigation projects and thereby intensifying salinity problems,

* Weather modification will be discussed later in this chapter.

southern Californians will be footing a larger and larger bill for salinity control.

According to the Bureau's initial plan, the irrigators will pay only one-half of the $240- to $300-million cost of the control program's irrigation system improvement component. That the irrigators should have to pay *any* part of the cost has nothing to do—from the Bureau's viewpoint—with their predominant role in creating the salinity problem. Instead, they will be paying for salinity control, the Bureau says, because they will be receiving "direct benefits," including:

> labor savings, more efficient water deliveries, reduced operational costs, and . . . a basis for more efficient layouts of irrigated fields.

Who is to pay the other half of the cost of the irrigation system improvement program—that is, the other $120 to $150 million? "The remainder of the cost is assumed to be allocated to salinity control and would be subject to cost sharing," the Bureau report declares.[36] In other words, the "beneficiaries" of salinity control, the municipal and industrial water users of southern California, will pay.

The seventh EPA conference on Colorado River pollution approved the Bureau's proposal:

> The salinity control program as described by the Department of the Interior in its report entitled "Colorado River Water Quality Improvement Program," dated February 1972, offers the best prospect for implementing the salinity control objective adopted herein.[37]

The conference also recommended that the Bureau of Reclamation have the "primary responsibility" for planning and implementing the program.[38]

INTERNATIONAL SALINITY PROBLEMS

Colorado River salinity problems have also had international repercussions. For years Mexicans have suffered from the high salinity concentration of Colorado River water caused by the Bureau of Reclamation's Wellton-Mohawk Irrigation

District in southwestern Arizona. They fear further damage unless the Bureau revises its irresponsible policies.

Water deliveries to Mexico from the Colorado River are governed by the "Water Treaty" signed by the United States and Mexico in 1944. Enforced by the International Boundary and Waters Commission, the treaty requires the United States to deliver to Mexico at least 1.5 million acre-feet (maf) of Colorado River water per year.[39] A major unresolved controversy about this treaty is whether or not it guarantees Mexico some minimum quality in the water that comes down the Colorado River from the United States.

Backed by the State Department, the Bureau of Reclamation maintains that the framers of the treaty intended that Mexico should accept the river water no matter how unusable it may have been made by saline return flows. Return flows are diverted waters which may have been used for irrigation and therefore have an increased salinity content, and which make it back to the main source from which they were diverted.

The highly saline return flows from the Wellton-Mohawk Irrigation District along the lower Gila River have long diminished the quality of Colorado River water, as it enters Mexico just above Mexico's Morellos Dam. The flows are unusually saline because the district lies atop a closed underground basin, called a salt dome, which lacks lateral drainage. As a result, repeated circulation of the same saline groundwater, plus use of the already saline downstream Colorado River water, reduces the usability of the return flows for drinking or irrigation.

Naturally, Mexico has strenuously objected to receiving 1.5 maf of what is in effect the runoff from the mining of Wellton-Mohawk salt.[40] After all, that water is essential to the livelihood and survival of the 10,000 Mexican irrigators in the Mexicali Valley—not to mention the 300,000 residents of Mexicali, Mexico, who depend on the Colorado River for municipal water.[41]

In the late 1950s, "severe seepage and drainage conditions in the [Wellton-Mohawk] District caused some land to go out of production, resulted in significantly reduced crop yields on other land, and limited availability of credit for crop financing and land improvement."[42] To cope with the growing salinity problems—in the district, not in Mexico— the Bureau of Reclamation constructed drainage wells and a canal to carry the briny return flows to the Gila River, which flows into the Colorado. When the works were completed, in early 1961, the Gila was contributing the bulk of the salt dissolved in the Colorado River at their confluence point just north of the Mexican border.[43] By the end of 1961, the salinity level of Colorado River water entering Mexico reached 2,700 parts per million (ppm)—virtually unusable for drinking or profitable irrigated agriculture.[44]

The Bureau of Reclamation, however, maintained that the quality of the water delivered to Mexico was irrelevant to the U.S. treaty obligation. According to former Interior Secretary Stewart Udall, Reclamation Commissioner Floyd Dominy went to some of his friends in Congress to convince them that "we could deliver sewage to Mexico," and, added Udall, "that was pretty much the Bureau's attitude."[45]

T. R. Martin, a State Department expert on Mexican affairs, explained how the United States justifies the abysmal quality of water that flows downstream: "We would hang our hat on Article 10 [of the Water Treaty], 'from any and all sources,' and on Article 11, 'waters . . . whatever their origin,' if we ever had to go to court."[46] An article in *Foreign Affairs*, however, claims that

> the available evidence seems to suggest that the words . . . were inserted primarily to give the United States maximum credit for return flow and only indirectly—if, indeed, at all— to cover the question of quality.[47]

Mexico did threaten to take the matter to the World Court when the Bureau showed no eagerness to control the salinity of Colorado River water following the crisis year of 1961. (In 1964, salinity levels still hovered around 2,500 ppm.)[48] Anxious lest Mexico make good on its threat, the United States agreed to negotiate the problem. On March 22,

1965, the two countries reached a five-year stop-gap agreement—the International Boundary and Waters Commission's Minute 218.[49]

The Minute stipulated that the United States would construct an extension of the Wellton-Mohawk drainage canal to convey part of the saline return flows to the Colorado River below Morellos Dam, where it would not affect the quality of the water used for drinking and irrigation in the Mexicali Valley. The United States agreed to divert below the dam about 50,000 acre-feet annually of the most heavily saline return flow, and to count none of it against the 1.5 maf which the United States is obligated to deliver annually to Mexico under the Water Treaty. In addition, the United States has agreed to divert the remainder of the saline return flows— about 220,000 acre-feet—to points above or below Morellos Dam, depending on Mexico's wishes. (Mexico has been reluctant to have this additional amount of poor quality water diverted below the dam, because this amount *is* charged against the United States's 1.5 maf obligation.)

Minute 218 was hardly a permanent solution. A new round of talks between the two countries during the summer of 1970 resulted in the extension of the Minute until November 15, 1971, to allow negotiators to search for a more lasting solution. The current dispute revolves around the definition of usable water. Mr. Martin, the State Department official, claims that "the water that we've been delivering to Mexico since Minute 218 was agreed to is perfectly usable for the type of crops grown on the type of soil present in the Mexicali Valley." The salinity levels of the water the United States has delivered to Mexico over the last five years have ranged from 1,280 to 1,330 ppm.[50] Indeed, reliable sources indicate that Mexico is willing to accept a 1,300-ppm level, but would prefer that salinity be reduced to about 1,000-ppm—the level that existed before the Bureau of Reclamation installed the Wellton-Mohawk drainage wells in 1961. Mexico is unwilling, however, to accept water with a salt content above 1,500 ppm.[51]

Still, the United States "hasn't acknowledged their claim," according to Mr. Martin.[52] The Bureau sees things differently from the Mexicans. "Growing cotton in the Mexicali Valley, you could use water with up to 3,500 ppm salinity and get away with it," claims Maurice N. Langley, chief of Reclamation's Water and Land Division and the regular representative of the Secretary of the Interior at the talks with Mexico.[53] What's good enough for the Mexicans, however, isn't necessarily good enough for the Americans. A forthcoming Environmental Protection Agency report on salinity problems in the Colorado River Basin notes that:

> In the Lower Colorado River present salinity concentrations [cited in the report as 760 ppm at Hoover Dam and 865 ppm at Imperial Dam] are above threshold limits for municipal, industrial, and agricultural uses. Some impairment of these uses is now occurring and future increases in salinity will increase this adverse impact.[54]

RECOMMENDATIONS

To remedy both the domestic and international salinity problems, we recommend that the Colorado River Basin states immediately set numerical criteria for salinity concentrations. We call upon Congress to authorize EPA to set maximum salinity concentration levels for these states, in case the state-established criteria are too lenient or too slow in coming. These levels, even for the Lower Basin states, should not exceed 1,000 ppm and probably should be less. The United States should then use these levels as the standards of acceptability of the water it delivers to Mexico. Only after such a revision in present policy will the United States again begin to fulfill its legal and moral obligations to its less affluent and less powerful neighbor to the South.

Until appropriate salinity levels are established and attained, the President and Congress should order a freeze on all Reclamation project construction in the Colorado River Basin—particularly the Central Arizona Project. Furthermore, Congress should authorize EPA to enforce the new water quality criteria and to plan and implement a basinwide salinity control program, perhaps with the technical assistance of the Bureau of Reclamation.

Before being allowed to resume project construction, the

Bureau—under the close supervision of EPA, the Office of Management and Budget, and the General Accounting Office —should subject all Reclamation planning efforts to benefit-cost criteria revised so as to place dollar values on salinity impacts. To date, the Bureau has displayed an alarming inability to quantify salinity costs, but has displayed great alacrity in quantifying benefits from any reductions in salinity in other Bureau projects. This double standard allows the Bureau to pollute the nation's rivers with projects of dubious worth and then to justify subsequent efforts to abate the very salinity problems it caused. By integrating water quality considerations into project planning, as we suggest, the feasibility of projects as well as their design and operation will begin to include proper recognition of the all too apparent salinity impacts.

c. Sedimentation Buildup

For millions of years the great Colorado River has borne mountains to the sea. As a part of its natural life cycle, it has carried the sedimentary wastes from the cutting of chasms and awesome canyons. It has swept away the dry land by the endless cycle of water rushing to the sea. In deep canyon stretches of the river at flood time one can hear the deep rumbling of boulders hurried along like marbles.

On the California side of the Colorado River, south of Boulder Canyon, lies a broad alluvial plain known as the Mohave Valley. On the banks of the river in this valley is the little desert town of Needles. In the 1930s and 1940s it was a railroad town, a division point of the Santa Fe Railroad, with a few shops and a large ice plant. It was and still is an important stopping place on U.S. Route 66, the transcontinental highway to Los Angeles.

Established in 1883, Needles existed in relative harmony with the river for years. Bank erosion and natural channel meandering had forced relocation of railroad tracks and of the railroad station, but only one serious flood brought significant damage to the town. In 1912 the river overflowed its banks and levees, but even this was attributed more to the effects of levee construction upstream than to natural flooding action of the river. Following this rather inconsequential flood "the river bank became stabilized."[55]

Into this natural setting came the Bureau of Reclamation. As a direct result of its construction of Hoover Dam (originally called Boulder Dam), the harmony between the town and the river was drastically changed. Acclaimed as the greatest dam in the world when it was built in 1935, Hoover Dam became the cornerstone of the Bureau's reputation. Commemorating the dam twenty-five years after its construction, a proud Commissioner Floyd Dominy declared that "flood control by Hoover Dam has been complete since it first stored water in 1935."[56]

Commissioner Dominy's statement is a remarkably vigorous editing of history. It is true that Hoover Dam has held back some flood flows of the river, but this does not mean that there have been no floods downstream from the dam since 1935, or that the immense project achieved complete control of the river—or that the river needed controlling in the first place. On the contrary, sedimentation problems caused by Reclamation dams have resulted in at least one major flood as well as other severe damage to the environment.

Flooding is a function of two characteristics of a river: the amount of water flowing down the channel at a given time and the carrying capacity of the channel. Carrying capacity is determined by variables such as grade, width, depth, and freedom from obstructions. While Hoover Dam helped control the first—the amount of water flowing down the river—it had an unintended, uncalculated, ruinous impact on the second—the carrying capacity of the Colorado—and thereby on the lives and property of people in the Lower Colorado River Basin.

First, the Dam created Lake Mead—a huge silt deposit basin in which the river's entire load of sediment was dropped. Although the Bureau claimed that one of the dam's benefits would be clear water issuing from its spillway, they didn't anticipate that the clear water coming out below Hoover Dam would quickly destabilize a river bed that had become adjusted over time to a heavily silt-laden river.[57]

The process of readjustment began immediately with the clear water scooping up huge amounts of sediment from the bed below the dam. Where the sediment would drop depended on the velocity of the river. Since the silt-carrying capacity of a river varies as the seventh power of its velocity, a small decline in the speed of flow will result in a large decrease in the amount of silt the river can transport. In short, the massive amounts of silt swept up by the river when it left the dam would drop wherever the river slowed down—namely at Needles.

The Mohave Valley around Needles is the first area below Hoover Dam that is not encased in a well-defined canyon. Gradual aggrading (rise in the river bed) of this valley had gone on since 1902, when record keeping was begun. When the gates of Hoover Dam were closed in 1935, releases were cut back to only the amount required to meet downstream users' needs—about one-third the normal flow of the river. The water level dropped in the Needles section and the rate of aggradation increased. Without adequate plans to flush out the river bed, plants proliferated in the shallow and newly exposed reaches of the bed. Thus during six years of low flow, an aggraded plain choked with a veritable jungle of plant life became a major impediment to the flow of the river.

Then in 1941, with Lake Mead partially filled, Hoover Dam releases began exceeding downstream consumption and power requirements. With the valley turned into an obstructing swamp, the heavily laden river dropped its silt. This, of course, slowed the river even more, thereby accelerating the aggradation. Very soon disastrous flooding occurred at Needles. A special report on the situation verified the Bureau's culpability for the flood and went on to describe the consequences:

> Water continued to rise at the rate of about one and one-half feet per year and by 1944, some 50 acres were rendered uninhabitable; over 100 families were obliged to move out;

the electric power plant and gas works supplying the town had to be moved, the Santa Fe Railroad shops were threatened and water raised into the turntable pit. The sewage disposal plant was put out of business and both water supply plants were surrounded by water and had to be diked and motors had to be raised.[58]

This tragedy is only a part of the disaster. According to the Bureau's files, the Mohave Valley was turned into a swamp.

As of December, 1944, the Colorado River had become a swamp or lake between Needles and Topock. This swamp was about 12 miles in length and from one and three-fourths to five miles wide. 125 acres within Needles were inundated or under a high water table. Within this area there were few, if any, sewers. Cesspools were flooded and an unsanitary condition bordering on an epidemic resulted from the polluted groundwater.[59]

Yet Needles was the town that was supposed to have been protected from floods by Hoover Dam. Instead, the Bureau structure resulted in widespread property damage and a severe health crisis.

To save its own reputation, as well as the town of Needles, the Bureau of Reclamation responded to the crisis with emergency corrective measures. In August, 1944, the Bureau established a permanent Office of River Control at Needles. During the next two years, this office had the responsibility of overseeing remedial works. Financed by various appropriations during 1945 and 1946 totaling close to $1 million, these works raised the existing levee four feet, extended it about three-fourths of a mile downstream, provided drainage ditches to collect seepage and return it to the river, and installed riprap* and pumping plants. Yet, the Bureau concluded that even "the above described work will not afford permanent relief."[60]

Although the situation was a disaster for Needles, it was

---

* Riprap is a foundation or wall made of broken stones thrown together.

an opportunity for the Bureau to build a new project. The Bureau determined that "a dredging operation of large magnitude, recreating a channel of sufficient capacity" was necessary to carry the river safely past Needles.[61] Large, indeed! A consulting engineer called in by the Bureau in 1945 estimated that some 5 million cubic yards of sediment had to be dredged between Needles and Topock to open a suitable channel. At about $5.75 per cubic yard, the project would cost $28,750,000. Since, in the engineer's opinion, "no existing equipment is available which would be suitable for the work involved," the Bureau decided to build a huge dredge, at a cost of over $1 million.[62]

In June, 1946, Congress authorized the massive Colorado River Front Work and Levee System (CRFWLS), which former Commissioner Dominy aptly described as "a general heading, a sort of catchall for problems that arise on the Colorado River."[63] By 1965 the total estimated cost of the system works was put at around $40 million, every penny of it nonreimbursable—that is, paid for by the taxpayers rather than by the direct beneficiaries of the system. Total federal expenditures on CRFWLS have since mushroomed to $70 million.[64]

CRFWLS is designed to channelize the river completely by dredging and levee building, from Davis Dam in California to the Mexican border. The hope is that, when completed, the artificial stabilization of the river's regimen will be permanent. Once the channel is "stabilized" below Hoover Dam, the only contribution of silt to the Lower Colorado Basin supposedly will be local. All the sediments from the Upper Basin will be trapped in Lakes Powell and Mead. For approximately the next hundred years, while those lakes are filling up with silt, the only source of silt to bother the lower river channels will be the runoff from the innumerable washes and intermittent streams of the desert below Davis Dam. Thus, if the scenario is followed, no further work will be required for a hundred years or more.

This prediction may or may not prove to be accurate. For one thing, while the amount of silt from these desert sources is small compared to what the river used to carry in its lower reaches, sedimentation is still likely to be a considerable problem, since increasing consumptive use will deprive the river of heavy flows. Furthermore, even these relatively small silt flows are usually very intense, since they result from harsh desert storms and flash floods.[65]

The picture that emerges from the history of CRFWLS shows the Bureau of Reclamation spending huge amounts of the taxpayers' money for a vast patchwork program to clean up the messes caused by their own projects. Bureau dam building has repeatedly disturbed the great river's silt—creating huge silt-catching swamps, aggrading the river bed to the point of flooding areas rarely damaged by floods, and consequently requiring immense protective and remedial works.*

d. Recreation, Fish, and Wildlife

"The Bureau of Reclamation is a great bunch of guys,"[68] claims Carl Stutzman, of the Bureau of Sport Fisheries and Wildlife. Notwithstanding Mr. Stutzman's glowing appraisal of Reclamation officials, the Bureau of Reclamation has demonstrated a capacity to plunder as well as to protect America's recreation and fish and wildlife resources. The story of the Bureau's performance on the Colorado River illustrates this problem.

As the great river of the Southwest, the Colorado is an aesthetic and recreational resource of immense value. It provides a habitat for countless birds, animals, and other wildlife. As a source of fresh water recreation for the huge populations of Los Angeles, San Diego, Phoenix, and many smaller desert communities, the river is unique.

It is hardly surprising, therefore, that conflict arose early over the impact of the Colorado River Front Work and

---

* The Bureau has also ignored the sedimentation problem on rivers other than the Colorado. A recent study on several Missouri River Basin Project dams, compiled by the Department of Transportation, found Bureau planning bereft of foresight: "Aggradation is extending further upstream than originally predicted and the deposition of the main river channel is causing excessive bank erosion."[66] A similarly unfavorable report was issued on sedimentation caused by Bureau efforts on the Middle Rio Grande River.[67]

Levee System (CRFWLS) on the unique aspects of the river. Much to the dismay of the Bureau, the first opposition came largely from Arizona. In a 1949 letter to Reclamation Commissioner Straus, the Arizona Game and Fish Commission voiced its belief that continued CRFWLS dredging would cause extreme losses of fish and wildlife.[69] California had similar reservations about the project.

After studies were done to evaluate CRFWLS's potential impact on fish and wildlife, the citizens' initial concern changed to something more akin to horror. It was estimated that a proposed channel cut through Havasu Lake National Wildlife Refuge would result in a 40 percent loss of fish and a 50–90 percent loss of waterfowl and other wildlife.[70] The California State Department of Fish and Game made a similar survey and reported in 1964:

> The results provided no basis for optimism. Very preliminary and conservative estimates indicated that the channelization project would result in the annual loss of approximately 1,000,000 waterfowl use days, 179,000 angler use days, and 85,000 hunter use days.* Upland game and dove losses were not estimated. The obvious losses to aesthetic and other recreational values were not assessed. We estimated that by the year 2020 the impact of channelization and vegetation control projects would result in 900,000 anglers and 200,000 hunters losing, each year, the recreation experience they might otherwise have enjoyed on the lower Colorado River.[71]

The uproar finally induced the Bureau to recognize the need to proceed more reasonably. Now Reclamation proudly claims it is busy making new side ponds and wildlife habitat areas to mitigate fish and wildlife losses. In fact, two of the three dredges it has working on the project are engaged in such mitigation efforts, according to Earl Walker of the River Basin Studies Office of the Bureau of Sport Fisheries and Wildlife (BSFW).[72] Although this effort adds to the expense of the channelization projects and is certainly good public relations for Reclamation, it is highly questionable whether it

---

* A use day is defined as any day *or part thereof* that the recreation, fish, or wildlife facility is used by one person.

really will rescue fish and wildlife resources from destruction by channelization, as California recognized. The same California report cited above criticized proposed mitigation measures in the Parker Division of CRFWLS:

> Even with these [mitigation proposals] our studies indicated we would still suffer extensive losses to fish and wildlife. The losses would be reduced but would still be in the range of 35 to 75 percent for the various species of wildlife studied and a reduction to an estimated 320,000 angler trips per year to this section of the river from a projected "without the project" annual use of 750,000 angler trips in the year 2020.[73]

California and Arizona's worst fears were justified. Before the Bureau of Reclamation built its projects along the Lower Colorado River, fish and wildlife existed in a delicate ecological balance. Aldo Leopold, in his famous *Sketches Here and There*, describes what once was the wilderness wonderland of the Colorado Delta:

> Dawn on the Delta was whistled in by a Gambel quail, which roosted in the mesquites overhanging camp. When the sun peeped over the Sierra Madre, it slanted across a hundred miles of lovely desolation, a vast flat bowl of wilderness rimmed by jagged peaks. On the map the Delta was shown bisected by the river, but in fact the river was nowhere and everywhere, for he could not decide which of a hundred green lagoons offered the most pleasant and least speedy path to the Gulf. So he traveled them all, and so did we. He divided and rejoined, he twisted and turned, he meandered in awesome jungles, he all but ran in circles, he dallied with lovely groves, he got lost and was glad of it, and so were we. . . .
>
> A verdant wall of mesquite and willow separated the channel from the thorny desert beyond. At each bend we saw egrets standing in the pools ahead, each white statue matched by its white reflection. Fleets of cormorants drove their black prows in quest of skittering mullets: avocets, willets, and yellowlegs dozed one-legged on the bars, mallards, widgeons, and teal sprang skyward in alarm. . . .
>
> All this wealth of fowl and fish was not for our delectation alone. Often we came upon a bobcat, flattened to some half-immersed driftwood log, poised for mullet. Families of rac-

coons waded the shallows munching water beetles. Coyotes watched us from inland knolls, waiting to resume their breakfast of mesquite beans, varied, I suppose, by an occasional cripple shore bird, duck or quail. At every shallow ford were tracks of burro deer. We always examined these deer trails, hoping to find signs of the despot of the Delta, the great jaguar, *el tigre*.[74]

Today the delta is a desert, with the jungles dried up and the wildlife virtually gone. As the Bureau banked and channeled the river, it cut off the water that kept the delta alive. For long stretches all the lakes and ponds are drained, and the green marshes are destroyed. Increased speed of flow has made canoeing more hazardous. Increasing consumptive use of the water upstream and consequent diminution of flows promise to destroy even further the recreational potential of the river. What was once a living, interesting river is now just another large canal.

In building its dams and lakes, however, the Bureau of Reclamation quite by accident partially offset the destruction of habitat in the delta. Before CRFWLS, the swamps and sloughs that resulted from poor planning of projects along the river provided some new homes for fish and fowl. Lakes behind Bureau dams became the inheritors of the waters of the green lagoons. The net effect was a massive unintended movement of some of the wildlife upstream from the delta to the American reaches of the lower Colorado River.

CRFWLS almost completely undid this accidental mitigation of losses. The Bureau achieved its goal of water salvage by "reducing waste and uneconomic uses of water from side channels, ponds, swamps, by improved drainage, together with a reduction in direct channel losses by improved conveyance characteristics."[75] But it is precisely these side channels, ponds, and swamps that served as scenic recreation areas and as the habitat so desperately needed by the remnants of the river's wildlife.

In viewing recreation and wildlife as an uneconomic use of water, Reclamation displayed its channel vision. Its goal was clear—to convert the Colorado River into a permanently stable, neat and tidy, rocklined irrigation ditch. Here was myopic planning at its worst: the Bureau of Reclamation looked at the lower Colorado River and saw a water supply and delivery system, nothing more.

MISCALCULATING RECREATION AND FISH AND WILDLIFE BENEFITS

The Bureau's narrow perspective is not limited to the CRFWLS project, for the Bureau systematically neglects environmental considerations in its most important decision-making procedure—the benefit-cost analysis. In a recent interview, one Bureau of Outdoor Recreation official observed:

> With all benefit-cost calculations there is a high percentage of individual personalities involved. There are some good apples, and there are bad apples.[76]

Evidently, the "bad apples" have been performing Reclamation's recreation and fish and wildlife benefit evaluations.

Benefit-cost ratios alone are used in determining whether a project passes the test of economic feasibility; all projects with ratios less than 1.0 are rejected by the Office of Management and Budget. The importance of the benefit-cost ratio to the Bureau's operations cannot be overestimated. Even the scale of a given project is determined by expanding a project until the marginal quantified benefits equal marginal costs. Benefit-cost ratios are used to rank projects. Thus, project impacts for which dollar values are not given rarely alter a project's feasibility, design, or priority. The Bureau of Reclamation recognized these political realities and determined that recreation and fish and wildlife benefits should be given dollar values even though they are difficult to estimate accurately.*

To calculate these benefits, President Johnson, on the

---

* Economist Otto Eckstein argued in an earlier study of the Bureau of Reclamation that "intangibles" such as recreation benefits should not be given "invalid benefit estimates."[77] The actual economic problem is to evaluate a user's willingness to pay for a recreation or fish and wildlife resource, plus the benefits to the nation from the mere creation and use of additional recreation and fish and wildlife opportunities.

recommendation of the interagency Water Resources Council (WRC), directed in Supplement No. 1 to Senate Document No. 97 that Reclamation apply a range of predetermined unit values to recreation and fish and wildlife activities.[78] General recreation experiences (such as boating, sightseeing, and picnicking) and general fish and wildlife activities (such as warm-water fishing and small-game hunting) take on value ranges from $.50 to $1.50 per activity-day. More specialized activities, including long cruises, wilderness pack trips, cold-water fishing and big-game hunting have daily unit value ranges from $2 to $6. Using these ranges of unit values, the Bureau of Sports Fisheries and Wildlife and the Bureau of Outdoor Recreation perform recreation and fish and wildlife benefit evaluations for the Bureau of Reclamation.

Although not developed through sophisticated economic studies, these unit values are preferable to earlier benefit estimation techniques which relied largely on the whims of the individuals performing the evaluation. The predetermined ranges of benefits are reasonable, even though less than precise. Reclamation can still make allowances for differences in the quality of certain facilities and for the uniqueness of a facility to a region, by adjusting the descriptive analysis section of project reports. Most important, the mere fact that recreational and other benefits are considered helps make the benefit-cost analysis more complete.

Still, there are serious problems with the current method of estimating recreation and fish and wildlife benefits. First, by giving higher values ($2–6) to activities "which often may involve a large personal expense by the user,"[79] Reclamation creates a bias in favor of projects that contribute to recreation and fish and wildlife opportunities for the rich. The necessary equipment costs for activities such as big game hunting and wilderness pack trips often prevent poorer individuals from participating in these opportunities. Decision-makers in Congress and in the executive branch should not only be aware of these distributional impacts, but also require the Bureau to modify its projects so as to help lower-income groups. For example, facilities benefiting poor city residents or Indians should be given unit-day values at least as high as those given to big game hunting. (See Chapter 4.)

Double counting of recreation benefits is a second problem. For example, a person who spends a few hours boating, an hour eating a picnic lunch, and a couple of hours hiking is credited with three recreation days of use, even though he may have spent only one day in these activities. The benefit data for the Mountain Park Project in Oklahoma display a typical case of this double counting (see Table 3-A). Over 88,000 activity-days were claimed for camping, water skiing, and boating. But these days had already been given a value of $.52 each under the category of general use. Boating, camping, and water skiing will bring no people into the project area who have not already been included in the evaluation of general use. Double counting, for which there is no justification, seriously distorts the analysis of the benefits of Reclamation projects.

The Water Resources Council, which establishes new benefit-cost standards for Reclamation and other water resource development agencies, should allow, at most, one recreation day to be credited to any one-day visit. The Bureau of Outdoor Recreation, which actually estimates recreation benefits for Reclamation, should give the single recreation day a value in the range of the highest-valued activity in which an individual participates, regardless of the number of activities engaged in. In addition to making adequate provision for a diversified experience by selecting appropriate unit values, the Bureau can make implicit adjustment by raising its estimates of probable attendance according to how many different activities are offered at the project. For example, a dam whose reservoir provides a diversified recreation experience including boating, fishing, and hiking is likely to attract more people than one that provides only boating.

The implicit recognition of the diversified experience occurs as more visitor days can be counted. The explicit recognition occurs by placing a higher unit-day value on the visitor days for persons engaging in a more diversified experience. For instance, a unit-day value of $.70 might be used for individuals who boat and fish as opposed to a $.60 unit-value for visitors who just fish. This provides more than adequate recognition of a diversified experience—with absolutely no need to double-count. The adoption of such a procedure would have the effect of reducing recreation benefits for the Mountain Park Project in Oklahoma, as noted in Table 3-A, by as much as one third.

A third problem with the Bureau's current procedures for calculating recreation and fish and wildlife benefits is that it omits significant costs and greatly overestimates benefits. While Reclamation officials frequently fail to calculate the lost opportunities and adverse effects of dams that injure recreational areas, they don't hesitate to take credit for any recreation or fish and wildlife "benefits" they can find around their projects.

For example, in the determination of present recreation benefits at the Mountain Park Project, the Bureau gave only brief mention of the preproject recreation opportunities by noting that "limited fishing was done" and "some picnicking occurred."[80] However, the Bureau evaluated the benefits it attributed to its own project much more meticulously, as Table 3-A demonstrates. Reclamation's failure to use tangible negative benefit values for existing recreation and fish and wildlife activities eliminated by the Mountain Park Project led to overestimation of the project's benefits. The Bureau of Reclamation used only gross—not net—project benefit estimates.

In another case, Reclamation systematically underestimated the value of recreation benefits which would have existed without its project. Bureau officials estimated that annual visitation in the Sun Teton area before the project was built equaled "15,000 recreation days with a value of 30¢ per day."[81] But 30¢ per day is below the minimum 50¢ unit-day value required by the WRC for the lowest quality recreation experience. Thus, Reclamation incorporated into its economic justifications an apparent bias in favor of its own project's recreation development.

The Bureau of Reclamation uses fish and wildlife benefit calculations which similarly undercount costs and overestimate benefits. The current procedure for calculating fish and wildlife impacts ignores many "intangible" values. By limiting fish and wildlife benefits and costs to the value of fishing and hunting, the economic analysis gives the preservation or extinction of unique species or other ecological and aesthetic goals no quantifiable value.

It appears that the Bureau of Sport Fisheries and Wildlife, which performs the fish and wildlife benefit evaluations for Reclamation, does not actually determine the net change of these benefits as directed by President Johnson. To do so would require subtraction of the project damages from the amount of fish and wildlife activities occurring with the project. Carl Stutzman, a leading official of the Bureau of Sport Fisheries and Wildlife, described the current evaluation process:

> We wouldn't evaluate the cost of losses in monetary terms for either recreation opportunities or the habitat. The emphasis is on preventing or mitigating it—to compensate by developing a substitute habitat. It's difficult to do though because what you lose may be irreplaceable in the same quality.[82]

The technique Mr. Stutzman described will lead to overestimation of fish and wildlife benefits in at least two ways. First, if mitigation does not totally compensate for losses caused by a project, then the unmitigated damages do not enter the benefit calculation. That is, if $1,000 worth of fish and wildlife are destroyed and only $250 worth of mitigation provided, society loses at least $750 worth of unmitigated fish and wildlife damages—but this is not shown in Bureau calculations.

Second, to the extent that damages are mitigated, fish and wildlife benefits become inflated over their actual value. Assume, for example, that a reclamation project will destroy $1,000 worth of annual fish and wildlife activities. Also, assume that Reclamation mitigates this damage and makes possible $500 worth of fish and wildlife activities annually at an annual cost of $250. Since project damages are not subtracted from project benefits, the project will be credited with a $500 project benefit and a $250 cost. Thus, it appears that the country is better off than before, since the benefits exceed the costs. In reality, however, society has suffered a net annual loss of $750, because the net annual dollar value of fish and wildlife activities has decreased by $500, and because taxpayers are being forced to bear an additional $250 worth of annual project costs.

Society also suffers an unmentioned loss of natural resources whenever the Bureau of Sport Fisheries and Wildlife (BSFW) is lax in its efforts to compensate fully for project damages. The damage resulting from ill-conceived projects should not be underestimated. A recent General Accounting Office report made the following observations concerning two Reclamation dams:

> Passage of anadromous fish up the Columbia River was permanently blocked by the Grand Coulee Dam and later by the Chief Joseph Dam . . . because it was not considered economical to construct fish passage facilities over the tremendous height of these dams and no practical way was known to prevent the young fish migrating downstream from passing over spillways and being mortally injured.[83]

An important observation is that mitigation measures were not undertaken because they were "not considered economical." Obviously, if the Bureau of Reclamation is able to direct BSFW officials to exclude unmitigated damages from economic evaluations of Reclamation projects, there is going to be little economic incentive for Reclamation to try to alleviate such harms. The present situation places Reclamation officials in a rather curious position. If they choose not to mitigate project damages, these damages will not be included in the benefit-cost calculation. If, on the other hand, they do try to make up for wildlife losses, the cost of doing so will be included in benefit-cost calculations. Fish and wildlife losses are real costs to society and should be recognized as such.

Finally, the Bureau of Reclamation shirks its legal obligation to enhance fish and wildlife resources by failing to make sure that efforts to mitigate damages are adequate and workable.[84] BSFW officials admit that "most estimates of wildlife mitigation don't come within 75 percent of making up the damage."[85] Even the damages that are "mitigated" might still occur. The difference between the proposed mitigation measures and those actually undertaken is significant. Often mitigation efforts are undertaken too late and in an inefficient manner.

A joint report by the Oregon Fish Commission and the Washington State Department of Fisheries describes their experience with respect to several Bureau dams on the Columbia River:

> Through their refusal to consider the importance of fishways, the U.S. Bureau of Reclamation ignored the protests of fish conservation agencies and as a result approximately 65% of the few fish ladders built were not constructed for some years after the dam was completed. Then, too, fish ladders constructed in the earlier part of the program were not efficient devices—a statement which is also applicable to early fish screens.[86]

Reclamation has displayed an alarming tendency to do too little, too late. Most fish and wildlife benefits are quantified in project reports under the assumption that the Bureau of Reclamation will follow the recommendations of BSFW regarding the operation of the project and the provision of facilities such as fish screens. Unfortunately, past experience demonstrates that there is no guarantee that the Bureau will undertake the steps needed to achieve the benefits that are claimed in project reports. The acuteness of this problem is increased by the failure of BSFW and Reclamation to return to the project sites during and after construction to estimate the extent to which the fish and wildlife benefits have been realized. Even the BSFW officials admit that "the follow-up program is weak."[87] Frank Dunkle, the Montana State fish and game director, recently summed up the problem:

> Congressional approval and funding is based on what is said and implied in paper planning, yet there is inadequate follow-up by your agency (BSFW) to see that accepted recommendations are put into effect. . . .
> Our experience with large water development projects

indicates that the plans we are given to evaluate are only tentative. They may bear little or no resemblance to actual project operations. There is no guarantee one project will not lead to another which will further alter the fish and wildlife habitat. To date we have found that when the Bureau of Reclamation must make a choice between irrigation, power or flood control on the one hand and fish and wildlife on the other; the irrigation, power or flood control needs are first fully served.[88]

RECOMMENDATIONS

To improve the deplorable state of current recreation and fish and wildlife evaluations, we recommend basic changes. Distributional weighting should be instituted to conform with the suggestions in Chapter 4. Double counting should be eliminated by permitting only one activity-day to be credited to a one-day visit and by clarifying the overlap between recreation and fish and wildlife activities. In the case of damage mitigation, the net loss to society which equals the cost of such mitigation should be recognized as a negative benefit and incorporated into projects' benefit-cost estimates. In the event that damages are not fully mitigated, the unmitigated losses should be evaluated (using the lost user days of fish and wildlife activities) and treated as a negative economic benefit of the project. Finally, there should be increased surveillance of Reclamation activities to guarantee that the proposed mitigation measures specified in project reports are successfully implemented.

e. Weather Modification

Americans in Vietnam are not the only people trying their hands at rainmaking. Westerners have been doing so for a long time. Like much else in the West, the attempt to stimulate precipitation by some artificial means has been taken over from the Indians by the Bureau of Reclamation. In light of the Bureau's dubious record regarding the environmental impacts of its projects, it is surprising that Congress has entrusted the major federal effort in weather modification research and development to the Bureau rather than to an agency with meteorological skills and responsibility.

According to the 1968 *Project Skywater Annual Report*, the Bureau got into weather modification when in the summer of 1961 "The late Senator Francis Case (South Dakota) approached Commissioner Floyd Dominy with an exciting challenge."[89] In fact, the approach was probably the other way around. Former Commissioner Dominy says that he and Senator Case were having lunch together "on another matter" in early 1961 when the senator happened to mention that a pilot in his state had been doing some cloud seeding work commercially and had sent some information and pictures to the senator to try to interest him in such undertakings. The pilot succeeded in raising the senator's interest. Commissioner Dominy quickly sensed an opportunity for the Bureau to get a new source of funds and work. "I'm not a stupid guy," he says. "Here was a senator interested in something so why shouldn't I encourage him a little?"[90]

Spurred on by Dominy, the Bureau's program in weather modification began with informal committee authorizations in 1961 that allowed diversion of some Bureau funds from other areas to finance a few small contract research projects. In 1962, Congress appropriated $100,000 specifically for weather modification research contracts.

The dominant characteristic of the program ever since has been growth. Appropriations for "Project Skywater," as it is optimistically called by Reclamation, have soared from $100,000 in 1962 to $6,692,600 in 1971. According to James Kerr, Washington Coordinator of Project Skywater, the program is well behind schedule even with its rapid growth.[91] In a 1966 report the Bureau spelled out its long-range plans for the program and anticipated an annual expenditure of some $10 million per year by 1970.[92]

Against this background of rapid expansion and grandiose plans, it is interesting to contrast Commissioner Dominy's 1964 testimony concerning expected levels of expenditure. In testimony asking for a nearly tenfold increase in program funding between 1964 and 1965, Commissioner

Dominy told the Senate Irrigation and Reclamation Subcommittee that the Bureau planned "the kind of program that we discussed with the Appropriations Committee starting out with a million dollars a year, and as we get it built up over a decade or two, perhaps up to as much as $3 million a year."[93] As so often before, and as with so many other federal agencies, once Reclamation got its foot in the door there was no stopping it. In the very next fiscal year (1966), Reclamation spent what Dominy had claimed would not be the level of expenditures for another "decade or two."

Perhaps the most significant aspect of the program was the fact that it grew so rapidly despite the scientific community's strong skepticism about the merits of weather modification research. Almost all published scientific evaluations reported that weather modification experiments from 1957 to 1963 showed no significant effects. Although commercial operators claimed to be able to increase rainfall, their claims were rarely if ever supported by published scientific data or subjected to independent scientific scrutiny.[94]

In 1961, Commissioner Dominy instructed the Bureau's Denver office to prepare a special report analyzing everything they could find on the subject of weather modification. After Dominy had read the report, he remarked, "It was all negative, all negative. Nobody had ever done anything." The report's criticisms of commercial cloud seeders led Dominy to conclude that one of the best-known commercial operators of the West was "a crook" who had "milked millions of dollars from innocent people."[95]

Thus when the Bureau pushed for a $1-million increase in Project Skywater appropriations in 1964, scientific evidence of the effectiveness of cloud seeding was still very limited. What little evidence did exist suggested that it might be possible to increase snowfall from certain types of mountain storms, but even this conclusion was put in guarded terms. The final report of President Eisenhower's Advisory Committee on Weather Control in 1957 found "a statistical basis to believe cloud seeding of winter storms in western mountains could increase precipitation ten to fifteen percent."[96]

Others remained unimpressed with the available evidence. The Committee on Atmospheric Sciences of the National Academy of Sciences reported in 1964 (the year that Dominy went after a million dollars for cloud seeding) that "it has not been demonstrated that precipitation from winter orographic storms can be increased significantly by seeding." The Committee went on to say, "the initiation of large-scale operational weather modification programs would be premature."[97]

Protests that the committee had not taken into account the evidence from commercial operations led to continued study and a revised report in 1966. This second report observed that "there is increasing but still ambiguous statistical evidence that precipitation from some types of clouds and storm systems can be modestly increased."[98] The committee admitted, however, that much of its evidence was gathered from the very commercial operations so vigorously denounced earlier by Dominy himself and by his own staff report.

The other major national spokesman for the scientific community at this time, the National Science Foundation (NSF), was equally pessimistic about the prospects for weather modification programs. The sixth Annual Report (1964) of the NSF Weather Modification Research Program noted that $1.1 million had been authorized in 1965 for Project Skywater, at a time when "many atmospheric scientists—perhaps the majority now engaged in research in this country—view the move toward large-scale engineering and development efforts in weather modification as premature."[99]

Nevertheless, in attempting to get a $1-million increase in funding for weather modification for 1965, Bureau officials overcame scientific doubts by ignoring them. They merely dangled extremely high, but purely speculative, benefits before the eyes of the project-hungry members of the Senate Irrigation and Reclamation Subcommittee. The senators snapped up the new idea without questioning in the least its advisability from a scientific point of view. As Senator Alan Bible (D-Nev.) noted:

> When the Bureau of Reclamation testified before our Appropriations Committee that an additional inch of precipitation above Glen Canyon would produce a runoff of 575,000 acre-feet, believe me, that sounded like something that should be accelerated without delay.[100]

Yet no independent scientific witnesses ever appeared before the subcommittee to corroborate the Bureau's earlier claim. Ultimately, the subcommittee approved the expenditure of a million nonreimbursable tax dollars for a project which lacked a formal benefit-cost analysis.

Even today the question of the effectiveness of weather modification attempts has not been resolved. Elwood Seaman, the Bureau's assistant to the commissioner for ecology, admits that the scientific community is split "about 50–50 on evaluation of results." The problem is that the changes anticipated from weather modification are difficult to distinguish from natural variations in precipitation. Even the most optimistic prediction of a 10–20 percent increase in mountain snowfall is well within the range of natural variation. "They know they aren't sure they make it rain or snow," says Seaman, referring to the Denver office's work on Project Skywater.[101] So fundamental are the measurement problems that Myron Tribus, chairman of the Federal Council for Science and Technology, recently wrote, "The fact is that the state of knowledge in precipitation modification is such that any announced specific goals are almost irrelevant. The output of current precipitation modification research is knowledge, not water."[102]

Knowledge is of course a valuable output, and the expenditure of a reasonable amount of federal funds to attain weather control information is thoroughly worthwhile. But the question remains, Is the Bureau of Reclamation the agency best suited to pursue such a goal? Should an agency with a demonstrated inability to act with sensitivity toward the environment be allowed the first chance to tinker with the weather? Until our knowledge is thorough, should not objective, purely scientific researchers be in charge of weather modification studies? Should the valuable goal of increasing knowledge about meteorological phenomena be subsumed under this particular agency's drive to attain an early operational status? An examination of some of the problems surrounding Project Skywater suggests that some other government agency might better administer federal research funds in this field.

The Bureau's Project Skywater is primarily touted as a research operation. However, since the Bureau does not have an in-house staff of trained meteorologists, it has created an Atmospheric Water Resources Research Division in Denver, headed by a meteorologist, Dr. Archie Cahan, to manage and monitor a contracting program. Former Commissioner Dominy explains why:

> We aren't a research outfit; we are an action outfit. I decided to leave all the research and study to others, to universities, the research firms. We'll put our engineering know-how at the top to guide it.[103]

The Bureau applied its political know-how at the top as well.

When Senator Case of South Dakota introduced legislation in 1962 to authorize the Bureau's official entrance into the field, he did so "with the understanding that a good portion of the work would go to South Dakota."[104] And it did. From December, 1961, to November, 1969, South Dakota received contracts worth $5,160,000—more than any other state. The second place money winner was Wyoming, with $3,923,000 worth of contracts; and third was Senator Bible's Nevada, with $3,306,000. As might be expected, the state with the greatest number of individual contracts was Colorado—the home state of Congressman Wayne Aspinall, chairman of the House Interior and Insular Affairs Committee.[105]

The story of South Dakota's honeymoon with the Bureau's program doesn't end with the contract sweepstakes. The Bureau's 1966 plan discussed the idea of "regionalization"—to develop regional or state centers to work in partnership with the Bureau's program. Curiously enough, the Bureau's 1966 plan confessed that "a regional research center has been established in embryonic form at South Dakota School of Mines and Technology."[106]

While such political wheeling and dealing is not unique or surprising, it is still cause for concern. Millions of dollars of nonreimbursable tax funds are going into a research program that has tremendous potential environmental, social, and legal consequences. It simply does not make sense for that research to be placed in an agency so traditionally prone to porkbarreling. Good science and political dealing don't mix.

A second serious weakness of placing this program under the Bureau's jurisdiction is the entirely unsatisfactory record that Reclamation has shown with respect to environmental side effects of its projects. Trained observers generally agree that the potential environmental effects of weather modification may be very great, and that knowledge from which to make good predictions is abysmally lacking. Yet the Bureau has never worried about predicting or guarding against these risks to the environment.

One of the first major attempts to identify potential environmental side effects of weather modification was made by the National Science Foundation in its 1966 report, *Weather and Climate Modification*. NSF warned:

> Anything that has a general and significant effect upon plants and animals, making some more abundant, others less so, is of primary concern to mankind, for it strikes at the very basis of human existence. Changes in weather and climate may be expected to have such effects.[107]

The report further noted that weather and climate fluctuations have been a molding influence on natural populations. Complex interrelationships of species depend not only on the normal levels of climate and precipitation, but also on patterns of weather variation. Thus, it is likely that changes in weather, even within the range of natural variation, would disrupt nature's balance if sustained over a period of years. Weather modification could change streamflow, thus altering nutrient levels and aquatic life and upsetting the competition among species.[108]

One of the most serious possible consequences of weather modification is its impact on pests and disease.

Many studies implicate unusual weather sequences for outbreaks of disease, insects, and weeds. Plant and animal
diseases, humidity-responsive bacterial and fungal diseases
of crops, and many insect outbreaks are possible consequences.[109] Any serious plan to modify the weather should
give these possibilities serious consideration.

The Bureau, of course, hopes that since two of its three
pilot projects are in sparsely populated high mountain areas,
these potentially damaging effects will be unimportant. But
the NSF report concluded that it is precisely such wild and
ecologically fragile areas that are most susceptible to damage
by weather modification. Wild natural areas are increasingly
confined and isolated so that migrations and inter-area transfers to replenish species or provide alternative habitat is generally infeasible.

All of these potential side effects are just that—potential.
No one knows exactly how weather modification will affect
the natural environment. No agency that has undertaken
weather modification research has devoted a very significant
amount of its research budget to these questions. The Bureau
of Reclamation has not done so. The simple lack of knowledge is the most serious environmental problem of weather
modification at this time.

Characteristically, the Bureau of Reclamation has taken
only small steps toward grappling with this problem. In May,
1968, the Bureau contracted with Drs. Charles Cooper and
William C. Jolly of the University of Michigan School of
Natural Resources to analyze the potential ecological impact
of weather modification programs. The budget for their study
was $31,625. A rough idea of priorities might be gained by
comparing this amount to the total of $17,997,000 author-
ized for the Bureau's weather modification research through
1968.

Yet the Bureau is very proud of the resulting report.[110]
James Kerr calls it excellent; Mr. Seaman describes Dr.
Cooper as "brilliant." In general the Cooper-Jolly report, a
genuinely fascinating document, was cautiously optimistic
about the kinds of programs that the Bureau is now considering. But the report was not an experimental or field investi-

gation and it left many questions unanswered. Its conclusions are tentative, more in the nature of suggestions. In effect, the report produced no new knowledge, but merely summarized present knowledge and recommended the kind of research that needs to be undertaken. It also warned against adopting new technologies, without sufficient understanding of their side effects. Finally the report observed that—

> there has so far not been a single biological field study completed and reported in the literature specifically designed to identify any aspect of the ecological effects of weather modification.[111]

Given this serious lack of information the report's recommendation for a research budget seems very reasonable indeed:

> Approximately 10% of the budget for any large-scale pilot project in weather modification, such as is now planned for the upper Colorado River Basin, should be allocated to a concurrent biological survey of the affected areas, to identify and evaluate conditions likely to be significantly altered by a deliberate change in climate. If the prospects of deliberate weather modification are good enough to justify field operations on the scale of the proposed Colorado River Basin Pilot Project, they are good enough to demand expenditures to develop procedures for identifying in advance some of the possible biological consequences of this new technology.[112]

The report further urged that serious attention be given to basic research on general ecosystem dynamics and the development of presently unavailable techniques for analyzing and predicting the subtle changes which may be caused by weather modification.

In view of the Cooper-Jolly recommendations, we examined the Bureau's program. Instead of evaluating the environmental risks before proceeding, the Bureau's weather modification program soars ahead precipitously. Since the start of Project Skywater, the Bureau has been developing a precipitation augmentation technology as rapidly as possible, "consistent with sound engineering practices."[113] The Bureau's program is now in a "transition phase," entailing a shift from basic research into an operational stage.

The main features of the new phase are large-scale, three- to five-year "pilot projects," designed to increase the usable water supply in the target regions while testing and evaluating new techniques. The three studies are: (1) the Colorado River Pilot Project, which will attempt to increase snow pack in winter mountain storms in the San Juan Mountains of Colorado; (2) the Pyramid Lake Project, which will attempt to increase snow pack and runoff in the water sheds of the Truckee and Carson rivers, which feed Pyramid Lake, Nevada; and (3) the Northern Great Plains Project in North Dakota, which will attempt to increase precipitation from rain storms.

A brief inspection of the Bureau's first three projects reveals Reclamation's apparent rejection of the Cooper-Jolly report, which the Bureau so eagerly praised. Of the three projects, only the Colorado River Pilot Project includes any ecological investigations. James Kerr claims that "all future pilot projects will probably have ecological monitoring —assuming that we can afford it."[114]

Dr. Cooper says that the Bureau of Reclamation responded to his report's suggestion for basic ecosystem research "about the way you would expect, that it is not their job."[115] The Bureau sees its job as supplying more water for the West as rapidly as possible. In this respect the Bureau is running Project Skywater consistently with former Commissioner Dominy's idea that "we are an action outfit, not a research outfit." Action apparently means making rain and snow in a hurry, ecology be damned.

Kerr is quite frank in admitting, for example, that the formulation of the Pyramid Lake "pilot project" came from political pressure to produce more water and not from a concern for scientific research.* The goal of the project is not experimentation or monitoring of effects of weather modifica-

* See Chapter 7 for more details about the Pyramid Lake controversy involving Indian water rights.

tion techniques, but simply "to get more water for the receding lake."[116] While the chief environmental effect hoped for is beneficial in the short run, there is no ecological investigation or monitoring planned in conjunction with the project. The excuse, of course, is that it was impossible to design an ecological research aspect of the project because of the short time allowed.

But this is exactly the point of criticism. The Pyramid Lake Project is a sterling example of how politics can make bad science. It is not a good investment of the taxpayers' research dollar to spend it on a hastily conceived project without necessary related fundamental research.

In essence, the Pyramid Lake Pilot Project is just another "rescue project," so common to the Bureau's history. The Newlands Irrigation Project has caused an intolerable set of environmental side effects to Pyramid Lake, and the Bureau has come in with a handy-dandy fix-it project to protect its own project interests and give it another job to do. This time the label is weather modification instead of drainage installation.

Former Commissioner Dominy sees a bright future for the Bureau "if they don't take weather modification away from us."[117] The Bureau jealously guards Project Skywater, as it does any program which produces another drop of water, as the source of more justification for its own existence. This situation itself causes one to doubt the objectivity and comprehensiveness of the science that will come out of the program in the long run. The 1968 Annual Report, for example, calls cloud seeding the total program:

> While other techniques have been suggested from time to time, Project Skywater does not now include research on these ideas because cloud seeding seems to be the technique most likely to attain early operational status.[118]

This attitude suggests that a broad range of alternative ideas is not receiving careful attention. Similarly, ecological research takes second place to the "action" goal of producing more water, and with water, more program funds.

In reviewing the Bureau's weather modification program, we find that the truly objective scientific analysis essential to successful weather modification development is missing from Reclamation's program. Political porkbarreling, shortsighted defense of the agency-empire, dubious benefit projections, and token recognition of potentially huge environmental side effects all discredit the Bureau's Project Skywater. Since weather modification is still a new science requiring extensive basic research, we recommend that Congress shift federal weather modification programs from the Bureau of Reclamation to a scientifically oriented agency like the National Science Foundation or the National Oceanic and Atmospheric Administration. Whichever agency sponsors such programs, however, it should delay pilot projects until sufficient research has been done to guarantee that such projects will not harm man and his environment.

f. Reclamation and Ecology

Despite the general belief that Western water is as valuable as gold, the Bureau still does not recognize water as a scarce resource. In other words, Bureau projects treat water as free for the taking, even though the scarcity of Western water is Reclamation's *raison d'être*. The economic value of water does not enter the Bureau's calculation of project costs. We recommend that the Bureau calculate the value of alternative future uses of water as an opportunity cost of Reclamation projects. Whenever water is used by a Bureau project, society is deprived of the enormous value of the water for alternative purposes. This value should not be blithely ignored.

The Bureau's blasé attitude extends to its general approach toward water quality. Reclamation projects continue to plague the West with severe problems of sedimentation, salinity, and undiluted waste. Despite the environmental-protection rhetoric continually spewed out in Reclamation press releases, the Bureau has made no major shifts in its basic practices. As a leading EPA official observed:

> There has been no change in the Bureau of Reclamation's attitude toward water quality as far as construction is concerned. There is still no operation of projects for the purpose of improving water quality.[120]

Even acts of Congress seem to have little effect on the Bureau of Reclamation. In the National Environmental Policy Act (NEPA) of 1969, Congress directed all federal agencies to "develop methods and procedures . . . which will insure that presently unquantified environmental amenities and values may be given appropriate consideration in decision-making along with economic and technical considerations."[121] Although the Bureau prepares environmental impact statements for prospective projects, its perception of what should be included in these statements is somewhat narrow. As the Environmental Defense Fund aptly noted, Reclamation's Four Corners thermal generating power plant would utilize 40,000 acre-feet of scarce water annually. Yet, the Bureau made no effort to discuss or evaluate the benefits that would have been reaped from alternative uses of that water. Such obliviousness to alternative resource development is hardly the "appropriate consideration" of environmental impacts which NEPA calls for. More important, the Bureau's environmental impact statement did not even recognize the unique scenic and cultural value of the territory affected by the Four Corners development. Further, the Black Mesa land has long had a deep religious significance to the Hopi and Navajo Indians; the Bureau of Reclamation did not discuss the deleterious impact of its efforts on this Indian heritage.[122]

The incompleteness of the environmental impact statements is only part of the problem. Even complete environmental discussions come too late to affect determination of project design or project feasibility. Reclamation undercuts its critics by waiting until the feasibility studies are underway before performing its comprehensive environmental studies; it then pretends that these projects are too far along to stop. If the critics continue to object, nothing prevents the Bureau from engaging them in a prolonged discussion while going ahead with the project.

We recommend that the Bureau of Reclamation prepare an extensive environmental impact statement for all projects during the initial reconnaissance investigations. Public hearings, announced through the local news media and in the *Federal Register*, should then be held in the project area and in Washington before beginning an economic feasibility study.

Even extensive discussion and review of environmental impacts is not a sufficient solution, however. The political reality of project development is such that only quantified benefits and costs significantly affect project design, operation, and economic feasibility. The Water Resources Council recognized this by setting unit dollar values for estimating recreation and fish and wildlife benefits. Although the WRC and the Bureau admit that these unit values are a crude way to estimate benefits, they recognize the political necessity of arriving at some dollar figures for those project impacts.

Why shouldn't environmental consequences of Reclamation projects also be given dollar values? Without such consideration, "tangible benefits" such as irrigation or power overshadow ecological effects. For example, in the 1960s the Bureau of Reclamation wanted to flood major portions of the Grand Canyon by building Bridge Canyon and Marble Canyon dams on the Colorado. As usual, the Bureau paid lip service to environmental considerations in the narrative section of its project reports. However, when it came to placing dollar values on project effects, environmental impacts weren't mentioned at all and played no part in the benefit-cost evaluation. Consequently, the Bureau of Reclamation added up the "tangible" benefits and costs of its projects, found that the dollar value of benefits exceeded the estimated costs, concluded that the projects were economically justified, and sent them on to Congress.

Fortunately, Congress blocked both projects. Significantly, the Bureau failed to get the dams authorized not because of unacceptably adverse environmental impacts. Instead, Grand Canyon was saved because Alan Carlin (of the RAND Corporation) and the Sierra Club successfully demonstrated to congressmen that the Bureau had incorrectly evaluated the project's power benefits. A correct benefit esti-mate, they argued, would have reduced the project's benefit-cost ratios below the necessary 1.0.[123]

The Grand Canyon controversy is not the only instance in which dollar estimation of ecological impacts would have helped to ensure rational project evaluation and design. Pres-ently, inadequate dollar values are placed on the nation's fish and wildlife resources. Except for the Bureau's spotty dam-age mitigation efforts, its only concern is to evaluate the fish and wildlife as a resource for fishermen and game hunters. However, unique habitats and breeding grounds for rare fish and wildlife species should receive prominent consideration as a valuable national resource—wholly apart from their value to hunters and fishermen.

Similarly, the ecological disturbances and disrupting effects on wildlife of Reclamation's weather modification programs should be studied and given dollar benefit and cost figures. Finally, the historical and cultural costs of desecrating sacred Indian lands and famed natural wonders should be systematically calculated instead of being neglected as an "intangible" effect.

A systematic set of economic values for such impacts should be drawn up by the Environmental Protection Agency and approved by Congress. While the primitive state of knowledge about ecological impacts might limit the accuracy of such estimates, this certainly does not diminish the need for them. An economic analyst is deluding himself if he thinks that somewhat inaccurate estimates of environmental im-pacts would reduce the precision of the benefit-cost esti-mates. The various systematic biases already incorporated in current benefit-cost estimates dwarf any new uncertainty cre-ated by attaching dollar values to ecological effects. Most benefits—like the unit day values assigned to recreation and fish and wildlife activities—are already estimated using fairly crude benefit indicators. It is probably better for benefit-cost estimates to be inaccurate and complete than to be inac-curate and incomplete. Political opposition—not a lack of expertise—is the principal stumbling block preventing eco-logical impact quantification. We recommend that EPA contract with several leading private economists—economists at Resources for the Future, RAND Corporation, Brookings Institution, and former members of the Harvard Water Resources Program (Professors Stephen Marglin, Robert Dorfman, Otto Eckstein, et al.) have expertise in this field —to make an intensive study of how ecological impacts can be quantified and included in future Reclamation benefit-cost calculations. Only then will the Bureau be able to make a rational allocation of the nation's resources.

Distorted Technical Criteria

a. Faulty Data

Perhaps the Bureau of Reclamation's greatest difficulty is a serious shortage of reasonably precise and relevant information. To estimate irrigation benefits with accuracy, for example, requires precise information concerning the quality of the land to be irrigated, the type of crops to be grown, and the amount of water to be supplied. Similarly, to estimate project costs correctly requires exact data on how much the federal government will have to pay for project construction and maintenance. We have already examined several of the shortcomings of Bureau data—overevaluation of irrigation benefits and a failure to take environmental data into account, for example. There are other, more general, indications that the information used by the Bureau to justify its projects is unreliable.

COST OVERRUNS

Since its creation in 1902, the Bureau has displayed an alarming inability to live up to its original cost estimates. In 1955, the Hoover Commission on Organization of the Executive Branch of Government observed:

The financial studies of the 90 projects involving irrigation (excepting the Missouri River Basin projects which are in the early stages) showed as of June 30, 1952:

The estimated total cost at the time of authorization	$1,580,000,000
The 1952 estimated total cost to complete	3,317,720,000
Total expended to June 30, 1952	1,968,933,800

The increase in estimated cost to complete construction over the estimates at the times of authorization can be attributed in part to the extension of original projects, and, to some extent, to rising prices. There can be no doubt, however, that there was serious underestimation in this 110-percent increase of cost and . . . at least some part would not have been authorized if the Congress had been better advised.[1]

Since the Hoover Commission's exposé of the Bureau's dismal record, the Bureau's performance has become even worse. Estimating cost overruns for 120 major projects, based on data provided in the Bureau's 1969 *Summary Report of the Commissioner*, we found the following:

Estimated total cost of projects at time of authorization	$1,392,142,000
Federal expenditure total as of June 30, 1969	3,968,436,000
Excess of actual over-estimated costs	2,576,294,000[2]

The rise in costs (reflected in the 1969 data) over those costs originally authorized is nearly 200 percent, far larger than the 110-percent figure for 1955. In short, even by this conservative estimate,* cost overruns are accelerating.

* While the Hoover Commission computed cost overruns in terms of the estimated total cost to complete the Bureau's authorized projects, we computed only the total actual federal expenditures to date for projects. This latter method should incorporate a conservative bias in cost overrun estimates since many of the projects considered are still under construction. More money will be spent on these, and the cost overruns are likely to rise. As in the Hoover Commission Study, we used the estimated total cost at the time of authorization as the base point for all cost estimates. To determine the cost overrun, we then subtracted the estimated costs at authorization from the total expenditures to date. All completed projects and unfinished projects for which costs had already exceeded original estimates were included in the computations.

These figures also indicate that original cost estimates were artificially low. Such inaccurate estimates inflated the benefit-cost ratios that were used to justify project authorization and appropriations. During the Senate Appropriations Committee hearings on the Bureau's 1971 budget, Senator Allen J. Ellender (D-La.) uncovered several instances in which original Bureau cost estimates failed to provide for eventual project needs. The San Luis unit of the Central Valley Project in California typifies the many Bureau cost overruns exposed during the hearings. Upon questioning Commissioner Ellis Armstrong, Senator Ellender learned that the San Luis project costs had increased by $45 million in a single year—almost 10 percent of estimated costs. Since it often takes ten to twenty years to build a Reclamation project, the completion cost of the San Luis unit could turn out to be double or triple the original estimate. Commissioner Armstrong's explanation for this cost overrun consisted of noting "miscellaneous increases" and that "some of the early estimates were too low."[3] These excuses, which hardly seem sufficient to justify the drastic cost increases, are indicative of the carelessness with which Bureau benefit-cost ratios are developed.

The General Accounting Office (GAO), the congressional unit which audits the activities of executive branch agencies, found that the Bureau also had failed to warn Congress of San Luis project cost overruns that Reclamation officials already knew were going to occur:

> The Bureau advised Congress that a decision had been made to substitute a more expensive detention reservoir for a siphon to provide increased flood control benefits and that the state of California would pay 55% of the additional costs. However, Bureau records showed that, at the time it so informed the Congress, the Bureau was aware that the State was not willing to share in the additional costs for the detention reservoir. Subsequently, the detention reservoir was constructed and all of the additional costs—about $2.7 million—were paid by the Federal Government.[4]

In addition to such blatant deception, the Bureau has been guilty of more subtle prodigality. The GAO cited recent instances in which the Bureau chose to replace defective rail-road facilities with improved facilities, while only equivalent replacement was needed:

> GAO believes that the improved facilities were provided because the Bureau had not clearly defined the Government's obligation for equivalent replacement facilities. . . . In those instances where sufficient information was available to estimate the costs involved, GAO believes that the Bureau could have saved about $436,000 by providing only those replacement facilities needed to meet the Government's obligation for equivalent replacement.[5]

Although some cost increases reflect annual inflationary price rises, these should be planned for in the original estimates; the project cost overruns are much too large to be explained away entirely by such considerations. The Bureau could—and should—have foreseen not only inflationary increases but also many later additions to projects.* Undoubtedly, a significant portion of the increased costs stemmed from the Bureau's failure to estimate costs accurately at the time of initial project authorization.

The problem of spiraling costs is not completely beyond the Bureau's control. Although it cannot, of course, constrain rising construction costs, it can certainly eliminate faulty cost estimates, "miscellaneous" cost increases, and simple extravagance—which together cause Reclamation projects to cost, on the average, almost three times as much as originally estimated.

IS THE BENEFIT DATA ALSO BAD?

The accuracy of the raw data on which the Bureau's project benefit estimations are based is more difficult to ascertain, because the Bureau never has conducted follow-up studies to determine if its benefit predictions have been realized. However, there exists some evidence that the benefits the Bureau hopes for are greater than the benefits it gets.

* See Chapter 3 for a detailed discussion of how the Bureau frequently fails to calculate for adverse consequences of its initial projects, which it should have anticipated, and then calls these created needs "benefits" to justify an expansion unit.

Several experts believe that irrigation benefit figures are greatly exaggerated. Neil Lane, the Soil Conservation Service representative on the Water Resource Council Task Force, suggested that Bureau of Reclamation officials "probably inflate their irrigation benefits."[6] William A. Green, former Department of Agriculture representative on the Water Resources Council Task Force, also admitted that "the quantification of the agricultural outputs themselves is also highly suspect. The original data itself is suspect."[7] As noted previously, the Bureau has made no attempt to collect data on the negative effects of its irrigation efforts. Further, Reclamation gathers information only on the amount and value of crops for acres receiving Bureau water without specifying what portion of these crops is directly attributable to this water. In Chapter 2's discussion of crop surpluses and displaced farmers, we had to rely almost entirely on data from the Department of Agriculture and a private study made by Professors William Easter and Charles Howe, simply because the Bureau has never checked its own figures.[8]

Reclamation statisticians responsible for collecting this data have no conception of the meaning of the data they have collected. Aldon Nielsen, chief of the Bureau's Economics and Statistics Branch, was able to offer the following insights:

> I have no idea of the percentage of the total amount of crops that were dependent on Reclamation water. I don't know whether it would be better to assume that all of the crops listed in our data were dependent on Reclamation water. I do know that Reclamation deserves some portion of the credit. . . . I don't know if it's half of that produced. . . . I don't know if it's a quarter of that produced. . . . I have no idea.[9]

In view of the Bureau's inability to comprehend the significance of its own crop production data, it is fortunate that Professors Easter and Howe independently attempted to determine the crop production directly attributable to Reclamation projects. If the Bureau can gather and present only meaningless and even misleading data regarding its projects, then there is no reason to waste the taxpayers' money in collecting it.*

In view of the dramatic cost overruns and the possibility that benefit data are also faulty, the GAO should attempt to determine project by project the extent to which the Bureau's benefit and cost estimates have been realized. The Bureau has not done so and shows no inclination to do so in the near future, and its poor record indicates that an outside study is needed.

Unlike the *theoretical* biases in the Bureau's benefit-cost techniques discussed earlier, the inaccuracy of project *data* cannot be eliminated by a simple revision of evaluation procedures. As long as the Bureau continues to collect faulty data, the General Accounting Office and the Office of Management and Budget should increase their supervision of Reclamation's benefit-cost estimates, by conducting more preliminary and follow-up studies of Bureau projects.

b. The Discount Rate

Compounding the built-in bias of the Bureau's benefit-cost analysis is the extraordinarily low discount rate included in the analyses. The discount rate is used to express society's preference for consumption now rather than later.

Consumers recognize the benefits of current as opposed to future income. The flexibility of having money now instead of later gives the consumer several major options. He can spend the money now to meet current needs or avoid

---

* While avoiding discussion of the accuracy and relevance of their irrigation benefit data, Bureau officials continually referred us to the evidence that their recreation benefits had been underestimated in the past, a point we concede about *past* recreation benefits. We do not accept this claim as a general defense of all their benefit estimates or even their current recreation benefits. The National Parks Service, which formerly estimated Reclamation's recreation benefits, was more conservative than the Bureau of Outdoor Recreation, which now makes these estimates. And it is still too early to know for sure how accurate the Bureau of Outdoor Recreation's data are, since there is no follow-up data on their recent estimates.

future inflation; he can keep the money readily accessible in a checking account to use for unexpected bills or to take advantage of a profitable investment opportunity that arises; or he may decide to invest the money in a savings account, stocks, or bonds in order to earn interest on it.

Individuals' preferences for present versus future income result in market interest rates. For the sake of simplicity, suppose that one interest rate establishes equilibrium in the capital markets of the economy. Furthermore, assume that capital markets are perfect and that the consumer is free to borrow and to lend at this prevailing interest rate. The classical result, derived by Irving Fisher,[10] is that an individual seeking the most satisfying pattern of consumption will choose his investments to maximize the present value of his money at the current market rate of interest. For example, if the prevailing interest rate is 10 percent, a consumer would need to invest only $82.64 today in order to get back $100 two years from now. It is for this reason we say that the present value of $100 two years in the future is only $82.64. The general formula businessmen use for the present value of any income Y_t at a future year t, where r corresponds to the interest rate, is:

$$\text{Present Value} = Y_t / (1+r)^t.$$

Or for the example presented previously,

$$\text{Present Value} = \frac{\$100}{(1+.10)^2} = \$82.64.$$

Like consumers, the government must also allocate its resources over time. Policymakers have to choose whether to build dams benefiting people living many years from now or to build projects that bring most of their benefits in the near future. Many current taxpayers who bear the real cost of the Bureau's projects won't even be alive to enjoy the future benefits. To meet this problem, the Bureau attempts to discount the future costs and benefits to a present value in a manner identical to a private businessman's present value computations. The only difference is that the "discount rate" replaces the interest rate in the calculation.

Most costs of Bureau projects occur in the first ten years of construction, while most benefits of Bureau projects ac-

crue between ten and fifty years after the initiation of construction. The higher the discount rate, the lower the present
value of benefits far in the future. Project costs, on the other
hand, are not as significantly affected by the discount rate,
since most of these costs are incurred in the near future. As a
result, the Bureau can jack up its benefit-cost ratios by using
a low discount rate, i.e., by placing little emphasis on the
needs and desires of present generations.

BUREAU OF RECLAMATION PRACTICES

It is not surprising, therefore, that the Bureau has attempted
to keep the discount rate as low as possible. Table 4-A
summarizes the discount rates used in economic feasibility
studies from 1959 through 1971. The rate from 1959
through 1961 was set at 2.5 percent.* Since this rate was set
arbitrarily by the Bureau of Reclamation before 1961, it is
not surprising that the rate never increased from 1959 to
1961. The Bureau kept the rate at the low level since a
higher, more appropriate level would have made justifying
projects difficult.

In 1962, Senate Document 97 (SD 97) was approved by
President Kennedy. This document revised the procedure for
determining the discount rate. The new procedure called for
the discount rate to be "based upon the average rate of interest payable by the Treasury on interest-bearing marketable
securities of the United States outstanding at the end of the
fiscal year preceding such computation which, upon original
issue, had terms to maturity of 15 years or more."[12]

This provision did not require that the new discount rate
be used in a feasibility study if this study had already begun,
so that—since many studies often require several years to
complete—this upward revision of the discount rate did not
affect a number of ongoing evaluations. Completed studies
were also exempt from this provision. The Bureau of Reclamation did not hesitate to advise its regional staffs to ignore
the discount rate change for current planning purposes. In a

---

*According to the Bureau of Reclamation, this discount rate
was intended to reflect what economists call the social rate of time
preference.[11]

Speedletter transmitted two weeks after SD 97 was approved, Assistant Commissioner William Palmer issued the following instructions:

> A new interest rate, which will very likely be higher, will become applicable shortly after the beginning of the next fiscal year. In order to avoid frequent revisions during the course of a given investigation, the interest rate which prevails at the time a given study is undertaken should be used throughout that study. This means that it will not be necessary to redo the project justification analyses each time the interest rate changes during the course of an investigation.[13]

Even if the discount rate specified in SD 97 had been used in all feasibility studies, this figure would still have been below the value it should have been. Interest rates on all long-term government bonds with over fifteen years till maturity from the date of issue were supposed to be averaged to determine the SD 97 rate. This permits the rates on government bonds which have only a year or two before they fall due to be included in the discount rate average; the interest rates on such bonds are thus usually much lower than the rates on more recently issued bonds. Even the Commissioner of Reclamation believed that the SD 97 formula understated the cost of long-term capital to the government—the principle upon which the SD 97 rate was based. In an internal memorandum to the Assistant Secretary of the Interior for water and power development, then Commissioner Dominy made the following admission:

> We agree that the current cost of long-term money to the federal government today is greater than the 3.253 percent interest rate we are now using and that, in estimating project effects, use of a higher rate would be appropriate.[14]

The chief of the Bureau of Reclamation's Economics Branch also found that a revision was long overdue:

> The discount rate was much lower than it should have been in order to have any relation at all to social time preference or the opportunity cost of capital.[15]

Recent revisions, however, have not yet affected the billions of dollars' worth of improperly justified backlogged projects. In 1968, the Water Resources Council revised the discount rate procedures for all project evaluations, while exempting previously authorized projects from these provisions.[16] No longer was the discount rate to be determined by the average of all outstanding long-term Treasury bonds that would fall due fifteen years or more *from the date of issue.* Now the discount rate was to be an average of the current rates on long-term Treasury bonds that had fifteen years or more *from today* before they fell due. Based on this 1968 procedure, the Bureau of Reclamation currently uses a 5.375 percent discount rate, which is still the lowest rate permitted in the federal government.[17]

WHAT SHOULD THE DISCOUNT RATE BE?

The Treasury bond rates do not reflect the true or present cost of capital—the principle upon which SD 97 was based. Because of rising interest rates, the Treasury has been reluctant to issue any long-term bonds since 1963. If current federal investments were financed by bond issues, the interest rate on long-term Treasury bonds would rise dramatically. The relevance of the Treasury bond rate is even more dubious when we note that the federal government does not finance the Bureau's projects through long-term bond issues but through taxes.

The opportunity cost of the private spending which is displaced by taxes is perhaps a more meaningful way to determine the proper discount rate. The private rate of return takes on added importance when it is realized that Bureau projects often displace private power and municipal and industrial water projects, all of which the Bureau evaluates in terms of financing at private interest rates. Thus, to rationalize the benefit estimation procedure and to reflect the true cost of capital to the federal government, one solution would be to use a long-term private riskless interest rate as the discount rate. The Joint Economic Committee's Subcommittee on Economy in Government conducted extensive in-

vestigations in 1968 into this discount rate issue and concluded that "the appropriate discount rate concept is the
opportunity cost of displaced private spending."[18] Most of
the economists appearing before the subcommittee recommended that the discount rate would then preclude the displacement of private investments that are more profitable
than the Bureau's projects.[19]

However, one major school of economic thought is not in
direct accord with this rationale. Professor Stephen Marglin
observes that the social rate of discount need have no
relation to any market interest rate.[20] Rather, Marglin con-
tends, the discount rate can be whatever the national policymakers believe to be the collective preference of society for
present as opposed to future consumption.

What is clear, though, is that a correct discount rate must
be the same for all federal agencies. It is not a parameter to
be manipulated at will to suit the whims of Reclamation
officials. If the discount rate were standardized across all
government agencies, there would be a substantial rise in the
rate used in evaluating Reclamation projects.

If any existing agency is capable of making this kind of
intertemporal judgment, it is the Office of Management and
Budget (OMB) in close consultation with the President and
Congress, not the parochially biased Bureau of Reclamation.
And the OMB maintains that the most appropriate indicator
of society's intertemporal preferences toward aggregate consumption is the real opportunity cost of capital.[21] Although
economists are in conflict as to the appropriate value of the
discount rate, one thing is clear: The discount rate should be
the same for all government agencies—including the Water
Resources Council and affected agencies like the Bureau of
Reclamation. If the current practice of setting a minimum
discount rate is replaced by requiring that all federal agencies
use the same rate, the OMB and Congress could finally rationalize the prolonged discount rate controversy.

Currently, the OMB is engaging in protracted negotiations with the Water Resources Council on the discount rate
question. The OMB's assistant director, Donald B. Rice,

stated the OMB position quite succinctly in a memo to the executive director of the Water Resources Council:

> In determining the discount rate for government investments in water resources, we believe that the real opportunity cost of capital should be used. We recognize that the rate of movement from the current level of 5⅛ % will have to be worked out but a significant increase from the current level should be made immediately.[22]

Appropriate revision of the discount rate should put the rate in the vicinity of 10 percent. A required rate of 10 percent would be equal to the discount rate currently used by the Department of Defense for its military construction program.[23]

The effect of such a revision would be significant. The example displayed in Table 4-B and Table 4-C demonstrates the effect of increasing the interest rate from 4⅞ percent (the rate used by Reclamation in 1970) to 10 percent (the rate used by the Defense Department). As expected, the increased discount rate reduces the benefit-cost ratio significantly. A project which once had a favorable ratio of 1.39 now displays a ratio of 0.58—well below the 1.0 cutoff point for acceptable projects.

The significance of this discount rate revision has not escaped the National Waterways Conference—the lobbyist for the profiteers discussed in Chapter 6. This conference commented on the previously cited OMB memo:

> In another shocker, OMB indicated that the "opportunity cost" principle should be the guide for establishing the discount rate. Such a rate would probably amount to between 10 and 15 percent, and would doom almost all water resource projects.[24]

We agree that an appropriate discount rate would weed out those projects whose benefits are not greater than their costs. If a meaningful discount rate will significantly decrease Bureau of Reclamation appropriations, so be it. Projects that are not in the national interest should not continue to be adopted under the guise of economic desirability.

c. Electrical Power and Municipal and Industrial Water Benefits

Without electric power and municipal and industrial (M&I) water benefits, very few Reclamation projects would be economically or financially feasible. Although the Bureau of Reclamation still perceives itself as primarily a water agency, it needs the revenues from power plants to justify and help pay for the large subsidies given to irrigation by Reclamation projects. Bureau officials also can be expected to claim more municipal and industrial water benefits as a means of justifying future projects. In fact, the President's Water Resources Council (WRC) predicted that municipal water requirements in the Reclamation states will more than triple and industrial water requirements in these regions will supposedly increase by more than 400 percent by the year 2020.[25] In light of the significance of these project objectives, we analyzed the Bureau's claimed benefits and procedures for estimating them to see if these benefits too are systematically overestimated.

THE ALTERNATIVE COST PRINCIPLE

The primary method used by the Bureau to estimate power and M&I water benefits is called the "alternative cost principle."* One weakness with this principle lies with its permissive ambiguity. In 1962 the Water Resources Council tried to clarify it:

> The usual practice is to measure the benefit in terms of the cost of achieving the same result by the most likely alternative means that would exist in the absence of the project.[27]

The key phrase is "most likely." Since the "most likely alternative" need not be the most economical, and since determin-

* Some municipal and industrial water benefits are also calculated by direct estimation technique established by the Water Resources Council in its 1962 Senate Document ⨣97. Under this technique, the Bureau can estimate M&I benefits by looking at "the average cost of projects planned or recently constructed in the general region."[26] To the extent that past project benefit estimates are distorted due to flaws in the alternative cost principle, the estimates based on this direct estimation technique will also be inaccurate. This procedure merely perpetuates past errors by letting the costs of past unjustifiable projects serve as surrogate benefit estimates for future projects.

ing which of several alternatives is most likely is necessarily subjective, Bureau power and M&I benefits tend to be exaggerated. In the absence of special congressional authorization, however, the alternative cost principle should be defined in terms of the "least cost alternative" instead of a "most likely alternative."

Two RAND Corporation economists, Alan Carlin and William E. Hoehn, studied the power benefits for the Hualapai Dam (formerly, the Bridge Canyon Dam) and the Marble Canyon Dam.[28] These were the Bureau's two efforts to dam up the Grand Canyon. Carlin and Hoehn concluded that proper consideration of feasible alternatives lowered the benefit-cost ratios of both projects from their former feasibility of 2.0 and 1.7 to ratios significantly below 1.0.[29]

In spite of these embarrassing revelations, the Bureau refuses to establish more rigorous guidelines for selection of the alternatives to their projects. Daniel McCarthy, chief of the Reclamation Planning Division, made the following response to our suggestion that more precise directives be issued:

> Planning still has a large element of judgment. You have to give the man in the field a chance to use his ingenuity. You can't tie him down with standards.[30]

It is difficult to share Mr. McCarthy's enthusiasm for the creativity of the persons responsible for the Bureau's economic evaluations. This ingenuity of the men in the field most often serves to promote only the interests of the Bureau of Reclamation. The imaginative nature of Reclamation officials does not appear to extend to consideration of alternatives which would lower a project's benefit-cost ratio.

PRIVATE ALTERNATIVES—THE RATE OF INTEREST

One method of computing the alternative cost is to look at possible private sources of power or water. Consideration of such private alternatives also biases the benefit evaluation upward. As was pointed out earlier in this chapter, Bureau projects are evaluated using very low discount rates. Private power projects or water supply projects, however, cannot now obtain financing at market interest rates as low as the Bureau's discount rate. David Flipse, chief of the Bureau's Economics Branch, pointed out that alternative projects are often assumed to have very high finance costs. In Mr. Flipse's words:

> The most likely alternative is usually privately financed at whatever the local rates happen to be. Sometimes these rates are Aaa [low-risk private interest rates], but often they tend toward the Baa [high-risk interest rates] end of the bond spectrum.[31]

Flipse's admission that private alternatives often must be financed at high interest rates indicates that the justification of many Reclamation projects is questionable. For example, if a power project was going to fulfill a predictably strong demand, financing at low-risk (Aaa) interest rates would be no problem. The necessity of high-cost financing indicates that the projected power or M&I demand is somewhat dubious.

The great disparity between the project's discount rate and the private rate of interest results in an overestimation of the alternative cost—a good deal of which is finance cost. The interest and discount rates should be treated uniformly for the private facility and Reclamation projects, respectively. Failure to evaluate Reclamation projects and private alternatives using the same rates distorts the efficient allocation of the nation's resources and biases the Bureau's power and M&I development.

MULTIPURPOSE ALTERNATIVES

Yet another objection to the present procedures is that multipurpose alternatives are not considered.[32] Instead, only single-purpose alternatives are evaluated. This biases the benefit evaluation of the Bureau project because almost any public or private alternative serves multiple purposes. It is difficult to imagine a power project which would not bring the same regional growth and indirect benefits claimed for Bureau projects. An alternative power or M&I project also might produce flood control and recreation benefits. Such benefits from alternative projects should be recognized.

Daniel McCarthy, chief of Reclamation Planning, took exception to such a suggestion:

> If you considered multi-purpose alternatives you'd get a lower value for your benefits. But everybody in the industry is convinced that the higher value should be the floor.[33]

The consensus of Reclamation interest groups is not a particularly compelling reason for overestimating project benefits. The Bureau should revise existing procedures to subtract miscellaneous benefits of alternative projects from their costs, just as it counts miscellaneous benefits in computing net desirability of its own projects, thereby obtaining the net alternative cost solely attributable to power or M&I water.

IGNORING POWER ALTERNATIVES MADE POSSIBLE BY TECHNOLOGICAL PROGRESS

The Study Group also found that the Bureau ignored technological progress in its electric power and M&I benefit evaluations. The Bureau of Reclamation assumes that annual power benefits are equal to the annual alternative cost of power over the life of the project, generally fifty to a hundred years. However, the alternative cost thirty or forty years from now may be much less than the alternative cost of current sources of power. Cheaper methods of generating electricity are constantly being developed. The Federal Power Commission recently concluded that the following advanced methods of producing electricity will be technically feasible by 1980: thermoelectric generation, thermionic generation, fuel cells, and magnetohydrodynamic generation.[34]

In its 1970 National Power Survey, the Federal Power Commission dealt with the effect of this changing technology on hydro power justifications. It concluded:

> The economic feasibility of a number of the potential installations are not currently firm and economic indicators are constantly changing. When alternative methods of providing peaking capacity are investigated, it may well be that

certain of the potential hydro projects will not be the economic choice.[35]

But what can be done to incorporate the effect of future technological advances into power benefit evaluation? Former member of the President's Council of Economic Advisors, Professor Otto Eckstein, has suggested that "a good rule of thumb would be to multiply the present benefit estimates of projects with economic lives of fifty years by 0.84, and projects with lives of a hundred years by 0.74."[36] This procedure would adjust power benefits to account for the fact that cheaper power sources will be available in the future. We concur with Eckstein's recommendation. The Bureau's present assumption of a stagnant technology diverts society's funds into sources of future power supply that may well be less efficient than alternative future sources.

RECOMMENDATIONS

In summary, current evaluation procedures consistently overestimate power and M&I water supply benefits. This problem is becoming particularly acute as the Bureau begins to utilize less promising sites for its projects. The Federal Power Commission even acknowledges that the Bureau has already exploited the most promising power opportunities:

> The best hydro sites in the [Western] region have already been at least partially developed; however, more will be developed incidental to irrigation and flood control projects.[37]

The Bureau should not be allowed to become further entrenched as an inefficient power and M&I water supplier. It appears that the bulk of the Bureau's justifiable efforts in this direction have been concluded. By adopting the revisions suggested in this section, unwarranted expenditures for hydroelectric power and for municipal and industrial water will be curtailed.

d. Secondary Benefits

In the previous sections of this chapter, we analyzed direct benefits associated with various project purposes. However, the Bureau of Reclamation does not restrict its benefit calculations to those effects specifically attributable to project functions. For each project purpose, it also claims credit for a series of secondary benefits.* Once money flows into a region, farm goods are produced; industries then enter the area to process the farm goods; unemployment usually decreases because of the influx of these new industries; service industries—grocers, clothiers, and the like—are drawn into the area to provide for the burgeoning population; and so on. It is our position that most of these benefits are not justifiably attributed to the Bureau's projects; nevertheless, the Bureau counts them in order to boost its benefit-cost ratios artificially. To substantiate this allegation, we focused mainly on secondary irrigation benefits, which constitute the secondary benefits quantified in dollar terms. A similar analysis could be made for power and M&I secondary benefits.

INDIRECT AND PUBLIC SECONDARY IRRIGATION BENEFITS

Secondary irrigation benefits are of two main types: "indirect" and "public" benefits.* Indirect irrigation benefits are "the increases in the net income of persons other than water users, as a result of the increased flow of agricultural products from the project."[38] In general, such indirect benefits consist of the growth of processing and marketing industries.

To determine these indirect benefits, the Bureau applies predetermined factors to each commodity expected to be grown with Reclamation project water. These factors, based more on custom than on theory, range from 6 percent for dairy products to 83 percent for cotton.[39] Thus, if the Bureau of Reclamation expects $100 of cotton to be grown with its water, the Bureau will claim a $100 direct benefit plus an $83 indirect benefit.

* The economic rationale for these secondary benefits is similar to the Keynesian multiplier concept.

* A third category of secondary irrigation benefits the Bureau calls "intangible benefits." Presently, the Bureau does not give any monetary values to these intangibles, but it does summarize them in project reports. For example, it calls the increase in garbage disposal necessitated by the project an intangible benefit to community facilities and services. In fact, this type of intangible benefit should be evaluated as a tangible cost of regional development.

The blind use of such factors is highly suspect. First, these factors are highest for crops in surplus, such as cotton and grains, and lowest for produce such as poultry and live-stock, which are not surplus crops. Thus the crops most likely to lie idle in a government warehouse are those with the highest indirect benefit factors—a clearly unacceptable system. These surplus crops may never even go through the handling and marketing process which is the justification for the indirect benefit. They may end up costing the government money, so that they should be considered costs, not benefits. This same objection to the indirect benefit factors was made in a 1952 report to Michael W. Straus, Commissioner of Reclamation.[40] In Chapter 2 we found that the main impact of produce from Bureau-irrigated lands was to contribute to crop surpluses or to displace crop production elsewhere. Hence, there can be no net increase in processing and mar-keting due to Reclamation projects. The only effect is to displace such industries elsewhere or to circumvent the marketing process altogether by storage in a government warehouse. As a result, the Bureau has no basis for claiming that its projects produce indirect (marketing, processing, and handling) benefits that are net national benefits. Professor Otto Eckstein of Harvard reached a similar conclusion.[41]

A second general category of secondary irrigation benefits is that classified as public irrigation benefits. These public benefits are supposed to relate to national benefits and are not intended to be limited to the project region at the expense of another area of the country.

Settlement Opportunity Benefits: The first subdivision of public irrigation benefits is that resulting from the opportu-nity to settle on irrigated farmland. The Bureau defines this settlement opportunity benefit as equal to the preproject earnings of farmers.[42] As Chapter 2 illustrated, direct irriga-tion benefits are computed by determining the net increase in irrigation benefits receiving Reclamation water. This net in-crease is determined by subtracting the preproject earnings of these farmers from their postproject incomes. The settlement opportunity benefit adds the preproject earnings back into the overall project benefit calculations, so that the earlier subtraction is nullified. The combination of these two procedures is equivalent to assuming that the income of farmers on Reclamation-irrigated lands would have been zero in the absence of the project. According to Professor Otto Eckstein, this assumption is contrary to the facts.[43] As a result, considering settlement opportunities as public benefits results in double counting of nonexistent benefits.

Writing Off Labor Costs: Increased employment opportunities due to Bureau projects form the second subdivision of public irrigation benefits.[44] In effect, this subdivision gives the Bureau a way to write off the labor costs of project construction and part of the labor costs of project operation and maintenance. By treating labor costs as employment opportunity benefits, the Bureau can cancel out the labor cost in its benefit-cost calculations.

The employment "benefits" are unjustifiable for several reasons. Not all of the people employed in the construction of Reclamation projects were previously unemployed. There is a significant time lag from project evaluation until the beginning of project construction—often as much as twenty-five years. Because of constantly changing employment patterns, there is no guarantee that a project will employ workers who would have been unemployed at the time of project construction and for the entire construction period. The Bureau makes no effort to determine whether project workers or other laborers would, in fact, have been unemployed if the project had not been constructed. Furthermore, when the end of project construction forces workers to return to the general labor market, they probably will experience temporary unemployment while looking for a new job.

There is yet another reason why these employment benefits are overestimated. Valuing the benefit of employing previously unemployed workers at the actual labor costs overstates the benefit which actually accrues. Unless an unemployed person places no value on his leisure time, the benefit from employing him will be less than the wages received. Also relevant is the willingness of other members of society to pay for more employment even though they might not be getting these new jobs. Reasons for this include the beneficial effects of employment in decreasing crime, welfare costs, and the like. Although the net effects of these considerations defy precise calculation, it is clear that the practice of writing off labor costs is not justified. The consequences of such a procedure would be disastrous. Any government project could be justified if labor costs could be written off. Virtually any government project costs can be traced to labor costs—if not in terms of project construction, at least so far as all project inputs (physical or human) involve labor costs in their production. Unless it can be shown that a Reclamation project creates more employment per dollar spent than alternative uses (either public or private) of the funds, then there is no valid justification for granting labor cost writeoffs to the Bureau. To do so only understates the real project costs, thus inflating the benefit-cost ratio.

In view of these considerations, we conclude that employment benefits are significantly overestimated. The Bureau should be required to demonstrate the magnitude of its employment benefits before it is allowed to blithely write off its labor costs. This method should be rigorous enough to meet the above objections to current Reclamation procedures.

Induced Economic Stagnation: The third measure of public irrigation benefits is the value of induced economic growth. These benefits consist of the increased regional development due to the investment stimulated by the project. Since these benefits cannot be determined directly, Bureau officials arbitrarily assert that regional development benefits equal 5 percent of project benefits. There is no existing support for the Bureau's claim that the 5 percent regional benefit represents a net gain to the nation.

Yet the Bureau, without valid justification, persists in contending that its regional benefits are net national benefits. In an attempt to justify this practice, Commissioner Ellis Armstrong recently cited a University of Nebraska study, financed by the Bureau of Reclamation, as proof:

> A more recent example of how irrigated agriculture contributes to the growth of an area is provided by a state-wide input-output study completed in 1968 by the University of

Nebraska. . . . While irrigation expansion in Nebraska has been largely a private venture by tapping the rich groundwater supply, this study nevertheless demonstrates how Reclamation's program has contributed to the growth of the Nation both by providing products needed to support an expanding population and by stimulating economic activity that results in job opportunities.[45]

A close look at the University of Nebraska study undermines Armstrong's claim that national benefits accrued. First, the study computed gross benefits to Nebraska, not net benefits to the nation. As the report admitted:

It should be noted here that a regional point of view—not a national point of view—was assumed with respect to impact measurement. Furthermore, the economic impact considered here is not net of the direct and indirect impact of alternative uses of resources outside of crop production.[46]

In other words, the Nebraska study overstates the regional benefits to Nebraska and does not even deal with net benefits to the Nation.

Earlier, we found that the Bureau's crops merely serve to displace crop production, thus causing regional harms elsewhere. These harms are ignored by the Bureau in computing its secondary benefits. But how significant are these displacement effects? Did the Nebraska crop production hurt farmers in other areas?

The University of Nebraska study actually found that most Reclamation-watered crops were shipped out of state. Assuming that Nebraska's farmers are not unique, and bearing in mind that farmers in many states sell their products locally, this situation reinforces our suspicions that Bureau crops displace farmers in other regions:

It was estimated that the Nebraska crop-producing sectors sold about 61% of their production outside the state in 1963. Most of the remaining 39% was sold to several processing sectors, which in turn exported substantial amounts of products from the state.[47]

What is really needed then is a study of what harmful regional and national impacts are caused by Bureau crops.

Needless to say, the Bureau of Reclamation has not funded such a study of the national impact of its projects.

REGIONAL GROWTH AND BUREAU PROJECTS

Even if the real goal is to spend federal money to promote a region's growth regardless of national effects, Bureau projects would not be the best choice. First of all, there is no significant correlation between the availability of water and economic growth. The most comprehensive study of this issue was done by Charles Howe, economist for Resources for the Future, in *Water Resources and Regional Economic Growth in the United States, 1950–1960*.[48] Dr. Howe was unable to find a significant correlation between regional growth and water navigation status, stream flow, or runoff:

> The evidence of the 1950–1960 decade . . . demonstrates that water did not constitute a bottleneck to rapid economic growth in the water deficit areas of this country, nor did its presence in large quantities in other regions guarantee the rapid growth of these regions. . . . The availability of abundant water and water transport is not a sufficient condition either for the attraction of rapidly growing industries or for attracting an increasing proportion of the slower growing and declining industries.[49]

According to another study, by economists Robert Haveman and John Krutilla, projects in the Reclamation states contributed even less to regional growth than similar projects in other states, except for Kentucky and Tennessee.[50] Haveman and Krutilla found that only 26 percent of the gross output resulting from projects in Montana, Wyoming, Idaho, Colorado, New Mexico, Arizona, Nevada, and Utah was retained in the project area. Projects located in California, Oregon, and Washington fared little better: 36 percent of gross project output was retained. The authors conclude that, except for the Mid-Atlantic and the East North Central states, "a relatively small percentage of total industrial and offsite labor demands is retained within the region."[51] Consequently, it is difficult to claim significant regional benefits for Reclamation projects since such a small percentage of the governmental expenditures remains in each Bureau of Reclamation project's region.

The contention that irrigation results in significant secondary benefits is untrue, for the claimed indirect and public benefits have not produced national benefits. While less specific provisions are made for the computation of the secondary benefits for power and municipal and industrial water uses, all these secondary benefit estimates should be omitted from the Bureau of Reclamation's computations.

e. Distributional Effects

While the Bureau's current secondary benefit calculations are misleading, there are two valid types of regional benefits which the Bureau should consider. On the one hand, the Bureau could justify pumping money into a region if building a project resulted in a higher GNP. However, these benefits are already counted in direct benefit estimates for project purposes, such as power, M&I, and recreation. There is no need to set up a specific regional benefit account for these effects.

Income redistribution is another valid justification for promoting a region's development. If Bureau projects raise the incomes of poor people in a region, a project may be justified even if the benefit-cost ratio does not exceed 1.0.

The Bureau currently ignores the importance of distributional effects in its project benefit estimates. However, it does matter who benefits and who is harmed by Bureau projects. If the rich are benefited at the expense of the poor, this fact should be made known in the measurement of project benefits and costs.

Policymakers should be informed as to who benefits and to what extent. The best method to incorporate distributional impacts into the Bureau's benefit-cost analysis would have the Bureau apply distributional weights that give appropriate preference to lower-income groups.[52] Since immediate implementation of this solution is politically overoptimistic, we recommend that the Bureau at least specify how projects affect the incomes of specific income groups.

The Office of Management and Budget should designate relevant breakdowns of the population into specific income groups, which encompass all members of society from the poorest to the richest. One reason for placing the task of defining relevant target groups in the OMB is so all government agencies can use uniform categories to assist Congress in comparing impacts of alternative government expenditures. Another reason is to prevent parochially biased agencies from designating income groups so broad that they hide the crucial distributional impacts.

For each project purpose, the Bureau should estimate the number of beneficiaries likely to fall into the particular income categories and how much members of these groups will receive. By making distributional considerations explicit, policymakers will be better informed as to who receives the benefits. Moreover, these officials will now have to confront the distributional considerations openly instead of playing with hidden subsidies.

Perhaps then the entire American public also will come to realize whom the Bureau really helps. The Bureau presently is displaying a marked preference for the rich and various special interest groups. Explicit recognition of distributional effects should go a long way toward bringing public pressure to bear on the type of perverse project effects that are discussed in the following chapters.

Part 2 | **Profiteers and the Damned**

Politics: the conduct of public affairs for private advantage.

—Ambrose Bierce

In politics I am sure it is even a Machiavellian holy maxim, "That some men should be ruined for the good of others."

—Jonathan Swift

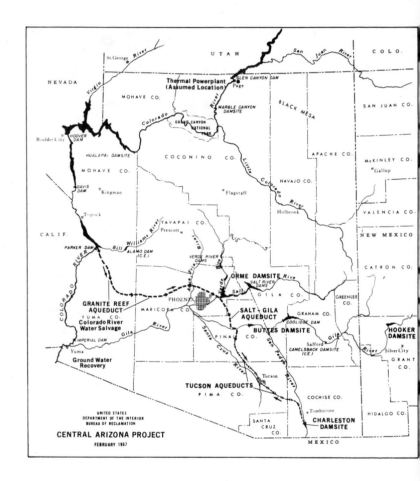

5

Politicians and Bureaucrats: The Central Arizona Project

INTERVIEWER: *What was the fundamental purpose of the Central Arizona Project?*

FORMER COMMISSIONER DOMINY: *Well—number one—Senator Hayden was a man that I loved.*[1]

The Bureau of Reclamation will soon begin construction of a Southwestern water project whose high cost and weak justification will caricature past Bureau endeavors. Upon completing repayment contracting with local water users some time in 1972, the Bureau will officially launch the billion-dollar Central Arizona Project (CAP).* The mammoth unit, which will take at least ten years to build, will divert Colorado River water to the Phoenix and Tucson areas for irrigation and municipal and industrial (M&I) use. "The basic plan," a Reclamation brochure explains,

* Though better known as the "Central Arizona Project," the central Arizona unit and the five Upper Basin projects authorized simultaneously by PL 90-537 are called the "Colorado River Basin Project" in the official act. The five satellite projects will cost $400 million, making the total cost of the Colorado River Project $1.4 billion.

calls for construction of a series of pumping plants and aqueducts, which will lift Colorado River water hundreds of feet from Lake Havasu [behind Parker Dam] and carry it to the Project service areas in Maricopa, Pinal, and Pima Counties. Construction of dams and reservoirs on the Salt, Gila, and San Pedro Rivers will provide needed regulatory, conservation, and flood control storage capacity, as well as additional recreational and water exchange opportunities. Federal participation in the Navajo thermal generation plant near Page, Ariz., will provide pumping power requirements for the project.[2]

CAP was authorized by Congress in 1968, after twenty years of political wrangling. It could turn out to be one of the Bureau's costliest boondoggles to date—what one Arizona observer has labeled "a billion-dollar raid on the U.S. Treasury."[3]

This chapter focuses on the politics behind the Central Arizona Project—the politics which explain why a largely unnecessary project was planned, authorized, and soon will be built at great expense to the nation's taxpayers; and why a small number of irrigators, politicians, and bureaucrats, not the majority of Americans or even of central Arizonans, will be the project's chief beneficiaries.

THE POLITICS OF WATER IN THE COLORADO RIVER BASIN

Water is a volatile issue in the politics of the Southwest. "If you're not a Westerner, it's hard to understand that water underlies every major decision made there," explains Edward Weinberg, solicitor of the Interior Department under the Johnson administration.[4] Western folklore abounds with tales of farmers and ranchers skirmishing over water rights.

As the West's water needs have spiraled in the past fifty years, states have clashed bitterly over rights to surface water. The Colorado River has been the scene of innumerable confrontations, because, although its flow is relatively small, it is the chief source of surface water in the Southwest.* At one point in the mid-1930s, Arizona even dis-

---

* The Colorado River is 1,440 miles long and drains a basin 240,000 square miles in area. The basin includes most of Arizona,

patched its National Guard to the east bank of the Colorado to halt construction of Parker Dam, a Reclamation project to divert water to the cities and farms of southern California.[5]

The water rights controversy among the seven states in the Colorado River Basin had become so explosive by 1921 that Congress sponsored negotiations to determine how the river flow should be allocated. The following year, all the Basin states except Arizona ratified the Colorado River Compact.[6] The compact divided the Basin into an Upper Basin and a Lower Basin, with the dividing line at Lee Ferry, Arizona. It allocated to each basin 7.5 million acre-feet (maf) per year for "beneficial consumptive use."*

Eager to put its share of Lower Basin water to use, California persuaded Congress in 1928 to pass the Boulder Canyon Project Act.[7] In return, the California legislature agreed to limit that state's use of Colorado River water to 4.4 maf annually. In 1930, the Bureau of Reclamation began building Boulder (now Hoover) Dam. Construction of an aqueduct to carry river water to southern California soon followed. The 1928 act also divided the remainder of the Lower Basin flow between Arizona (2.8 maf annually) and Nevada (0.3 maf annually).

Complaining that California had received favored treatment, Arizona nevertheless ratified the Colorado River Compact in February, 1944. At the same time, it entered into a contract with the Secretary of the Interior to arrange for the delivery of Arizona's share (2.8 maf) of the river water. The contract failed to specify, however, when, where, or how the water would be delivered for Arizona's use.[8]

---

parts of California, Nevada, Utah, Wyoming, Colorado, and New Mexico, and a piece of Mexico. The river's average annual virgin flow of 15 million acre-feet (maf) is small in comparison with the 180 maf of the Columbia or the 440 maf of the Mississippi (an acre-foot is the amount of water necessary to cover one acre of land to a depth of one foot—approximately 326,000 gallons).

* "Consumptive use" is the difference between the amount of water withdrawn from a stream or groundwater supply and the amount returned to it.

EARLY EFFORTS TO AUTHORIZE CAP

A combination of local pressure groups and the self-interest of the Bureau of Reclamation provided the initial impetus behind CAP. For decades, Arizona irrigators, backed by bankers, food processors, and local merchants, have reasoned that if only Arizona's water supply could be augmented, then the state's economy could continue to prosper.[9] Seeking government assistance to alleviate their own irresponsible depletion of the state's limited water supply, the farmers and businessmen went to local Reclamation officials in the 1940s for support.

The Bureau responded with precipitate speed. It was only too happy to start a major new project in the Colorado River Basin. The fight for authorization of Davis Dam was nearly over, and the Bureau engineers and officials in Region 3, which includes Arizona, needed another major project in the Lower Basin to keep themselves busy. Furthermore, the wishes of the late Senator Carl Hayden (D-Ariz.), the project's chief sponsor, were not easily neglected. As a powerful member of the Senate Appropriations Committee, he had repeatedly befriended the Bureau. Now it was time for the Bureau to do him a good turn.

Late in 1940, the Bureau launched a preliminary investigation into various plans for diverting Arizona's share of Colorado River water into the central part of the state. In 1944, the Bureau reached agreement with the state of Arizona providing for joint financing of feasibility investigations.[10]

Meanwhile, on Capitol Hill, the members of Arizona's congressional delegation responded to the same local pressure by prodding their fellow legislators to authorize CAP. As early as 1944, both Arizona senators, Hayden and Ernest McFarland, introduced bills to authorize CAP. Although both senators possessed substantial influence in Congress, their initial bills never got beyond the committee-hearings stage.

Feasibility Report: On its own initiative and without formal congressional authorization, the Bureau went ahead from 1944 to 1947 and spent $660,000 to study CAP's feasibility.[11] Throughout the long authorization battle, Senator Hayden repeatedly used his senior position on the Appropriations Committee to obtain funds to keep Bureau planning of CAP alive. In December, 1947, the Bureau released its feasibility report on the Central Arizona Project.[12] The hundred-page document, bulging with maps, tables, and graphs, presented detailed evidence to demonstrate the project's engineering feasibility, economic feasibility (benefits greater than costs), and financial feasibility (water users' ability to repay their assigned construction costs). Specifically, the report called for the construction of Bridge Canyon Dam on the Colorado River to provide hydroelectric power for the Lower Basin states and energy for pumping water from behind Parker Dam through a 240-mile aqueduct to the irrigated lands of central Arizona.[13]

Official Objections to the Report: Early in 1948, the Secretary of the Interior routinely circulated the feasibility report among the affected state governments and federal agencies for comments. Their responses, however, were anything but routine.

The Department of Agriculture, for instance, lambasted the Bureau's benefit-cost analysis. In particular, it criticized the Bureau for using gross rather than net crop figures in computing the benefits accruing to irrigators using CAP water. The error, USDA pointed out, inflated benefit estimates, thus creating a mistaken impression of the project's desirability.[14]

The Federal Power Commission charged that the burden of the irrigation costs was considerable and that the proposed charges for electric power consequently approached a level where such power could not be classed as low-cost.[15]

The state of Nevada rightly questioned the justification of spending $1,469 per acre in net irrigation construction costs to salvage farmland valued at only $300 per acre, even with irrigation.[16]

The state of California, Arizona's historic adversary in matters concerning the Colorado River, sent its comments to the Bureau in December, 1948, in the form of a highly critical report by the California Department of Public Works. Its critique was almost as long and complex as the Bureau's own study.[17] California's objections were generally valid. It argued that the Bureau's feasibility report on CAP suffered from inaccurate estimates of water supply and demand, benefits, costs, and repayment capability.

The First Authorization Fight: Throughout the initial four years of the twenty-year fight to gain authorization for CAP, the Bureau remained steadfastly on the side of Arizona, except for the specific water rights controversy between Arizona and California, in which it remained publicly silent. The Bureau's allegiance to Arizona stemmed first from its devotion to Senator Hayden, a long-time friend of the Bureau in its frequent congressional struggles. Its loyalty to Arizona also derived from its natural devotion to the Central Arizona Project, in which it had invested considerable funds, time, and political capital. Even if outside critics gave the Bureau second thoughts about CAP's feasibility, it would very likely have continued to back the project out of loyalty to Senator Hayden and to its own bureaucratic apparatus. Evidence of such inertia came later, when the Bureau continued to support the major idea of CAP with a new set of reasons, a new set of project components, and a new calculation of financial and economic feasibility. The old rationales had become unpalatable even to Congress.[18]

Arizona v. *California:* In 1952, Arizona filed suit against California in the United States Supreme Court to gain adjudication of its rights to Colorado River water. *Arizona* v. *California* dragged on for eleven years. Hundreds of hydrologists, Reclamation officials, state water experts, irrigators, and politicians appeared before a special master assigned by the Supreme Court. Their testimony filled thousands of pages.

Through the courts, Arizona hoped to obtain a final determination of its rightful share of Colorado River water. Through CAP it hoped to gain federal assistance for its delivery. Arizona felt it deserved the same shot in the arm that the federal government had administered to California by building Hoover Dam, Parker Dam, and the All-American Canal to the Imperial Valley. The Bureau tended to agree, especially following the long court battle. As Daniel V. Mc-Carthy, chief of the Planning Division, noted: "The Southwest hasn't gotten its share of water-resource-development funds, due to the ten-year period of court suits. It's only equitable that we build CAP now."[19]

The special master reported his findings to the Supreme Court in January, 1961, and the Court declared in 1964 that Arizona was entitled to 2.8 million acre-feet, California to 4.4 million acre-feet, and Nevada to 300,000 acre-feet annually, if sufficient mainstream Colorado River water is available to supply 7.5 million acre-feet to the whole Lower Basin. When that amount is not available, the Court empowered the Secretary of the Interior to divide the shortage burden among the three states in the same proportion as their water rights.[20]

Arizona considered the verdict a victory because the Court also declared that the 1.5 million acre-feet available to the state from Colorado River tributaries within its borders was not to be considered a part of Arizona's allotment of Colorado River water.

NEVER SAY DIE: THE SECOND AUTHORIZATION FIGHT

The Proponents: The day after the Supreme Court delivered its ruling, Senator Carl Hayden, by then chairman of the Senate Appropriations Committee and a powerful figure in Congress, introduced S.1658 to authorize CAP. From that day until President Johnson signed the CAP authorization act into law, September 30, 1968, the state of Arizona and the Bureau of Reclamation fought unceasingly for CAP.

Arizona's congressional delegation, led by the venerable Senator Hayden, made up for its small size (five members) by uniting behind the CAP effort. Their rallying cry was not that the project would benefit the nation as a whole or even that it would pay its own way. Instead they reminded their colleagues that while Arizona sat in court for ten years, other sections of the country, with the help of Arizona's senators and congressmen, were receiving federal water projects right and left. Now it was Arizona's turn.

A lobbying group assisted the state's congressional delegation in pushing CAP. The Central Arizona Project Association (CAPA), with offices in Phoenix and Washington, D.C., was formed in 1947, and is still in existence. Its membership has always been weighted toward farmers and those involved in farm-related industries. In 1971, for example, CAPA's fifty-five-member board of directors included seventeen men involved in farming or farm-related businesses, seven bankers, several lawyers and representatives of utilities, the mayors of Tucson and Phoenix, and State Supreme Court Justice Ernest McFarland—the former United States Senator.[21]

The Interior Department and the Bureau of Reclamation also mobilized behind CAP authorization. In early 1963, Secretary of the Interior Stewart Udall designated his deputy solicitor, Edward Weinberg, to head a special administration task force from the Interior Department to push for immediate authorization. Weinberg and other top Bureau officials guided Senator Hayden's bill through five years of sticky negotiations among conflicting states and congressmen. Secretary Udall, himself an Arizonan, took a special interest in the CAP fight.[22]

However, one of the most effective lobbyists was former Commissioner Dominy. "Dominy was very strong-minded, very tough, and one of the ablest commissioners ever," notes Udall, his one-time boss.[23] Dominy knows how good he was:

> I became Reclamation, and I'm proud as hell of the fact that for thirteen years, I ran the damn place. And I was running it long before that, but they wouldn't admit it.[24]

"It was exciting working for Dominy," notes a former Bureau official. "He terrorized his staff, which kept them working at their peak."[25] He did so by keeping almost as informed about their work as they did.

Unlike most top-ranking Reclamation officials, Dominy

was not an engineer. He got to be commissioner in 1959 because he did his homework so well. His predecessor, Commissioner Dexheimer, apparently did not, and he "was under orders not to go up to the Hill, although he was a Republican in a Republican administration."[26] According to agency lore, Dominy was appointed commissioner because he was the only Reclamation official who knew the facts at a late-1950s appropriations committee hearing. "What had happened," notes Daniel A. Dreyfus of the Senate Interior Committee staff,

> was that the present commissioner and his regional directors could not answer the questions. The chairman was so inflamed that he asked if anyone in the room knew any more. Dominy raised his hand, came to the front, and testified.[27]

From that point until his retirement in 1969, Dominy not only managed the Bureau of Reclamation aggressively and efficiently, but also skillfully guided Bureau legislation through Congress. He was personally close to Senator Hayden, chairman of the Senate Appropriations Committee, and the late Congressman Michael J. Kirwan (D-Ohio), then chairman of the House Appropriations Subcommittee on Public Works. "Dominy used to work the appropriations committees like an artist works an organ," former Interior Department solicitor Weinberg recalls.[28] If a piece of legislation was proceeding too slowly, "Dominy himself would buttonhole congressmen, or if necessary, build fires under their constituents."[29]

Asked what he felt was the fundamental purpose of CAP, Dominy once said, "Well—number one—Senator Hayden was a man that I loved." He also felt that Arizona had "won the right to [Colorado] River waters" and therefore deserved a Reclamation project to deliver it to the water users.[30] Though Dominy's attempt to gain authorization of the Grand Canyon dams was thwarted by conservationists, his effort to gain congressional approval of the larger CAP package reached fruition in 1968.

The Opponents: There would have been no need for the special attention of Commissioner Dominy, a united Arizona congressional delegation, a state lobbying group, or a special administration task force to champion CAP, if there had not been considerable opposition to the project on Capitol Hill. Oddly enough, the 1963 Supreme Court decision by no means cleared the way for CAP authorization, as project proponents had hoped it would. Open resistance to the project had increased since the first CAP authorization fight.

For one thing, Congressman Wayne N. Aspinall (D-Colo.), then chairman of the House Committee on Interior and Insular Affairs, opposed the project. Aspinall, a crusty political wizard, exerted tight congressional control over Bureau activities; his opposition constituted a seemingly insurmountable obstacle to authorization. Generally, through his close relationship with Commissioner Dominy, he was one of the Bureau's best friends in Congress. However, in the case of the Central Arizona Project, Aspinall balked at the idea of making Colorado River water available to Arizona before his state of Colorado and the rest of the Upper Basin had a chance to make use of their share. Without the chairman's support, CAP's floor leader in the House, Congressman Morris K. Udall (D-Ariz.), was unable to obtain committee approval of Senator Hayden's bill, S.1658.

The second major impediment to quick House committee action on the bill was the continued opposition of the state of California. Five out of the thirty-three members of the House Interior Committee were from California (compared to one out of the seventeen members of the Senate committee). They derailed the proposed Senate authorization bill by opposing it in committee and threatening concerted opposition by the full forty-member California delegation on the House floor.

Negotiations: Talks between CAP proponents and their two adversaries began in the Eighty-eighth Congress while Senator Hayden's bill died without even being brought to a vote. Aspinall's price for supporting CAP was reserving the Upper Basin's share of Colorado River water, lest CAP and existing Lower Basin projects absorb the Upper Basin's share. As a result, Aspinall got Congress to tack the Animas–La Plata, Dolores, Dallas Creek, San Miguel, and West

Divide Projects onto the CAP authorization bill. All five of the projects, worth a total of $392 million, were to be located within his own congressional district.[31]

It is highly dubious that any net benefit to the nation would accrue from this mammoth political payoff. The five projects were intended to provide water for irrigating short-season, high-altitude cropland. The inefficiency of such irrigation led the Bureau of Reclamation to find that the projects had direct benefit-cost ratios* barely exceeding 1.0, even under Reclamation's distorted criteria. The San Miguel Project actually had a direct benefit-cost ratio significantly less than unity (0.89 to 1). Figured under the revised criteria we have recommended, the ratios would be even smaller. All the projects were expensive; the cost per acre for irrigation ranged from $630 to $1,710 and the investment per farm ranged from $140,000 to $273,000. The irrigators would be capable of repaying only 10–15 percent of the projects' irrigation costs.[32]

The Office of Management and Budget's negative reaction to three of the five proposed Upper Basin projects led the Bureau to send reports to Congress only on the Animas–La Plata and Dolores Projects, in 1962 and 1964, respectively. According to Senate Interior staff economist Daniel Dreyfus, Congressman Aspinall realized that the three marginally feasible projects would never be authorized on their own. Wishing to see them approved, if only thereby to protect the Upper Basin's share of Colorado River water from use downstream, the committee chairman demanded that their authorization be packaged with CAP's.

To support his demand, Aspinall refused to hold House Interior Committee hearings on CAP until the Bureau of Reclamation sent him feasibility reports on the Dallas Creek, West Divide, and San Miguel Projects. At that point Senator Hayden himself wrote into the CAP bill authorization of all

---

* The direct benefit-cost ratio excludes secondary, or indirect, benefits such as regional project impacts. Since such regional effects are usually offset by project impacts elsewhere, the Office of Management and Budget requires the Bureau of Reclamation to submit both a direct and a total benefit-cost ratio for each project investigated.

five Upper Basin projects.[33] How did Aspinall gain such a concession? "As committee chairman," former solicitor Weinberg explained, "he was powerful enough to get them."[34]

The California Compromise: While the Aspinall deal was being negotiated, officials of Arizona and California talked water rights. Theoretically, the 1963 Supreme Court decision had finally resolved the feud between the two states over the division of Colorado River water in the Lower Basin. California, however, had received a smaller share through the Court's decision than it would have liked. It sought to rectify the situation by employing what Reclamation planning chief McCarthy somewhat bitterly called "political blackmail."[35]

Marshaling its huge congressional delegation, California vowed to kill the CAP bill on the floor of the House unless Arizona agreed to a provision in the bill guaranteeing California its Court-allocated 4.4 million acre-feet of Colorado River water annually—even in years of shortage. If Arizona succumbed to the blackmail, it would do so knowing that CAP would be able to deliver to central Arizona far less than Arizona's own Court-allocated share of 2.8 million acre-feet, since Colorado River flow had been decreasing every year since 1930. If Arizona did not succumb to the deal, however, then California's mammoth congressional delegation would most certainly act on its threat. Accepting the Bureau's questionable assurance of an adequate Colorado River flow well into the next century, Arizona capitulated to California's demands in late 1967. The state had little choice, if it ever wanted to see a Central Arizona Project built—however poorly supplied with water.

New Resistance: The compromises emerging from the negotiations were reflected in HR 4671, a more comprehensive bill introduced in the House Interior Committee in August, 1965. The bill authorized CAP and the five Upper Basin projects. However, its additional authorization of Hualapai and Marble Canyon dams, and of transbasin water augmentation studies, touched off new resistance to CAP.

Senator Henry M. Jackson (D-Wash.), chairman of the Senate Interior and Insular Affairs Committee, reversed his position on CAP and opposed HR 4671. He vigorously objected to the bill's authorization of studies on transbasin augmentation of water supplies in the Colorado River Basin. He read the provision as an invitation to the Colorado River Basin states to raid his home state's sacred water preserve, the Columbia River System.

That, of course, was exactly what the Bureau of Reclamation and Congressman Aspinall's committee had intended the provision to mean. Noting the scarcity of water in the Pacific Southwest, even with full utilization of Colorado River water, the writers of HR 4671 wanted to augment the water supply in that region by importing water from the Columbia River—a river that every year pours over ten times the Colorado's annual virgin flow into the Pacific Ocean.

Rarely do states and regions act in such insular and self-protective ways as they do when water is at stake. Senator Jackson and fellow Columbia River Basin congressmen fought the water importation provision so strenuously and successfully that later versions of the CAP authorization bill included a ban on transbasin importation studies for ten years following passage of the act.

CAP authorization bills had always included at least one "cash register" dam on the Colorado River, in the Grand Canyon. The original feasibility report called for construction of Bridge Canyon Dam, later called Hualapai Dam. To permit the production of even greater revenues and to help subsidize irrigation costs, HR 4671 proposed the construction of Marble Canyon Dam, in addition to Hualapai Dam. The Bureau eagerly supported both dams, since the dams greatly improved the financial feasibility of CAP.

For one thing, the dams would produce the electrical energy necessary for pumping Colorado River water through the 240-mile aqueduct to central Arizona. Second, the excess revenues accruing from the sale of hydroelectric power produced at the dams would help repay the tremendous costs of irrigation.

The Sierra Club and other conservation groups opposed the Grand Canyon dams. The groups justly claimed that the dams would disrupt the ecology of a section of the Colorado

River and diminish the aesthetic value of the Grand Canyon. In the early 1960s, the same groups had lost the battle to save Glen Canyon from Reclamation inundation. This time they were determined to win. Through their regular publications and special mailings, the groups mobilized a prolonged national barrage of conservationist opinion against the Bureau's plan to build the dams.

The Bureau, however, resolutely resisted the pressure and continued to push for the dams. Commissioner Dominy went to the extent of flying over the future damsites and taking pictures to convince Congress that the reservoir behind the proposed Hualapai Dam would not impair the beauty of Grand Canyon. On viewing the Marble Canyon damsite, however, he did agree with the conservationists that Marble Canyon Dam should be scrapped. Meanwhile, Congressman Aspinall continued to support the construction of both dams.

The deafening public uproar over the Grand Canyon dams eventually caused Aspinall and Dominy to alter their positions. In February, 1967, Secretary Udall issued a report to Congress to get the administration off the hot seat. Instead of pushing for authorization of the Grand Canyon dams, the report called for approval of a prepaid federal share in the output of a private thermal generating plant that would provide power for CAP pumping operations. The proposed Navajo Power Plant, to be built at Page, Arizona, and to be fueled with coal mined on an Indian reservation fifty miles away, would provide no surplus revenues to subsidize CAP irrigation costs.* Under the new scheme, higher municipal and industrial water charges and a special property tax levied on land in the CAP area would subsidize the irrigation costs which farmers were incapable of repaying themselves. The secretary's report also eliminated from the administration's previous proposal the controversial provision authorizing transbasin water import studies.[36]

* As noted in Chapter 3, opposition to the Navajo Plant, which is now under construction, has arisen among environmentalists concerned about potential air pollution and among Hopi Indians determined to stop the mining of coal at Black Mesa, which they claim is desecrating their sacred grounds.

Following quick House and Senate passage of a bill based largely on the administration's proposal, President Johnson signed the Colorado River Basin Project Act into law on September 30, 1968. By gaining congressional authorization of the Central Arizona Project, its proponents had won a major battle, but not yet the war.

ADVANCE PLANNING

Before construction can begin, a project must undergo "advance planning." To finance advance planning, the Bureau of Reclamation needs congressional appropriation of funds and OMB approval to spend them.

In its 1971 budget, the Bureau received $850,000 for advance planning of CAP. To speed this stage of development, the state of Arizona provided $650,000 in loans eventually to be repaid by the Bureau.[37]

Much of the advance planning has involved repayment contract negotiations with representatives of the state of Arizona and future CAP water users. The talks have proceeded slowly, although initially the Bureau had no trouble finding enough claimants for CAP water. By June 30, 1971, over a hundred irrigation districts, Indian reservations, municipalities, and government agencies had expressed interest in four times as much water as would be available. They did so, of course, before they found out how much CAP water would cost.

The setting of water charges and the allocation of project water are the subjects of continuing negotiations between the Secretary of the Interior (represented by the Bureau of Reclamation) and the state of Arizona. The talks are stalled over the amount of CAP water to be allocated to Arizona Indians. When that issue is resolved, the Secretary of the Interior will make the final allocation and price decisions.

A LAST-MINUTE INDICTMENT

As soon as the water-allocation issue is resolved, *or before*, the Secretary of the Interior can initiate construction of CAP. Nevertheless, it is not too late to stop this $1.4 billion boondoggle. There is still time, before the major construction funding becomes available, to convince the President and Congress to terminate the Central Arizona Project.

In addition to the objections raised during the two authorization fights, CAP is still vulnerable to four major criticisms. We believe that any one of these criticisms justifies scrapping the project.

1. An Insufficient Water Supply: Twenty years ago, Bureau plans showed CAP diverting 1.2 million acre-feet of Colorado River water annually to central Arizona. Since then, the average annual virgin flow of the river has decreased markedly and newly constructed projects have begun to withdraw more water from it. Congressman Aspinall's five projects, due to be completed simultaneously with CAP, will enable the Upper Basin to withdraw a greater portion of its share of the river flow.

As a result, the Bureau itself estimates that in the year 1979, which was to be the first year of CAP operation, only 1,105,000 acre-feet would be available for diversion to central Arizona. In the year 1990, only 500,000 acre-feet would be available; in the year 2000, only 360,000; and in the year 2030, only 284,000.[38] But, according to the Bureau:

> The minimum average annual amount of water necessary [during the anticipated repayment period, 1979–2030] to the economic and financial feasibility of the Central Arizona Project is about 450,000 acre-feet.[39]

In view of the fact that CAP is intended to divert 1.2 million acre-feet annually from the Colorado River, the feasible figure of 450,000 acre-feet, supplied by the Bureau, seems highly suspect. Even if the figure is accurate, the project will be feasible for less than twenty years.

And, again assuming the accuracy of the Bureau's estimate, the project still will not be feasible unless M&I users—whose payment of inflated water charges will finance much of Arizona's repayment obligation—contract for a large amount of CAP water now, when the project's water supply is great, as well as later, when it is not. However, according to a March 17, 1971, letter from Assistant Secretary of Interior

James Smith to the Office of Management and Budget, the cities are reluctant to bankroll CAP in this way:

> On the Central Arizona Project, letters of intent have been filed for some 5 million acre-feet of water annually, which is far in excess of that which will be available. There is little doubt that all of the water could be marketed for irrigation at a price range of $10 to $12 per acre-foot. Financial integrity of the project, however, is dependent upon marketing an average of 300,000 to 400,000 acre-feet annually for M&I purposes at a price of $50 to $60 per acre-foot. *We do not have adequate assurances by municipalities that they are now prepared to contract for such quantities at that price.* [emphasis added][40]

Statements by Arizona city officials back up Secretary Smith's observation. Larry Woodall, deputy city manager of Tucson, has said, "It would be ridiculous for Tucson to pay $50 for CAP water and stop pumping $9 water." And William Stephens, director of the five-city Municipal Water Users Association, noted, "We're not sure, but it looks as if we may not need CAP water."[41] If the cities will not buy large amounts of CAP water now, then present revenues will be insufficient to balance the small revenues accompanying later reductions in Colorado River water supply.

A rapidly diminishing Colorado River water supply may wreak havoc in CAP repayment arrangements, but it will benefit the Bureau by providing it with an excuse to seek congressional authorization of still another major project—this time to import water from the Columbia River Basin. Such a project would be anathema to Senator Henry M. Jackson, powerful chairman of the Senate Interior Committee. During the authorization fight, he successfully sidetracked a proposal for transbasin importation studies. If he had realized at that time that CAP would be unable to function efficiently with only Colorado River water to draw on, he probably would have blocked CAP authorization permanently. By 1978, when the ten-year ban on transbasin importation studies expires, the Bureau will be only too eager to renew its insistence on such studies. And the game will begin again.

2. *M&I Alternatives to CAP:* Under the Bureau's plan, the Central Arizona Project will provide the water which Phoenix and Tucson need in order to reduce groundwater pumping. Lacking access to sufficient surface water resources, the cities as well as the irrigators have been pumping groundwater at an alarming rate. Former Secretary of Interior Stewart Udall observed that Southern California, west Texas, Colorado, and even his home state of Arizona have greatly depleted underground water supplies, as if water were an inexhaustible resource. In his view, the Arizona "water crisis" was "self-caused."[42] As a result of the huge overdrafts, Arizona's groundwater bank account of 700 million acre-feet of economically recoverable water has dropped by 100 million acre-feet. Each year, water users withdraw 3.5 million acre-feet more than they return to the groundwater supply.[43]

In spite of the Bureau's allegation that CAP is "basically an M&I project," M&I water users in the project area will be expected to subsidize the construction costs assigned to irrigation by paying higher water charges. While irrigators are paying $10 to $20 per acre-foot of water, the M&I users will have to pay $50 to $60 per acre-foot. Phoenix now pays only $3 per acre-foot for water obtained from the Salt River project. Tucson pays only $9 per acre-foot for its water, which is pumped from underground.[44] Thus CAP will raise the price of water by over 1,000 percent—a politically distasteful fact that has been concealed from Phoenix and Tucson taxpayers. CAP should be exposed for what it really is—a water steal by the irrigators. At $60 per acre-foot, the cities simply cannot afford a billion dollars' worth of additional water.

Under politically favorable circumstances, the central Arizona cities could augment their water supplies sufficiently without expensive CAP water. For one thing, they could accelerate the transfer of Arizona water from irrigation to municipal and industrial use. That transfer is now occurring automatically as the cities envelop the agricultural lands surrounding them. For instance, the Bureau's Salt River project supplies almost three-quarters of Phoenix's water because the city has expanded onto former project-irrigated lands. Theoretically, the cities could speed up the process by purchasing rights to water on adjacent irrigated lands. But a 1969 Arizona Supreme Court ruling prohibits the pumping of water from irrigated lands in "critical water areas" into the cities.[45] And the whole state of Arizona could probably be classified as a critical water area. The Arizona cities might skirt the court decision by purchasing irrigated lands and piping their water to municipal users. However, without zoning and financial aid from what so far has been an unwilling state legislature, the cities could never afford the tremendous cost of such an action. According to one commentator on Arizona water problems,

> the law on which this case is founded will be changed, but it will be a long haul in overcoming agricultural interests that are entrenched in the various boards and commissions that would have to provide the impetus or at least be neutralized in a legislative showdown.[46]

The Bureau has frequently singled out Tucson's water problems as the key to the area's need for CAP. Since Tucson, unlike Phoenix, does not own enough irrigated lands to meet its domestic water needs, the Bureau claims that it needs CAP water to avoid exhausting its existing groundwater supply. The Bureau's argument, however, ignores several additional sources of water available to Tucson.

First, if the Arizona Supreme Court ruling is overturned by subsequent court review or a state constitutional amendment, Tucson can begin contracting for the water currently used for irrigation in the nearby Alter-Avra Valley. The 33,000 acres of cropland in the valley absorb more water annually than the entire Tucson population consumes in a year. Second, the depletion of Tucson's groundwater supplies is not so rapid that this source should be ruled out in filling the city's water needs. Indeed, according to a forthcoming report by the U.S. Geological Survey, the Tucson Basin has subterranean water supplies that could last more than 380

years, at the current rate of depletion.[47] Shifting irrigation
water to M&I use and reusing waste water could guarantee
Tucson an adequate water supply much further into the future. Third, if the state made water exchanges legal, Tucson
could avail itself of yet another source of water. Several copper companies on the Santa Cruz River between Tucson and
Nogales withdraw large quantities of fresh water from the
river for smelting operations. Waste water would serve such
industrial purposes just as well. Conceivably, Tucson could
negotiate the exchange of treated city effluent water for the
copper companies' rights to drinkable downstream Santa
Cruz River water.[48]

Oddly enough, despite the high project M&I water prices,
the cities have been supporting CAP. Not so oddly, however,
their support has not been altogether voluntary. Constrained
severely by their inability to exploit, on their own, water
supply alternatives cheaper than CAP, the cities have been
forced to accept CAP as the answer to their future water
needs. The state legislature could make things easier for the
cities, but it seems unlikely to do so as long as agricultural
interests retain a decisive influence within it. Repeatedly,
these interests have blocked the cities' attempts to get the
legislature to enact a groundwater code to conserve and real-
locate existing water supplies.[49]

The Bureau of Reclamation has remained anything but
neutral in Arizona water squabbles, despite what its officials
claim.[50] In a typical alliance with the irrigators, the Bureau
has lent support to Arizona agricultural interests. Perhaps
more than any other force, CAP and its enthusiastic advocate, the Bureau of Reclamation, have consistently prevented
the development of cheaper water augmentation plans in central Arizona.

3. *Better Alternatives for Arizona's Economy:* The Bureau defines the larger purpose of every Reclamation project
as the stabilization of the project area's economy. CAP's
1947 feasibility report declared:

> Unless additional irrigation water is made available to the
> project area, the equivalent of a 30 per cent reduction in the
> presently cultivated lands in the area must eventually be

effected. *The central Arizona project is needed to sustain the agricultural economy of the area.* [emphasis added][51]

Likewise, in 1971, Daniel V. McCarthy, veteran chief of the Bureau's Planning Division, explained: "The larger purpose involved in CAP is to maintain a healthy economy in central Arizona."[52]

Contrary to the Bureau view, however, the Arizona economy is thriving in spite of the continuing decline of its agricultural sector.[53] According to the *Arizona Statistical Review*, Arizona ranks among the five leading states in each of six important indices of economic growth.[54] Today, agriculture—crops and livestock—accounts for only 12 percent of total personal income in the state.[55] At the same time, however, crops alone consume 90 percent of the state's water.[56]

In an effort to deny that the central Arizona economy can continue to prosper without CAP, the Bureau exposed its weak reasoning during the 1963 Senate hearings on CAP authorization:

> MR. DOMINY [Commissioner of Reclamation]: During the 1950 decade, when activity on the Central Arizona Project was dormant, Arizona experienced the fastest population and economic growth in the Nation.
> SENATOR [CLINTON] ANDERSON [D-N.M.]: What does that prove, that if we kill this project, Arizona will grow faster?
> MR. DOMINY: It proves that without this project, the economy of that area is going to dry up almost as fast as it expanded.[57]

Suppose that the decline of agriculture in Arizona does promote the economic stagnation of the area, as Bureau officials have claimed for years. If the aim of federal assistance is, as chief planner McCarthy says, "to maintain a healthy economy in central Arizona," then is a major Reclamation project like CAP the only way to fulfill it? If not, is it even the *best* way to fulfill it?

A recent report by the National Academy of Sciences concluded that $1 billion invested in Arizona industry, education, other government services, or a combination of the three might stimulate economic growth more effectively than the $1 billion which is to be invested in CAP.[58] Of course, no one ever expected the Bureau of Reclamation to propose non-Reclamation federal aid programs to stimulate the economy of central Arizona. Other federal agencies are better suited for that task. Nevertheless, the Bureau of Reclamation prevented the national decisionmakers—the President and Congress—from choosing intelligently among the Reclamation and non-Reclamation alternatives before them, in two ways.

First, the Bureau of Reclamation painted an artificially bright picture of CAP by using inadequate and at times erroneous project data. Its survey of future water supply and water requirements in central Arizona was incomplete; its benefit and cost estimates were inaccurate because of faulty criteria; and its investigation into the water users' ability to repay costs was sketchy and undependable. (See Chapters 2, 3, and 4 for a discussion of the Bureau's faulty benefit-cost calculations.)

Second, since the Bureau failed to investigate Reclamation alternatives to CAP, the decisionmakers could not tell whether CAP was the most efficient and equitable way to achieve their objectives in Arizona. For instance, the Bureau has never proposed using Arizona's share of Colorado River water to irrigate croplands adjacent to the river—rather than in the middle of the state—despite the idea's advantages over CAP. As Daniel Dreyfus, Senate Interior Committee staff member, explained:

> With no expensive, permanent public works, like aqueducts, the plan would have been more flexible for the future. It could have absorbed the Phoenix agricultural industry without hurting anyone and it would have benefited the whole state by generating a second major urban area.[59]

Furthermore, it would have been far less expensive. Construction costs might even have been low enough for the water users to repay completely. But the Bureau never took the idea seriously because "the political power in Arizona has always resided in the Phoenix area; that is where the irrigators and most other Arizona people have always lived."[60]

4. *Repayment: A Raid on the U.S. Treasury:* CAP's proponents argue that even if the project's economic feasibility and overall worth are subject to strong doubt, CAP should nevertheless be built, because it allegedly pays for itself. In the opinion of Congressman John J. Rhodes (R-Ariz.), an influential Republican and long-time sponsor of CAP, "the only question that should be considered when a project is being studied is its repayment capability, not its benefit-cost ratio, or anything else."[61] We disagree. Even if beneficiaries repay all reimbursable costs, they are getting a significant subsidy in the form of long-term, low-interest-rate repayment obligations, as discussed in more detail in Chapter 6.

In the case of CAP, however, water users may not pay even this subsidized obligation. To repay reimbursable construction costs completely, Arizona water users will have to buy CAP water at an average price of about $35 per acre-foot, according to Bureau figures.[62] M&I users can probably afford to pay such a price, though they are now receiving water at a much cheaper rate. Irrigators, who of course require much larger quantities of water, cannot afford this average price. The Bureau calculates that the irrigators will be capable of repaying only about $96 million, or less than 30 percent of the $322 million in costs assigned to them.[63] As a result, the irrigators will be charged only $10 to $20 per acre-foot of CAP water.

Under project proposals advanced as late as 1966, excess revenues from the sale of hydroelectric power produced at Hualapai Dam were to have subsidized construction costs assigned to irrigations. When the dam was eliminated from the final authorization legislation, the Bureau suggested several possible solutions to the repayment problem.

Under the Bureau's first suggested repayment plan, M&I users could be required to pay $50 to $60 per acre-foot to make up for the much lower price to be paid by the irrigators. Under the second plan, the three counties in the CAP area, Maricopa, Pinal, and Pima, could form a water conservation district with the power to levy property taxes to repay all project costs. Under the third plan, the federal government could sell water to M&I users at cost and to irrigators at the price they could afford to pay. It would then supply the difference in direct subsidy of the irrigators.

Neither Congress nor the administration ever considered the third plan seriously, because it would make the subsidy too open to public view and criticism. The Bureau of Reclamation, which has been representing the federal government in the preconstruction negotiations with Arizona water users, favored either the first plan or a combination of the first and second.[64] Recently, however, the Bureau has expressed more interest in beginning project construction than in resolving the water contracting problems.

Agreeing with the Bureau, Congress appropriated $1.5 million in 1971 to fund the first phase of construction. The OMB, however, aware of the almost unstoppable momentum a project develops once it receives its first construction funding, impounded the funds. It demanded that the state of Arizona and the Bureau of Reclamation come up with a satisfactory repayment contract before the first spade of earth was turned.

The OMB made known to representatives of the state of Arizona that it would look favorably on a solution to the repayment problem combining above-cost municipal and industrial water supply charges and a property (ad valorem) tax levied on land within the project area.[65] Bowing to the OMB's desires, the Arizona legislature enacted a bill in April, 1971, establishing a tax-levying water district which includes all of Maricopa, Pinal, and Pima counties.[66] The legislation placed an upper limit of 1 mill (1/10 of a cent) per dollar of assessed valuation, but left the annual setting of tax levies to the district's board of governors. Judging from Governor Williams's first nine appointees, the board is going to be weighted heavily toward agricultural interests.[67] As a result, the board is likely to set a high tax rate in order to minimize irrigation water charges. Neither the tax rate nor the water charges have yet been set. Before any taxes are levied, citizens within the tri-county water district ought to challenge the constitutionality of this *appointed* board imposing a general tax on them.

It is naïve to think that the citizens of Phoenix and Tucson will be willing to pay for CAP water at more than ten times the price they pay for water now. The prospect of having to pay such high rates is bound to drive the cities to investigate cheaper ways to augment their water supplies. As noted earlier, indications are that they will be successful, if—and it is a big if—the state legislature cooperates with them.

Then who will pay for CAP construction, if not the irrigators or M&I water users? Who else but the lender of the funds with which CAP will be financed—the federal government. That means the nation's taxpayers will be paying for a project which does not benefit the nation.

The story of the Central Arizona Project is more colorful and pronounced than that of most Reclamation endeavors, but it is nonetheless typical. Most projects originate, as did CAP, in the self-interested planning of local politicians and businessmen. Often Bureau of Reclamation planners are involved in initial project discussions. If not, they soon become involved, eagerly adopting the proposed project as their own—frequently at the request of the local congressman. After investigating the project idea from a technical standpoint, the Bureau goes to Congress to push for its authorization. With the help of the friendly, predominantly western House and Senate Interior Committees and the bipartisan congressional affinity for public works projects, the Bureau gains authorization of the project. Frequently, as CAP illustrates, the project receives congressional approval *before* the Bureau has determined whether the project is really necessary and whether potential water users will be capable of repaying project costs.

CAP is atypical of Reclamation projects in the length and ferocity of congressional debate over authorization. Most projects, though equally unjustified economically, sail through Congress faster and with none of the public uproar which surrounded CAP. The Central Arizona Project must be stopped, to prevent a massive waste of federal funds. If Congress will not repeal the 1968 authorization act, then the citizens of Arizona should urge legislative action and bring suits to halt the project.

6 | Hidden Subsidies

Some large farmers push for irrigation projects even though their farms are too large to benefit from the irrigation water. They're just concerned about the public interest. It really restores your faith in democracy and human nature. It really gives you a good feeling inside.[1]

Loren Holt, Economics Branch,
Bureau of Reclamation

The owners of the big estates cannot get what they want by state action alone. They also need federal help, and they think they can come to Washington, with no one greatly concerned over the issue, and push their proposal through Congress on favorable terms to themselves.[2]

Former Senator Paul Douglas

a. Tricky Accounting

Commissioner Armstrong likes to boast that "Reclamation projects, to a large extent, pay their way."[3] In fact, the Bureau's projects do no such thing. Although Bureau officials frequently and repeatedly tout repayment as a virtue of Reclamation projects, their repayment schemes actually hide enormous subsidies.

In order to gain congressional authorization of a project, the Bureau must demonstrate that project beneficiaries are able to repay all "reimbursable costs." The Bureau of Reclamation labels most project costs as "reimbursable," including irrigation, electric power, and municipal and industrial water supply.

As the first step in measuring repayment capacity, the Bureau determines the amount of project costs which are to be repaid by the beneficiaries of each project function. To accomplish this cost distribution, the Bureau uses the "separable costs–remaining benefits" method.

The operation of this method is explained in the *Reclamation Instruction* manual:

> In this method each project purpose is assigned its separable cost [cost which could be omitted from the project if the purpose were excluded] plus a share of joint costs proportionate to the remainders found by deducting the separable cost of each purpose from the justifiable expenditure for that purpose.[4]

The "justifiable expenditure" is the benefit for a given purpose or the alternative cost of a single-purpose project to obtain the same benefit, whichever is less. And thus, the extent to which this method of cost allocation is equitable depends on the accuracy of the original project benefit estimates. Since Reclamation's benefit estimates bear little resemblance to the actual benefits accruing, as our study demonstrated in Chapters 2–4, it is unfortunate that the Bureau relies on them in allocating costs for repayment. Nevertheless, having made these distorted cost allocations for different project purposes, the Bureau of Reclamation then assigns repayment obligations to the project beneficiaries. It is in this latter phase of the process that Reclamation buries huge subsidies in complicated accounting procedures.

IRRIGATION SUBSIDIES

The history of irrigation project repayment is a history of increasing subsidization. The Reclamation Act of 1902 required recipients of project irrigation water to repay the construction costs in ten annual interest-free installments.[5] When ten years proved to be too short a period for the farmers to repay these costs, Congress lengthened the irrigation repayment period to twenty years, through the Reclamation Extension Act of 1914.[6] Since the irrigators were still unable to meet their repayment obligations, the Fact Finders' Act of 1924[7] authorized the use of Reclamation power revenues to subsidize project irrigation costs. Even with such direct assistance, the irrigation repayment period had to be extended to forty years by the Omnibus Adjustment Act of 1926.[8] The Reclamation Project Act of 1939 authorized irrigators to use project water for ten years following project construction before even beginning their forty-year repayment obligation—in effect making the repayment period fifty years.[9] Present Reclamation policy continues the ten-year period, but has extended the interest-free repayment period to fifty years,[10] for a total repayment period of at least sixty years.* Thus, Reclamation projects offer irrigators two types of subsidies—direct revenue transfers from other project functions and a subsidy resulting from the long-term interest-free obligations.

Direct Revenue Transfers: The most obvious of the two subsidies is the direct transfer of electric power revenues and municipal and industrial water revenues to repay costs assigned to the irrigators. Although the Bureau of Reclamation allocates the bulk of project costs to irrigation, it does not assign this whole burden to the farmers who will benefit from project water. Instead, the Bureau determines the amount per acre which an average farmer in the project area can afford to pay toward construction costs; it then multiplies this amount by the number of acres in the area to be irrigated to arrive at the total sum to charge the irrigators.

For example, the Bonneville unit of the Central Utah project has allocated $220,409,000 (or $1,408 per acre) to irrigation out of a total project cost of $413,250,000. Yet Reclamation has assigned only about $16,400,000 (or $105 per acre) to irrigators for repayment.[11] Hence, the irrigators

* The Missouri River Basin Project permits a 60-year wait before repayment starts, for a total of *110 years.*

get a direct capital subsidy at the outset of $1,303 per acre, or a total of over $204 million for all the irrigated farmland in the project area. Collection of a special property tax (an ad valorem tax) is expected to return $64,691,000, or $414 per acre of this initial capital subsidy. Of course, whatever share of this tax the irrigators pay reduces their subsidy accordingly; but in no case will the average direct revenue transfer subsidy to irrigators in the Bonneville Unit fall below $800 per acre.*

This example of a direct transfer subsidy is neither extreme nor unusual. In fact, Senator Allen J. Ellender (D-La.), chairman of the Senate Appropriations Committee, discovered during hearings on 1972 appropriations that ten new Reclamation projects cost $1,045 to $2,803 per acre to irrigate while the farmers themselves are repaying as little as $77 per acre. (See Table 6-A).

To make these direct transfer subsidies, the Bureau of Reclamation depends heavily on the use of revenues from its hydroelectric power plants. For the twenty-three projects listed in the Reclamation publication, *Power Systems: Average Rate and Repayment Studies, FY 1969*, $1,420,705,465 in repayment aid to irrigation was given from power revenues.[12] Future transfers of power revenues make this $1.4-billion figure seem insignificant by comparison. For the Central Utah and Deedskadee participating projects of the Colorado River storage project, the Bureau has apportioned over $1 billion of future power revenues for irrigation assis-

---

* In arriving at this $800 per acre direct transfer subsidy we recognized the fact that costs allocated to irrigators may overstate somewhat the direct subsidy. Currently, irrigators are assigned all separable projects costs, plus a proportion of all remaining non-separable costs—where the proportion depends on the amount of irrigation benefits. Since the irrigation benefits category includes secondary irrigation benefits that don't directly increase farmer income, the resulting portion of costs allocated to irrigation should instead be distributed among all the project purposes in proportion to the amount of benefits claimed. Our analytic neglect of this secondary benefit problem results in a slight upward bias in the subsidy figure—which should be more than outweighed by the downward bias created in our treatment of ad valorem taxes.

tance;[13] for the Missouri River Basin project, it has apportioned over $2-billion worth.[14]

Reclamation officials frequently claim that it is only right for power and municipal and industrial (M&I) water users to subsidize irrigation costs since M&I users supposedly reap indirect benefits from irrigation. Or, in the words of Reclamation Commissioner Ellis Armstrong:

> By participating in irrigation repayment, the power user, the user of municipal and industrial water, and the payer of ad valorem taxes contribute to social payout in return for the economic and social benefits they receive.[15]

Armstrong's logic is deficient in several respects. Admittedly, there are some regional benefits from Reclamation projects. Reclamation irrigation probably helps expand local economies, thus helping power users and others in the same project area. By the same token, however, electric power and municipal water provisions promote regional growth, thus increasing the local markets in which Reclamation irrigators can sell their goods. Thus, the indirect benefits work both ways. It is unclear that power users are receiving more regional benefits from irrigation than irrigators are receiving from electric power.

Furthermore, power revenues from a project located hundreds of miles away often are used to subsidize irrigation costs. When projects produce power or M&I revenues in excess of their repayment obligations, the Bureau often uses the revenues to help repay irrigation costs for basin projects several states away. For example, such basin accounts are in operation for the Central Valley project, the Upper Colorado River storage project, the Colorado River Basin project, and the Missouri River Basin project.* This use of basin accounts gives the illusion that a project is paying for itself when, in fact, it is being subsidized by other projects in the basin. The distant power users who help pay this subsidy to irrigators experience virtually no indirect effects of Reclama-

---

* The Missouri River Basin extends into ten states, seven of which have irrigation projects.

tion projects, except the displacement effect of Reclamation agriculture on farmers in their region. In short, there is little or no justification for irrigators to be subsidized by power and M&I water users.

THE INTEREST SUBSIDY

What repayment the irrigators do have to make need not start for ten years, and then is spread out over fifty years, and no interest is paid on the outstanding debt. This is the second subsidy. To get a feeling for the extent of the interest subsidy over the entire repayment period, consider the following example. Suppose that there are no interest costs during project construction* and that irrigation repayment begins ten years after the original outlay of construction funds. Also suppose that the irrigators will repay their obligation in equally sized annual installments over a forty-year period. If an irrigator repays a reimbursable cost of $100 per acre in the above fashion, then he really is repaying an amount with a present value of $9.42.† Thus, irrigators are getting a 91 percent interest subsidy on their repayment obligation. It should be noted that this 91 percent figure is very conservative. The example used assumed that the repayment period began ten years after project funding instead of the sixty years required in the Missouri River Basin area. Moreover, irrigators were assumed to repay their obligation in forty years—ten years faster than required. These two biases in the Bureau's favor make 91 percent a conservative estimate of the hidden interest subsidy given to irrigators.

Thus while the hidden subsidies to irrigators vary from project to project, a rough, but conservative, formula for estimating the hidden subsidies is as follows: First look for the direct transfer subsidy, that is, the cost allocated to irrigation minus the irrigators' repayment obligation, minus any ad valorem tax; next, add to this direct transfer figure 91 percent of the irrigators' remaining repayment obligation, which represents the interest rate subsidy. These numbers can be

* An equivalent assumption is that project construction is instantaneous.

† Present value was computed using a 10 percent interest rate.

calculated on either a per-acre or project-wide basis. The sum is the total subsidy.

Using this formula for the Bonneville unit, we found a total subsidy of $985 per acre of $154,245,000 for the whole project area.* To find the annual subsidy, we divided this per-acre total by a factor of 9.91 (which we got by assuming the total subsidy was taken over a fifty-year period and discounted at a rate of 10 percent to its present value). So the *annual* subsidy to irrigators getting water from the Bonneville unit will be about $99 per acre or a total of $15,600,000.

Economists Howe and Easter in a study for Resources for the Future found comparable figures. They noted that Western farmers served by Bureau of Reclamation water pay $35–$135 less per acre per year than the full cost of supplying the water.[16] If computed for a fifty-year period and discounted to its present value, this yearly subsidy range would yield a total over the fifty-year assumed life of the project of $347 to $1,133 per acre.

One observation should be made at this point. The fact that irrigators have consistently fallen short of their interest-free repayment obligations, which can be paid off with money worth only a fraction of the initial obligation, implies that either irrigation benefits have been grossly overestimated or Reclamation farmers are reaping a huge profit. Whether irrigators are able to fully capitalize on all of this subsidy is really a peripheral consideration. The crucial point is that the taxpayer—not the irrigator—bears the huge cost of Reclamation's irrigation facilities.

*			$1,408 per acre, or $220,409,000
1. Allocated to irrigation:			$1,408 per acre, or $220,409,000
2. Irrigators' repayment:	Minus	105	16,400,000
		$1,303	$204,009,000
3. Ad valorem tax:	Minus	414	64,691,000
		$ 889	$139,318,000
4. 91% of irrigators' repayment:	Plus	96	14,927,000
Total subsidy		$ 985	$154,245,000

Lines 1, 2, and 3 are used to compute the direct transfer; line 4 represents the interest subsidy.

SUBSIDIES TO OTHER BENEFICIARIES

In addition to subsidizing irrigators, the power and M&I beneficiaries have to repay their repayment with interest. Even though power and M&I revenues help pay for irrigation construction costs, power and M&I users may still get a subsidy of their own, for the interest rate is so low as to substantially understate the true cost to society of building these projects. The General Accounting Office reached the same conclusion:

> GAO found that the interest rate criteria used by federal agencies in determining the cost of financing the Federal power program result in the use of interest rates that are not representative of the cost of funds borrowed by the Treasury during the period of construction of a power project.[17]

The Bureau of Reclamation is particularly guilty of understating this interest rate. The Comptroller General of the United States pointed out in a 1970 GAO report that "unless legislation directed otherwise, the Bureau of Reclamation has used a 3 percent interest rate."[18] Examples of projects using the three percent rate are: the Boise project, Minidoka project, Columbia Basin (Grand Coulee Dam), Hungry Horse project, Palisades project, and the Yakima-Roza division.[19] The only major exceptions to this practice are the Yakima-Kennewick division power project (2.5%) and the Grand Coulee third powerplant (3.125%).[20] As a result of these low interest rates, power and M&I users may get enough of a hidden subsidy on some projects to outweigh the share of irrigation costs they must repay. In either case, however, the federal taxpayers are subsidizing the projects as a whole.

RECOMMENDATIONS

Although there is no panacea to this complex problem, some constructive suggestions can be made. First, all subsidies should either be abolished or made openly. Direct project beneficiaries should be required to pay all the reimbursable costs with interest for the project outputs they receive; if Congress wants to subsidize needy beneficiaries it should do so more candidly and without loopholes and smokescreens that hide them. Project costs should include an annually compounded interest charge, computed on an interest rate equal to the discount rate. All transfers of power revenues and M&I water revenues to help pay off irrigation costs should be prohibited. Finally, the General Accounting Office should be funded to do more comprehensive studies of Reclamation projects and given the authority to determine the repayment obligation of the beneficiaries in cases where the Bureau does not do so appropriately.

b. *160-Acre Limitation and the Excess-land Law*

I grant you, you start kicking the 160-acre limitation and it is like inspecting the rear end of a mule: You want to do it from a safe distance because you might get kicked through the side of the barn.[21]

Senator Claire Engle

While all irrigators receive special subsidies through the Bureau of Reclamation's repayment practices, only a few of them receive the largest share of this enormous hidden payout. The Bureau is again to blame for this inequitable distribution of Reclamation project windfalls.

The source of the problem is simple. In 1862, to encourage settlement in the West, Congress passed the Homestead Act, which sold 160-acre parcels of land for a nominal sum to families that had lived on the land for five years. Forty years later, in the Reclamation Act, Congress reaffirmed its desire to promote homesteading in the West by providing that no landowner could receive Bureau water for more than 160 acres. The statute reads as follows:

No right to the use of water for land in private ownership shall be sold for a tract exceeding 160 acres to any one landowner, and no such sale shall be made to any landowner unless he be an actual bona fide resident on such land, or occupant thereof residing in the neighborhood [i.e., within 50 miles].[22]

In 1914, Congress added an anti-land speculation provision requiring that no contract be let or construction started on any federal Reclamation project until the owners of excess land within the project area agreed to dispose of their excess land holdings at the value it would have been worth, if the government had not decided to build an irrigation project.[23] Congress intended by this provision to prevent large landowners and speculators from capitalizing on any unearned increment which would result, or had already resulted, from the federal investment in the project.

To tighten the language of the excess land law and to facilitate effective enforcement, Congress included a new provision in the Omnibus Adjustment Act of 1926. After 1926, excess lands could legally become eligible to receive Reclamation project water only if the landowner executed a recordable contract with the United States, obligating him to sell his excess lands at appraised prices excluding incremental values added by the proposed Reclamation project. The act stated explicitly that "no such excess lands held shall receive water from any project or division if the owners thereof refuse to execute valid recordable contracts."[24] However, the law did not clearly stipulate when the excess land must be sold; consequently, the Secretary of the Interior determined that the sale must occur within ten years after the signing of the contract and that, if the owner defaulted on the contract, the Secretary of the Interior had a power of attorney* to sell it.[26]

All these early provisions have been carried forward and reaffirmed in recent Reclamation laws and decisions. In a 1958 opinion, the Supreme Court gave a clear summation of the purpose of these laws:

> The claim of discrimination in the 160-acre limitation, we believe . . . overlooks the purpose for which the project was designed. The project was designed to benefit people, not

* The Secretary of the Interior has used this power of attorney only once, although as of December 31, 1970, there were 9,501 acres under the Secretary's power of attorney since the owners have failed or refused to sell their land as promised. Yet they continue to receive water.[25]

land. It is a reasonable classification to limit the amount of project water available to each individual in order that benefits may be distributed in accordance with the greatest good to the greatest number of individuals. The limitation insures that this enormous expenditure will not go in disproportionate shares to a few individuals with large land holdings. Moreover, it prevents the use of the federal reclamation service for speculative purposes.[27]

Through lax and ineffective enforcement, the Bureau of Reclamation has enabled certain large-scale irrigators to evade the 160-acre limitation on farms receiving Reclamation water.

INTERPRETATION AND ENFORCEMENT

While the purpose of these laws may now be clear, the interpretation and enforcement of all their provisions is not. How do Bureau of Reclamation officials and the courts define "any one landowner"? How do they read the antispeculation clauses, including the residency requirement, and the pre-project appraisal stipulation?

"Any one landowner" does not mean "any one farm or farm family." Thus a husband and wife may each own 160 acres that are eligible for Reclamation water. They may even give ownership of parts of their farms to their children; a family of four, for instance, may own a 640-acre farm eligible for subsidized water from a Reclamation project. With an annual subsidy of $35 to $135 per acre,* each 160-acre landowner can rake in from over $5,000 to over $20,000 per year. But a family of four may get from over $20,000 to over $80,000 per year.

Similarly, a family or close-held corporation—one with only a few shareholders, often from the same family—can divide its landholdings into several eligible blocks as long as it adheres to three rules by which multiple ownership using the corporate device are to be tested. These rules are:

1. No corporation may own more than 160 acres in a single Reclamation project as eligible land for project water.

* These figures were noted by Howe and Easter and described in the previous section.

2. The corporate farm may be disregarded to determine whether any stockholder, as a beneficial owner of a pro rata [proportional] share of the corporate land holdings owns land in excess of 160 acres.

3. The corporation must not have been created for the primary purpose of avoiding application of the excess land laws.[28]

If all three of these rules were enforced, corporate farmers would have difficulty hiding their evasion of the 160-acre limitation behind a facade of corporate fronts. But the Bureau of Reclamation prefers to give them cover by effectively ignoring the third rule, as illustrated in a recent case.

In early 1965, the A. Perelli-Minetti Corporation broke up its 1,909-acre holding into twenty-six separate corporations, with a different former stockholder owning each new corporation. Since each of the new corporate entities has less than 160 acres and is technically owned by a single stockholder who doesn't "own" any other project lands, each new corporation is eligible for project water. According to J. Lane Morthland, the Interior Department's associate solicitor for reclamation and power:

> The fact that each of the new corporations has identical officers and boards of directors at this time is unimportant. . . . The identity of officers and directors goes to the question of operation and management and not to ownership.[29]

The fact that the total acreage continues to be operated as a unit under essentially the same management, and in the same manner as before it was divided, is also ignored.

Mr. Morthland concluded that fraud is the only grounds for invoking the third rule of multiple ownership. He did not find fraud in the fact that the owners of this corporate farm of nearly 2,000 acres rearranged its corporate structure in order to receive a subsidy of from $70,000 to $270,000 per year.* If the Perelli-Minetti Corporation didn't defraud the

---

*The figures are based on the same $35–$135 per acre annual subsidy noted by Howe and Easter and described in the previous section of this chapter.

public of these funds, then the Department of the Interior did.

Publicly owned corporations and large individual land-owners cannot disguise attempts to evade the excess-land provisions as easily as the Perelli-Minetti Corporation did, since the second rule applies only to family and close-held corporations. It is too difficult to identify all the ultimate owners of a large publicly owned corporation, and the second rule was never meant to apply to individually owned land. Instead these landowners have other methods of evading the 160-acre limitation and hiding the huge subsidies they get from Reclamation projects.

First, they get outright exemptions from the law. The private land residency requirement of the 1902 Reclamation Act has "long been discarded,"[30] although one long-time corruption fighter, Ben Yellen, has sued in California to get the residency requirement enforced. If Yellen wins and if Congress does not then repeal the residency requirement, his victory could drive the big growers out of California. One official involved in the case admitted, "Interior is scared stiff; we're going all out on this one because if Yellen wins, all hell could break loose."[31]

Other exemptions have been granted by legislative or administrative fiat to special irrigation districts. A 1971 un-published report from the Bureau of Reclamation describes twenty-four different exemptions, modifications, waivers, and special provisions applicable to the excess-land laws.[32] These exemptions cover a total of 2,022,500 acres of land.[33]

For example, in the Small Projects Reclamation Act, large landowners succeeded in obtaining the privilege, known as the Engle Formula, of making interest payments in lieu of other compliance with acreage limitations. That is, as long as the big landowner pays back the cost of construction with a low interest rate, he can receive project water for as many acres as he desires.[34]

In addition to this privilege, the Small Reclamation Projects Act provides interest-free loans for private irrigation of less than 160 acres.[35] Such loans follow the simple formula of no money down, fifty years to repay, and no interest—a far cry from the annual 18 percent rate consumers pay for credit card privileges. To date, the Bureau of Reclamation has made over $157 million of these no- or low-interest and long-term loans to private individuals and groups for private projects specifically benefiting only these private interests.

Large landowners on the Kings and Kern rivers have also sought Congressional and administrative acceptance of full payment of their repayment contracts as a means of discharging their obligations to comply with the 160-acre limitation. According to Paul S. Taylor, professor emeritus of economics at Berkeley, former consultant to the Bureau of Reclamation, and author of numerous law review articles on the 160-acre limitation issue:

> The demand of excess landholders that full payment be accepted as "full satisfaction" of acreage limitation is a spurious claim that final payment of a fraction of the construction cost should extinguish a public policy that does not depend on cash.[36]

Even when large landholders can't get some kind of exemption from the 160-acre limitation, they still have plenty of ways to circumvent the law and reap undeserved and excessive benefits from Reclamation projects. Although the 1914 law specifically required excess landowners to negotiate recordable contracts even before construction begins, in practice the Department of the Interior ignores this stipulation and says that the excess landowner "must volunteer" and "has an unlimited time" to sign—or not to sign—a recordable contract.[37] On all Reclamation projects there are less than eight hundred recordable contracts covering 164,000 acres of excess land. About 65,000 acres of this has actually been sold and an additional 992,250 acres of excess land in project areas is not even under contract.[38]

The Bureau of Reclamation also ignores the 1926 statute that prohibits giving *any* water to landowners who refuse to place their excess land under recordable contract for sale. The Bureau gave away $14 million worth of Shasta Dam water before signing any contracts at all. As Table 6-B illustrates, many big landowners in the Westlands Irrigation District are receiving Reclamation water in spite of the fact that little—or none—of their excess land is under recordable contract.

Furthermore, over sixty excess landowners receive Reclamation water on several 160-acre plots within the same project or division. For example, Southern Pacific gets Central Valley project water from five districts besides Westlands.[39] If the landowners get the 160-acre minimum irrigated in each district, they get a total annual subsidy from $28,000 to over $100,000.* By administering the excess-land law on a contract-wide rather than a project-wide basis, the Bureau permits these excess landowners to split up their holdings into several "eligible" 160-acre plots which can circumvent the intent of the law.

In addition to permitting this blatant evasion of the law, the Bureau of Reclamation participated in a more subtle giveaway of federally subsidized water. While the Bureau concedes that the 160-acre limitation applies to surface deliveries of project water, it argues that the excess-land law does not apply to pumping of underground waters that have been improved by deep percolation losses from surface water applications—including surface applications of project water.[40] In short, owners of ineligible excess lands get a water windfall from the raising of the underground water level due to the federal water project.

Even those landholders who do execute recordable contracts have nothing to lose—and everything to gain. These excess lands under a recordable contract are still eligible to receive subsidized water for up to ten years before they must be sold. And the value of this subsidy is considerable. Anderson Clayton and Company, for example, as noted in Table 6-B, has over 25,000 acres of excess lands under recordable

* Again, these figures are based on Howe and Easter's $35–$135 figures, as verified by our calculations from the previous section.

contract; these acres receive a direct subsidy of over $2 million per year in cheap water. No wonder Harry Horton, a lawyer for big southern California growers, stated:

> I will give you my own opinion of Jack O'Neill's [a big landowner in the Westlands District of the San Luis project] willingness to sign the 160-acre limitation. He thinks if he gets water for ten years on there without having to sell, he can make enough money out of it so he can afford to sell the land at any old price.[41]

But Jack O'Neill and other big landowners don't have to sell their excess land at "any old price." The Bureau's assessment policies see to that. Instead of appraising land values prior to project construction and without project benefits as the law requires, the Bureau's trick is to compare land receiving project water with nearby land not receiving the water, claiming that the difference in sales price represents the project's value to the land. But San Luis has helped nonproject land in the area a great deal by replenishing the fast-dwindling groundwater supply, by raising its value, and by relieving the general demand for its water. Contrary to the intent of federal law, the Bureau's assessment technique permits O'Neill and associates to cash in on an unearned increment in land value created by the San Luis Project.

The absurdity of this assessment technique is indicated in a case cited by a Westlands realtor, Jack Molsebergen.[42] The Bureau approved the sale of land receiving San Luis project water for $425 an acre.* Its appraised value at the time of sale was $450, but the Bureau considered that twenty-five dollars' worth of value came from the San Luis project, and in conformity with the law requiring sale at prewater prices, marked the land down to $425. In other words, by the Bureau's own straight-faced estimate, the United States was spending nearly $1,000 an acre to confer benefits which it valued at only $25 an acre.[43] Of course, the Bureau's $25 figure was phony, and anyone selling for $425 an acre re-

---

* One Bureau official indicated that the range of Westlands land values is about $400–$1,000 per acre, so the example we are using is on the low end of the spectrum.

ceives an unearned incremental land value added by the project. In 1960, when the project began, the land cost $150 and its value was declining rapidly as groundwater levels plummeted from over-pumping. Westlands was "mining" 900,000 acre-feet a year from a basin with an estimated replenishable yield of 190,000 acre-feet, dropping pumping levels ten feet a year. The San Luis project is the only change throughout Westlands since 1960 that could possibly affect land values.[44] Even adding a factor for inflation, based on the average increase of all farms during the period, we calculated that the land would yield a price of only $190 by the time of its sale in 1968. But with the water levels dropping, it probably wouldn't have been worth $100 an acre without the project.

In fact, sales figures in Westlands show an appreciation of about $300 an acre.* As Table 6-B shows, this appreciation confers a potential windfall of more than $23.5 million on the Southern Pacific Company; $13.4 million on the Giffens; nearly $7 million on Boswell's Boston Ranch; and over $9 million on Anderson, Clayton and Company. The district's total land value has increased over $167 million. This is the capitalized value of the subsidized water, which the law is supposed to prohibit large landowners and speculators from getting.

By permitting a high selling price like $425 per acre, the Bureau sometimes gives the landowners a way to avoid selling at all. Since the fraudulent assessment technique of the Bureau puts the postsubsidy land value in the "presubsidy assessment" for sales purposes, no one wants to buy. So the large landowners in Westlands, some of whom, like Southern Pacific, never wanted to sell in the first place, get to keep their land and the subsidies that go with it.

The Westlands case discussed above is the most conspicuous and well-documented example of how large landowners circumvent the excess-land law with the Bureau's help. Westlands has about one-third of the excess acreage on all Bureau

---

* The $300 figure is less than our computations in Table 6-B showing a total subsidy of $847 per acre, since landowners could only capitalize on part of the total.

projects. But there are still over 858,000 acres of excess lands outside Westlands. Unfortunately, there is no way to determine whether similar evasion takes place on other project areas. Reclamation officials did not have—or at least would not admit to having—the information they would need to enforce the law effectively. The data they did have on Westlands were incredibly difficult to dig out and organize; the data they have on other projects are even more fragmentary and confusing—and are largely irrelevant. The absence and inaccessibility of these data are strongly suggestive of the Bureau's desire to avoid enforcing the law. Data on each project or major unit within a project, naming each excess landowner, should be gathered by the Bureau and made easily available. Likewise, Reclamation should know, but does not, how much subsidy is in each acre-foot of Reclamation water, and exactly how much water (and hence subsidy) each landowner receives. If public welfare recipients must give much more detailed and personal information to qualify for meager benefits, why shouldn't the few big irrigators who soak the government for millions of dollars be required to give their names and the amount of federally subsidized water they receive? Congress is entitled at least to a list of all the landowners receiving Reclamation water, the estimated subsidy per acre-foot of this water, and the total amount of water and subsidy they receive. Then Congress can better evaluate where the excess-land law is being evaded and where profiteers are receiving excessive and undeserved benefits.

The Bureau also fails to give enforcement of the law a high priority. They have fewer than twenty-five people working on the problem and only six are technically full-time compliance officers.[45] Worse still, the Bureau has rarely cut off water as a penalty for violation of the law, so irrigators know they can evade it with impunity.

RECOMMENDATIONS

Governor Reagan's Special Task Force on the Acreage Limitation Problem recommended that the federal excess-land provisions be raised to 640 acres; but others such as Bill

Kinsey, agricultural economist with Stanford University's Food Research Institute, and Paul Taylor, professor emeritus of economics at Berkeley and noted expert on the 160-acre limitation, strongly disagree. Without taking a position on the current debate over whether 160 acres is still a viable size for profitable farm operations, we support the continuation of a low-acre limitation—if for no other reason than to set a limit on the federal subsidy one landowner can receive from a Reclamation project. In fact, we recommend that Congress revise the excess-land laws so that one landowner cannot receive Reclamation water for more than 160 acres—counting water received from *all* Bureau of Reclamation projects. To be effective the excess-land law must at least be more vigorously enforced.

If the Bureau of Reclamation really wanted to enforce the law, it would buy up the excess land itself *before* building the project, and either lease or resell it at cut-rate prices to small land operators. Or it could sell it at the market price, which would include the capitalized value of the project water subsidy. The government—rather than private profiteers—would then receive the "unearned increment," which it could use to help the hard-pressed Treasury or redistribute in the form of other government programs, such as education or conservation efforts. Representatives Robert Kastenmeier (D-Wis.), Jerome Waldie (D-Calif.), Ronald Dellums (D-Calif.), Don Edwards (D-Calif.), George Danielson (D-Calif.), John McFall (D-Calif.) and Edward Roybal (D-Calif.) have introduced legislation to achieve this objective.

At the very least, the Secretary of the Interior should require that all excess-landholders sign recordable contracts before the project is built and that they sell all their excess land before receiving any water on *any* of their lands. Furthermore, their land values should be assessed *before* the project is built to ensure that the appraised value excludes project benefits. Finally, the Bureau of Reclamation should compile data in more relevant form (as illustrated in Table 6-B) for each and every project, showing the excess-land-owners, the amount of their land that receives Reclamation water, the direct annual subsidy they get with this cheap water, the total amount of their excess land in the project area, and the unearned increment they may capitalize on by selling their land.

The Secretary has ample authority to make these procedural revisions, which are in keeping with the original intent of the laws. It was the administrative discretion of past secretaries that established the current loopholes, allowing landholders to evade the excess-acreage laws. Unless the hidden subsidies that sneak through these loopholes are exposed and eliminated, a privileged few will continue to profit at the expense of the general public.

7

Indians Sold
Down the River

a. Water Law and Indian Rights

In the previous two chapters, we discussed how Reclamation projects are built for special interest groups—not for the poor or the nation's general welfare. Nevertheless, it is often said on Capitol Hill that a Reclamation project has a better chance of passing if it is presented "under an Indian blanket" —in other words, if the project includes some benefit for Indians. Unfortunately, it is usually true that Indians get *only* a "blanket"—a token. The Bureau of Reclamation and its allies use the Indians for their own political purposes and, at the same time, infringe upon the Indians' rights and ignore the Indians' needs.

The Bureau of Reclamation has never tried to serve the Indians, because it has never needed to. Traditionally the servant of the large Western land and water magnates seeking government water to enhance their economic power, the Bureau of Reclamation has always viewed the Indians and their water rights as obstacles in the path of Reclamation projects. The following case studies* describe how the Bu-

* In addition to the examples presented, there are other significant cases which we did not fully investigate but which merit more critical analysis. For example, the Bureau of Reclamation treatment of the Shoshone and Arapaho Indian tribes' land claims around the

reau of Reclamation has either circumvented or run rough-
shod over these human obstacles in order to build their dams.
To appreciate the legitimacy of the Indians' grievances and
outrage against the Bureau of Reclamation, and to put the
issues in perspective, it is first necessary to understand some
principles of water law and the Indians' legal rights.

In the western United States, there are two major legal
principles regarding private and corporate rights to the use of
water. In California, and to some degree in other western
states, there is adherence to a greatly modified *riparian doctrine* that originated in the more humid areas of the eastern
United States. Broadly speaking, the riparian doctrine has
been described as follows:

> Rights to the use of water in a stream are created by owner-
> ship of land which is riparian [i.e., land touching the river
> bank and within the watershed] to that stream. The water
> right is an incident of landownership, and it cannot be lost
> by mere disuse.[1]

Riparian rights are held in common with others who own
land which is riparian to (i.e., touching) the stream in question.

The *prior appropriation doctrine*—predicated upon compliance with state law respecting the diversion and use of
water for beneficial purposes—is the second, and predominant, water rights principle in the western United States. This
doctrine differs markedly from the riparian doctrine and is
more suitable to the arid and semiarid regions. The prior
appropriation doctrine has been summed up as follows:

> A right is obtained simply by taking water and applying it
> to a beneficial use, and it may be lost by ceasing to make
> such use. . . . As between competing appropriators from the
> same source, priority in time is determinative.[2]

If water users compete for the use of the same water, the
doctrine of prior appropriation provides, "first in use, first in

Riverton project, its policy toward the Pueblos in the Rio Grande
Basin, and its involvement in the Navajo Steam Power Plant and
the Black Mesa controversy should be examined further.

right." A senior appropriator of water, if his claim has been filed with the state, has absolute rights over a junior appropriator.

In 1908, a third doctrine of water rights was propounded by the U.S. Supreme Court in the case of *Winters* v. *United States.* At issue in that case were the legal rights to the use of the waters of the Milk River, which constitutes the northern boundary of the Fort Belknap Indian Reservation in Montana. The Indians used this water for irrigation on their reservation. When Henry Winters, an upstream farmer, diverted the stream's water for his own use, the Indians were deprived of the amount of water they needed; consequently, the Indians sued. In 1908 the Supreme Court ruled in their favor. It is useful to quote at some length from the decision in order to clarify the Court's reasoning:

> The case, as we view it, turns on the agreement of May 1888, resulting in the creation of Fort Belknap Reservation. In the construction of this agreement there are certain elements to be considered that are prominent and significant. The reservation was a part of a very much larger tract which the Indians had the right to occupy and use, and which was adequate for the habits and wants of a nomadic and uncivilized people. It was the policy of the government, it was the desire of the Indians, to change those habits and to become a pastoral and civilized people. If they should become such, the original tract was too extensive; but a smaller tract would be inadequate without a change of conditions. The lands were arid, and, without irrigation, were practically valueless. And yet, it is contended, the means of irrigation were deliberately given up by the Indian and deliberately accepted by the government. . . .
>
> The Indians had command of the lands and the waters—command of all their beneficial use, whether kept for hunting, "and grazing roving herds of stock," or turned to agriculture and the arts of civilization. Did they give up all this? Did they reduce the area of their occupation and give up the waters which made it valuable or adequate? . . . If it were possible to believe affirmative answers, we might also believe that the Indians were awed by the power of the government or deceived by its negotiators. Neither is possible.

> The government is asserting the rights of the Indians. . . .
> On account of their relations to the government, it cannot be
> supposed that the Indians were alert to exclude by formal
> words every inference which might militate against or de-
> feat the declared purpose of themselves and the government.[3]

In short, the Court ruled that the Indians reserved, by infer-
ence, their rights to water in the Milk River in the 1888
treaty—even though water rights had never been mentioned
in the document itself. Furthermore, the Court said explicitly
that such a reservation was not repealed by the subsequent
admission of Montana into the United States in 1889:

> That the government did reserve them [i.e., the water rights
> for the Indians against appropriation under state law] we
> have decided, and for a use which would necessarily be
> continued through the years.[4]

More generally, the Court was saying in the *Winters* case
that when the Indians reserved rights to use of water for
themselves or when the Congress or the executive branch
reserved it for them, the rights thus reserved were enough to
make the reservations livable.

Later decisions established that Indians have prior and
superior rights to any beneficial uses of water, both at the
present time and in the future. The Supreme Court stated this
position most clearly in *Conrad Investment Company* v.
United States, where it said:

> Whatever water of Birch Creek may be reasonably necessary,
> not only for present uses, but for future requirements, is
> clearly within the terms of the treaties as construed by the
> Supreme Court in the Winters Case.[5]

These early decisions were reaffirmed by the Supreme
Court in subsequent cases, including the 1963 case of *Arizona* v. *California*. In this case the Court said:

> Most of the land in these reservations is and always has
> been arid. If the water necessary to sustain life is to be had,
> it must come from the Colorado River or its tributaries. It is
> impossible to believe that when Congress created the great

Colorado River Reservation and when the Executive Department of this nation created the other reservations they were unaware that most of the lands were the desert kind—hot, scorching sands—and that water from the river would be essential to the life of the Indian people and the animals they hunted and the crops they raised.[6]

The *Winters* doctrine has been muddied by a recent Supreme Court decision in the consolidated cases of *Eagle River* and *Water Division No. 5*, which held that federally reserved water rights are subject to the jurisdiction of state courts.[7] This decision raises a serious question as to whether Indian water rights are now also subject to state court adjudication. While the Indians can still claim their *Winters* doctrine rights, they will have an onerous burden if they must fight the costly battles to protect these rights in all the states as well as in the federal courts.

The Indians are particularly perturbed that the federal government, the Indians' legal trustee, inadequately defended their interests in these cases. Although several Indian tribes and their lawyers specifically and repeatedly requested that the federal government clarify the Indians' rights in these cases, the government's brief stated—in a footnote the Indians and their lawyers consider false and inadequate—

> To the best of our knowledge, none of the reserved water rights claimed by the United States in Water Division No. 5 relate to Indian lands. In the event this Court should rule that 43 U.S.C. 666 subjects federal reserved rights in general to state adjudication, there would remain the further question (not presented by this case) whether the consent statute covers water rights held by the United States in trust for specific Indian tribes—frequently pursuant to treaty—rather than for the benefit of the general public.[8]

In fact, the Department of Justice failed in the presentation of the case at all levels of the proceedings to distinguish between the Indians' *private* rights to the use of water held in trust for them by the United States and the *public* rights to the use of water reserved by the United States for *public* use.

The Indians object particularly to the definition used by the United States of "reserved rights" which includes Indian private rights:

> Reserved rights entitle the United States to use as much water from sources on lands withdrawn from the public domain as is necessary to fulfill the purposes for which the lands were withdrawn, with a priority as of the date of withdrawal, subject only to water rights vested as of that date. *Winters v. United States*, 207 U.S. 564, 577; *Arizona v. California*, 373 U.S. 546, 598, 601.[9]

For support of this definition the Justice Department cited the *Winters* doctrine and *Arizona* v. *California*. However, *Winters* relates exclusively to Indian—not federal—rights, and *Arizona* v. *California* relates primarily to Indian rights. By melding the private rights of the Indians with the public rights of the United States this definition subjects them to the same principles of law, with severe damage to the Indians. Furthermore, if the language of the decisions is followed strictly, it will force the Indians to have their rights adjudicated in state court proceedings, which will greatly add to their legal costs.

Indian tribes from Arizona, California, Colorado, Nevada, New Mexico, and Utah passed a resolution requesting congressional investigation of the "shocking and deplorable failure of the Federal Government to make any good faith effort to present the Indians' case to the United States Supreme Court."[10] In addition, Raymond G. Simpson, tribal attorney for the Fort Mojave tribe, filed a motion with the Supreme Court requesting that the Court consider the Indians' argument and vacate its March 24 decision. This motion was denied. Meanwhile, Senators Alan Cranston (D-Calif.) and John Tunney (D-Calif.) and Congressman Jerry L. Pettis (R-Calif.) wrote Interior Secretary Rogers Morton and Attorney General John Mitchell expressing their interest in and support for the Indians' position.

We recommend that either the Supreme Court on its own

motion or the Congress investigate the Justice Department's failure to distinguish between public and private rights under 43 USC 666, and clarify and reaffirm the Indians' special private water rights and their unique relationship with the federal government. In particular, it must be made clear that the Indians' *Winters* doctrine rights are not subject to state court jurisdiction without specific Indian consent.

It is important to understand how the Bureau of Reclamation interprets Indians' water rights, for their opinions have vital implications for the Indians' supply of water. The Bureau, as might be expected, defines the *Winters* doctrine as narrowly as possible. Edward Davis, Assistant Solicitor for Reclamation, claims that the *Winters* doctrine can be applied only to agricultural and domestic uses—i.e., irrigation and household uses.[11] Others within the Bureau conceptualize it slightly differently by saying that the *Winters* doctrine can be used for the purposes for which the reservation was founded. Though that sounds broader, in practice it is just as narrow as Davis's interpretation, for they interpret the "purposes" of the reservation as agriculture, or, in some cases, fishing.

Yet, what constitutes the "purpose" of a reservation? And what, if anything, have the courts said or implied about the uses to which the *Winters* doctrine applies? The treaties themselves are vague about establishing "purposes." The Navajo Treaty of 1849 speaks of the "prosperity and happiness of said Indians."[12] Surely that cannot be interpreted reasonably as limiting the Navajos to the pursuit of agriculture. Many of the treaties speak of teaching the Indians the "arts of civilization." Undoubtedly, industry and mining are included among the "arts of civilization" as we understand that term now.

Every important court case concerning the *Winters* doctrine has involved irrigation or fishing uses, so there has never been any explicit ruling on the applicability of the doctrine to—for example—industrial uses. However, that does not mean that there are no implications to be drawn from court decisions. The phrase that seems to have been most popular with the courts is "beneficial use": a water right can be maintained if the water is applied to some "beneficial use." To repeat part of the *Winters* decision:

> The Indians had command of the lands and the waters—command of all their beneficial use, whether kept for hunting "and grazing roving herds of stock," or turned to agriculture and the arts of civilization. Did they give up all this?[13]

No, the Court answers. The Indians did not give up the command of the lands and the waters for "all their beneficial use"; by implication, then, the Indians still have that command. Furthermore, the Court distinguishes between "agriculture" and "the arts of civilization." They are not presented as synonyms. The *Winters* doctrine therefore seems clearly to refer to more than just agriculture, and the Bureau of Reclamation's interpretation is indefensibly narrow.

How faithfully does the Bureau of Reclamation apply even its very narrowly defined version of the *Winters* doctrine? When asked this question, Assistant Reclamation Commissioner Gilbert Stamm replied, "You're talking about a doctrine as compared to a law. . . . We are obligated to carry out the laws as passed by Congress."[14] When asked further whether a doctrine propounded by the Supreme Court might have the force of law, he said that that was a technical legal point which he, not being an attorney, was not qualified to answer.[15] Not only was he ignoring the fact that, in most cases, the Bureau actually writes and lobbies for the laws that Congress passes, but he was also revealing how little attention the Bureau gives the *Winters* doctrine in its planning of projects. As George Myron, former Associate Solicitor for Reclamation, said, the Bureau "tries to ignore" the *Winters* doctrine; it tries to "nibble at the [water] right."[16] The following case studies serve as evidence of this allegation that the Bureau of Reclamation consciously evades and infringes on the Indians' water rights.

b. *Pyramid Lake: Down the Drain*

Pyramid Lake is a beautiful lake in western Nevada, approximately 30 miles north of Reno. It is the lifeblood of the Pyramid Lake Indian Reservation, inhabited by the Northern Paiute Indians. The fish that the lake provides have been the Northern Paiutes' prime economic resource for centuries. The Truckee River, which flows east into Nevada from the California Sierras, is the lake's only source of water.

Since 1905, the level of Pyramid Lake has steadily dropped because of the diversion of water from Truckee River. In that year, the Bureau of Reclamation established the Newlands Reclamation project in Nevada. The construction of the Derby Dam on the Truckee provided the water necessary for the project. Without the approval or consultation of the Northern Paiutes, the Bureau of Reclamation developed the irrigation project and the dam.[17]

The results have been catastrophic for Pyramid Lake. Every year the water level drops more than a foot and the shoreline recedes about 10 feet. The lake's surface area is 50 square miles smaller than in 1905, and sandbars at the south end of the lake prevent the fish from swimming up the Truckee to spawn. The lake's shrinkage plus the increased salinity due to the dropping water level have seriously reduced the fish population and threatens to wipe it out altogether.[18]

Since Pyramid Lake is the basis for their economic survival, the fortunes of the Northern Paiutes have receded with the water level. About 75 percent of the tribe's income is derived from the sale of fishing and boating permits.[19] Now, however, they are forced to stock the lake with fish—a process that cuts deeply into their profits. Although the tribe would like to increase its income by developing the lake area for recreation, it cannot do so until the level of the lake is stabilized.

The situation threatens to deteriorate further. Only a limited quantity of water is available from the Truckee River; all parties cannot be completely satisfied. The Bureau of Reclamation is still constructing part of the Washoe project, another Nevada irrigation development, which would divert even more water from the Truckee—and which would mean even less water for Pyramid Lake. Moreover, because part of the Truckee flows through California, that state has been trying to claim part of the river's water for its own use. And Nevada and California have negotiated a water compact that, if approved by Congress, would not only recognize California's right to Truckee water, but would also require that all users seek state approval of water claims.

Where has the Department of the Interior stood during this controversy? In every instance, the department has sided with the non-Indian claimants who have illegally been stealing Indian water for sixty-seven years. The department has consistently supported the Bureau of Reclamation's actions. In 1963, when the Indians objected fiercely to Reclamation's plans for the Washoe project, Interior Secretary Udall appointed a task force to investigate the matter. Although the government task force's report gave the Indians vague assurances that the department would make "every effort to maintain the greatest practicable flow of water into Pyramid Lake,"[20] it refused to specify any definite amount of water which would be reserved. In March, 1969, Secretary Hickel assured the Northern Paiutes that Pyramid Lake would not be destroyed, but scarcely four months later he approved a proposal which would have "stabilized" the lake by lowering its water level another 152 feet.[21]

The Northern Paiutes have been betrayed by the federal government—their legal trustee—every step of the way. They have found no relief in the Department of Interior, the Bureau of Reclamation, the Justice Department, or anywhere else in the government. They have been the victims of political power plays on both the state and federal levels. In August, 1970, the Northern Paiutes brought suit against Secretary Hickel and Attorney General Mitchell in the United States District Court in Washington, D.C.

Justifiable as they may be, such lawsuits are a long, costly, and uncertain avenue to relief. To correct the injustices more directly, we recommend that the Secretary of the

Interior use his administrative authority to (1) claim sufficient waters from the Truckee River to stabilize the present level of Pyramid Lake so that it can be maintained as a fishery and a viable, stable body of water; (2) oppose any usurpation of the Indians' water rights, such as the proposed Nevada-California interstate compact; and (3) ensure that the Washoe project, and in particular the Watashemau Dam on the Carson River, does not proceed as long as it threatens the Northern Paiutes' water from the Truckee River and hence from Pyramid Lake. In addition, Congress can and should (1) hold hearings on the Pyramid Lake controversy; (2) refuse to approve the Nevada-California interstate compact; and (3) refuse to appropriate any more funds for the Washoe project.

c. Kennewick Extension: Misrepresenting the Facts

The Kennewick irrigation district, connected with the Yakima project in southern Washington, has been in operation for several decades. When the Bureau of Reclamation built the Kennewick division in the 1920s, it constructed a large enough irrigation system to serve 25,000 acres—6,000 acres more than the irrigation district needed at the time. About 1960, the board of directors of the Kennewick irrigation district recommended to the Bureau of Reclamation and the Department of the Interior that the 6,000 additional acres be developed by using the existing irrigation system at full capacity. Such a proposal was supported by the important local agricultural concerns. As an intra-Bureau memorandum stated:

> You will observe that the bulk of the pressure for the immediate development of the Extension area is coming from a "corporate type" farm operation.[22]

One of these operations was Balcom and Moe, who are growers and shippers of wholesale potatoes. This firm, by its own statement, represents "ownership interests of over 1,100 acres."[23]

The new project, known as the Kennewick division extension, would require pumping units, a siphon, canals, wasteways, and drainage works. The total cost of the project is now estimated at over $7.5 million.[24] Finding the necessary water for the project was the major problem.

The Yakima River has its source in northwest Washington, and flows into the Columbia several hundred miles southeast. The river forms much of the northeastern border of the Yakima Reservation. Its water is drawn from numerous smaller rivers and streams, among them Toppenish and Satus Creeks, which arise upon and join the Yakima within the borders of the reservation. The Kennewick irrigation district and the extension area are both downstream from the Yakima Indian Reservation.

According to the Interior Department's report on the Kennewick extension, written by the Bureau of Reclamation, the water needed for the irrigation project will come from the overflow of the dam next upstream (Sunnyside Dam) from the diversion dam (Prosser Dam), and from the water flowing into the Yakima between the two dams.[25] However, because the overflow from Sunnyside is reported to be unreliable, the project is expected to depend on the more reliable inflow between the two dams. This inflow has two sources. First, and particularly during the late irrigation season (July and later), there is the return to the river of the water from the Yakima Reservation and elsewhere that was diverted for upstream irrigation uses, but which was not consumed; this is the return irrigation flow. The second source is the natural flow from the streams and creeks which are tributaries to the Yakima between Sunnyside and Prosser dams, such as Toppenish and Satus creeks. These creeks will be the main reliable source of water supply during the early irrigation season, before the return flows are large enough to be significantly useful.

It is the proposed reliance on these two creeks that poses the problem for the Yakima Indians. These two creeks, which arise upon, traverse, and join the Yakima River within the reservation, will be used for downstream irrigation. For over fifty years, the Yakimas have been trying to get three small irrigation projects approved by Congress and built by the Bureau of Reclamation—projects which would use the water from Toppenish and Satus creeks. The three projects have been pending since 1914, 1916, and 1920, but not one penny has yet been appropriated for any of them. "We could not even get approval," wrote the Yakima tribal chairman to Senator Henry Jackson, chairman of the Senate Interior Committee, "for $500,000 for the irrigation of 5,000 acres."[26] The Yakimas are afraid that if their creek water is used for the Kennewick extension, they will never regain its use if and when their projects are eventually built. Even though they would still possess legal rights to the use of the water under the *Winters* doctrine, they would lose the water from the two creeks for all practical purposes. Even former Secretary of the Interior Hickel "agreed absolutely" that "as a practical matter, if the Indian water was committed for the Kennewick Division, it would mean that the Indians—irrespective of their legal rights to that water—would lose it."[27]

Yet the Bureau of Reclamation and others in the Department of the Interior insisted on misrepresenting the facts of the case. Only one month after Hickel "agreed absolutely" that the Yakima would lose their water if the extension were built, he wrote in a letter to Senator Jackson:

> The project is not dependent on water from the Yakima Reservation. . . . There is nothing in our opinion in the language of S. 742 [the bill which would build Kennewick extension] or its legislative history which we would construe as adversely affecting the Indian interests.[28]

After William Veeder, water conservation and utilization specialist of the Bureau of Indian Affairs, sent the Bureau of Reclamation a detailed memorandum documenting Kennewick's reliance on Indian water, the Bureau of Reclamation replied:

> The construction and operations of Kennewick Division Extension will not affect the Indians' water rights. . . . Together the two creeks account for only 2 percent of the total natural flow of the Yakima River in that reach during the period July through October. Even if the entire flow of

the two were lost to the project, the effect on Kennewick would be inconsequential.[29]

While the Bureau's statement is technically accurate, it is quite irrelevant and even misleading. The period at issue is not only the late irrigation season, but also the early months; these are entirely ignored in the Bureau's statement. One must assume from their refusal to defend their plans that Yakima Reservation return flows and the two Indian creeks are crucial to the necessary water supply during the early irrigation season. Consequently, the plan for the Kennewick extension is based upon a malicious and intentional disregard for the legal rights of the Yakima Indians.

Why didn't the Department of the Interior make these objections apparent to Congress before 1969? It wasn't until the final set of hearings and right before Congress voted on the Kennewick extension bill that the Yakimas' interests and objections were placed before the respective Interior Committees. The Bureau of Indian Affairs (BIA) and the Department of the Interior were responsible for this inaction. Both the department and the Bureau of Reclamation were two-faced in their reports on the Kennewick extension. One example was Hickel's two contradictory statements cited above. Furthermore, the Bureau of Reclamation would tell one story to the Indians of how the project would use solely non-Indian water, while initially telling Congress the opposite. And when the Indians tried to clarify their position for Congress, the Department of the Interior squelched their efforts. According to Chairman Robert Jim of the Yakima tribe:

> When S. 742 was before the Senate Interior Committee the objection of the Yakimas to the project were brought to the attention of the Department of the Interior. Those objections were totally ignored and the Senate was not informed of them.[30]

This breach of trust was not merely another case of the Bureau of Reclamation triumphing over the BIA; in this particular incident, the BIA failed to push on the Indians' behalf. A staff member on the Senate Interior Committee said that "the BIA suppressed itself."[31] Any opposition to the Kennewick extension within the Indian Bureau was "suppressed somewhere in BIA's hierarchy."[32] The first two times Congress considered the proposal, the BIA commissioner was asked for his comments on the measure. However, "he had no comments to make, and said so."[33] The third time it came before Congress—in 1969—he was not asked again; it was assumed there was still no objection on his part. According to Senate Interior and Insular Affairs staff man Daniel Dreyfus, any meaningful effort BIA made to oppose the project came "too goddamned late."[34]

One of the problems highlighted by this case, then, was the utter failure of the Bureau of Indian Affairs to make a concerted effort to protect the Yakimas' interests. Believing that "there are no Indian interests involved" in the Kennewick extension,[35] BIA never bothered to reevaluate or revise this judgment until nothing could be done to rectify the Bureau of Reclamation's theft of Indian water.

While the above indictment describes injustice already committed, corrective action can still be taken. Congress can refuse to appropriate any money for the construction of the Kennewick extension, until and unless the Bureau of Reclamation irrefutably proves that this project will not deprive the Yakima Indians of water that is legally theirs and essential to them. Furthermore, the Congress should hold public hearings on this project to ensure that the Indians' side of the story is heard and to determine how to prevent the Bureau of Reclamation from taking such callous actions in the future.

d. Yellowtail Dam: A Snow Job?

In 1944, Congress authorized Yellowtail Dam, situated on the Crow Indian Reservation in Montana.[36] In 1946, the Bureau of Reclamation began negotiating with the Crows to buy the 6,000–7,000 acres of land needed for the dam site and for part of the reservoir the dam would create. Dam construction began in 1961. The intervening fifteen years was a period of intense maneuvering, characterized by the government's coercion and failure to fulfill its trusteeship obligations to the Crows. The role of the Bureau of Reclamation merits special criticism.

For eleven years, the Department of the Interior negotiated with the Crows, seemingly in good faith. However, from the very beginning, the federal government sought a way to take the land without the Indians' consent. As early as 1949, the Secretary of the Interior asked the department's solicitor if it were possible for him to acquire the Indian land by condemnation. In response, the solicitor advised that legislative authority for such a seizure did not exist.[37] Later in the year, after a new solicitor had been appointed, the secretary repeated his request, but the new solicitor reiterated the previous decision that "there is no existing legislation under which the Secretary of the Interior may acquire from the Crow Tribe the site needed for the Yellowtail reservoir and dam."[38]

In 1950, the department asked the Bureau of Reclamation and the Bureau of Indian Affairs to appraise the value of the Indian land which was needed for the dam. Robert F. Herdman, for Reclamation, and S. L. Alin, for the Bureau of Indian Affairs, each concluded that a fair price for the 6,846 acres of Indian land in question was $1.5 million—approximately $38,000 for the value of the land itself, and the rest for the value of the Indian interest in the dam site.[39] Yet even this appraisal was made in apparent bad faith, for it was conducted at a time when snow covered the ground. As a memorandum written several years later (when the issue was being decided in the courts) admitted, "Our expert would be quite vulnerable were it necessary for him to admit that he had examined the ground at a time when it was snow-covered."[40] It was this questionable appraisal, then, that formed the basis of the government's negotiating position for the next several years.

The tribe employed an engineering consultant, named Barry Dibble, to make an independent appraisal of the value of the land. He determined that a fair price would be $5 million. Consequently, on February 23, 1951, the Crows passed a resolution rejecting the government's offer of $1.5

million for their property, and making a counteroffer of $5 million based on Dibble's report.[41]

Meanwhile, political pressure on the Indians was building. Headed by the former chairman of the Senate Interior Committee, James Murray of Montana, and supported by the chambers of commerce of Billings and Hardin, Montana, and other powerful organizations, opposition to the Crows' demands increased. The Secretary of the Interior again asked his solicitor whether he had sufficient authority to institute condemnation procedures, and for a third time was refused.[42] This refusal was based on Section 9 of the act of June 28, 1946, which stated:

> No further construction work on the Crow Indian Reservation shall be undertaken by the United States without the prior consent of (1) the Crow Tribe, (2) the irrigation district or districts affected, and (3) the Congress of the United States. . . . The consent of the Crow Tribe shall be obtained by a majority vote of the general council of the tribe expressed at a duly convened meeting.[43]

"It will be noted," the solicitor ruled, "that the prohibitions contained in these statutes are sufficiently broad in scope to cover the construction of the proposed Yellowtail project."[44]

Also during this time, a split developed in the ranks of the Crow tribe. A faction headed by Robert Yellowtail, tribal chairman, worked in staunch opposition to the government's offer. Yellowtail was working toward offering the government a fifty-year lease on the dam site—at the end of which time the dam site and the dam would revert to Indian ownership. He also demanded rent of $1 million a year, a figure based on an offer by Montana Power Company and Pacific Power and Electric Company whereby the two companies would build the dam and the transmission lines in exchange for payment to the government of $1,142,000 annual rent. Yellowtail reasoned that if these companies could pay such a rent and still plan on making a profit, the government could pay a comparable figure to the Crows for the lease of the dam site and reservoir lands.

Yellowtail's faction, still in control of the Crow Tribal Council, favored authorization of the dam, and opposed further negotiations until Congress passed the de-authorizing bill sponsored by then Senator Edward Martin of Pennsylvania. By taking such a position, Yellowtail was resisting not only the combined power of the federal government (both the Bureau of Reclamation and the Bureau of Indian Affairs, often working in concert), but also the ruling groups of nearby Montana communities and the Montana congressional delegation.

Having failed to win their way in the tribal council meetings, the government forces and their supporters searched for other ways of bringing the Crows around. The regional directors of both Reclamation and the BIA considered the possibility of holding a plebiscite among all the Crows:

> The advantage of a plebiscite would be that it would present a better picture of the thinking of all of the Crow Indians than would the tribal council meeting or the [also proposed] closed meeting with Indian representatives. The principal disadvantage of the plebiscite would be its failure to abide by the specific language of the act of June 28, 1946. . . . This, admittedly, would not be a "majority vote of the general council of the tribe expressed at a duly convened meeting."[45]

Their efforts to skirt the law frustrated, the Bureau once again tried to pressure the Crow Tribal Council. At its meeting of December 28, 1953, the tribal council again considered the government's offer of $1.5 million. According to the Bureau of Reclamation regional director's account of that meeting:

> The meeting of December 28 was conducted in a very orderly and friendly manner. . . . While much of the discussion was in the Crow language, the exact purport of which could not be followed, careful and courteous attention was given to the statements of the governmental representatives. . . .
>
> I then described the plan for the Yellowtail dam and reservoir and further described the basis upon which the $1,500,000 offer was made. I then outlined the benefits which

would accrue to the Indians from dam construction. . . .
Most of these benefits were not seriously challenged, at least
by those members of the Crow tribe who spoke English.
However, one of the first tribal members asking the floor
was a young woman, whose Indian extraction was not apparent, who read what purported to be an editorial of the
Hardin *Tribune* which excoriated the Indians for refusing to
endorse the sale of liquor on the reservation and characterized
them as a foreign element in the community. I am afraid
this editorial set the tone for subsequent discussions since,
thereafter, frequent references were made to social affronts,
discrimination, and incidents of white avarice. Emphasis
was placed particularly on the fact that the dam was eagerly
sought by the Hardin and Billings communities, on which
communities no Indian love is apparently lost.

Opposition to the dam was expressed principally by
Crow tribal members who appeared to be primarily white in
racial origin, and by the older Indians, one of whom was 87,
and one of whom recalled the Custer massacre. Two of the
three Crow tribal members who spoke in favor of the dam
were apparently full-blooded Indians of the younger and
better educated group. However, their efforts and mine to
reach a sound basis for negotiating the Yellowtail right-of-
way acquisition were apparently inadequate to overcome
either preconceived views or views based upon the emotional
conditioning provided by a recitation of white affronts to
Indian dignity. Only one member of the tribal members
present voted to approve the acceptance of the $1,500,000
offer and an obvious majority of the members present
voted against endorsing construction of the dam.[46]

The Bureau's representatives just could not understand
why the Indians were suspicious of their motives, why the
Crows might think the building of the dam was a means of
getting a foothold on the rest of their reservation. Reclamation's regional director wrote that Crow opposition to the
dam "appears based on a deep-seated aversion to further
white intrusion on the tribal reservation."[47] No doubt he
considered such an attitude irrational.

As a result of this meeting and of increasing political
pressure, the secretary asked his new solicitor for the fourth
time if condemnation procedures were possible. At long last,

he got the answer he wanted. Taking the same set of laws as the previous solicitors, Solicitor Clarence Davis ruled differently:

> There can be no question that the United States possesses the inherent right of eminent domain in the lands required for the construction of this project, even though they be tribal lands of the Crows. To hold otherwise is to say that the Crow nation holds land in a more sacred title than do any other landowners in the United States, including the States themselves and their political subdivisions.[48]

At last, the government had acquired a new weapon in its arsenal of coercion. The government now held the upper hand.

In July, 1954, BIA area director Paul Fickinger reported that a more favorable attitude existed among the Crows toward the construction of the dam. He gave five reasons for such a conclusion: (1) A letter written by Assistant Secretary Fred Aandahl to House Speaker Joseph Martin on January 6, 1954, which concluded:

> Being unable to arrive at a negotiated settlement with respect to the tribal lands required for the Yellowtail undertaking, it appears that a fair and just settlement can most expeditiously and surely be had through a judicial determination of the amount to be paid the Crow Tribe. It is our recommendation that consideration be given this course of action;

(2) The Solicitor's Opinion of February 3, 1954, described above; (3) The May 4, 1954, resolution by the Subcommittee on Irrigation and Reclamation of the House Interior and Insular Affairs Committee recommending that Yellowtail be immediately programmed for construction; (4) The same subcommittee's opinion that "immediate steps be taken to reach a settlement with the Crow Tribe in accordance with the opinion of the Interior Department solicitor Clarence Davis dated February 3, 1954, and in accord with the letter of Fred Aandahl, Assistant Secretary of the Interior, dated January 6, 1954"; and (5) The Crow tribal elections of May

19, 1954, in which Robert Yellowtail was defeated for re-election by William Wall, Jr.[49]

In other words, the prospects were better for a settlement with the Crows largely because the combined power of the executive branch and the Congress held the threat of condemnation procedures as the final trump card.

While everyone kept assuring the Crows that there was no desire to "deprive the Indians of fair compensation for their lands,"[50] the political pressure was further increased by the appropriation of funds to begin construction. The pressure began to resemble blackmail. For example, at the Crow Tribal Council meeting of July 29, 1955, the Indians agreed to open negotiations for granting a right of way, largely as a result of a telegram sent by Senator Murray threatening condemnation procedures. As the president of the Big Horn County Chamber of Commerce told Murray in a subsequent letter:

> Your wire, dated July 27, to Mr. William Wall was the turning point and actually the important factor in bringing the Indians to the negotiating table.[51]

At that meeting, the Crows elected a fifteen-man negotiating committee, and offered the land to the government in exchange for (1) $5 million or (2) a sixty-year lease with an annual charge of $150,000, with the dam and lands reverting to Indian ownership at the end of the lease period.

The Crow Tribal Council meeting of November 12, 1955, destroyed any optimism the government might have been harboring. Not only did the Crows refuse to approve a proposed three-man appraisal board, but they also passed Robert Yellowtail's resolution calling for a lease with an annual charge of $1 million. This demand was passed easily, by a vote of 114 to 63.

The government, of course, was not in accord with such an offer (although the Montana Power Company and Pacific Power and Electric Company had repeated their offer, and had again been refused). Indeed, the tribe's action caused a good deal of anger in high places, as this quoted portion of a subsequent letter from the Commissioner of the Bureau of Reclamation to the tribal chairman indicates:

> At a conference on Friday, December 9, with the Senate Interior and Insular Affairs Committee, the position of the Interior Department and the Bureau of Reclamation were, I believe, made entirely clear. We are processing the papers to proceed with a condemnation suit on the Crow tribal lands for the site of Yellowtail Dam. We expect these papers to be filed with the Court within the next few weeks. In this connection, it should also be pointed out that the usual position of the United States Government in condemnation proceedings is that no allowance would be made for power site value and that the land values with appurtenant grazing, timber, or mineral rights would constitute the valuation to be placed on the lands by the government. As pointed out in my testimony before the Senate committee, this was about $35,000 in 1951 and might be slightly increased to bring those values up to date.[52]

In other words, not only was the government threatening condemnation proceedings, but they also insisted that such proceedings would net the Indians $35,000 or just a little more.

On December 29, 1955, the Crow Tribal Council—being ripped apart by internal division and outside pressure—reversed their position on Robert Yellowtail's resolution. By a vote of 119 to 63 that resolution was rescinded by the tribe. The government was, of course, pleased, but decided not to relieve their pressure. As Secretary of the Interior Douglas McKay wired to Chairman William Wall:

> I understand that the Crow Tribe will hold a council meeting on January 11. I strongly urge the council at that meeting to take action authorizing the calling of a referendum election for the purpose of obtaining the consent of the tribal membership to a grant by the Secretary of the Interior of a right-of-entry to the United States upon the lands needed to permit the early start of construction on the dam and appurtenant works. A majority vote at the referendum election in which at least 30 percent of the eligible voters of the tribe participate would be acceptable. At the same time, I

strongly urge also that the council at the meeting on January 11 authorize appropriate negotiating procedures looking toward a prompt reappraisal by a jointly constituted appraisal board of the value of the land needed for both the dam and reservoir with a view toward arriving, if at all possible, at a negotiated determination of equitable compensation agreeable to both parties that can be jointly recommended to the Congress for its approval.

Should the council take these steps and the required consent be given at the referendum, I am prepared to pursue that course as an alternative to proceeding in condemnation.[53]

In effect, the tribe was being told: if you play it like we tell you, you'll get $1.5 million; but if you fight back, you are getting only $35,000.

But the tribe did not accede to the secretary's demands. At their meeting on January 12, 1956, they reaffirmed their request for $5 million and took no action to authorize a referendum or grant a right of entry. Consequently, on January 25, the secretary formally asked the attorney general to initiate condemnation proceedings against the Crows:

For use as construction site and reservoir area in connection with the construction and operation of the Yellowtail Dam and Reservoir of the Yellowtail Unit, Missouri River Basin Project, by the Bureau of Reclamation of this Department, I have determined that it is necessary and in the interest of the United States to acquire by judicial proceedings certain property on the Crow Indian Reservation located in Big Horn and Yellowstone Counties, Montana. The property is ostensibly owned by the Crow Tribe of Indians of Montana.[54]

When the tribal council, at its meeting on January 28, almost unanimously denied right of entry to the government to begin construction, the Bureau of Reclamation apparently decided to use more direct methods of persuasion. On February 27, 1956, the commissioner of BIA received the following telegram from his area director:

During business conference late in November or early in December 1955, Matt Tschirgi stated to me he had acted as intermediary in substantial offer to Robert Yellowtail if he would work for instead of against Yellowtail project. Tschirgi said he was sworn not to divulge name of person making offer. This indefinite information not then considered materially different from recurrent and unsubstantiated rumors that other members of Crow Tribe were profiting by their position in controversy.

Friday, February 24, Yellowtail telephoned me to protest ruling that Crow meeting that day not official. He said he would obtain name of intermediary in offer to him from Tschirgi and "break the case wide open." Early Saturday morning in another telephone conversation, Yellowtail told me he had learned Carl Sloan, Bureau of Reclamation employee, residing Hardin, Montana, was man who had approached Tschirgi. Said he regretted situation since Sloan was a good friend of his but he had advised FBI and press representatives. Yellowtail also stated he had evidence Wall, Kronmiller, et. al., received payment for supporting dam assumedly from business interests in Hardin and Billings. . . . Sloan and Tschirgi have different opinions as to nature of proposition to be made to Yellowtail through Tschirgi. Sloan maintains he only discussed possibilities of education work among Indian opponents of dam and employment of other engineers and attorneys.[55]

When we sought information on the results of the Bureau of Reclamation's investigation of this case of alleged bribery, Bureau officials "could not find" the relevant files either in Washington, or in its Denver, Billings, or Salt Lake City field offices. The only further information that could be found is that Carl Sloan is still working for the Bureau of Reclamation, employed now in the Salt Lake City office.

Despite the Bureau's unconscionable pressure, including possible bribery, Congress prepared to act in the case, and in the Crows' interest. On February 3, 1956, Senators Mansfield and Murray introduced Senate Joint Resooution 135, a bill to grant the Crow tribe $5 million in exchange for the land needed for Yellowtail Dam and Reservoir. The Resolution was passed by both the Senate and the House relatively quickly, and sent to the President. On June 7, 1956, however, President Eisenhower returned the bill to Congress without approval. His veto message stated in part:

> The standard of payment for land acquired by the Government is just compensation or fair market value. However, I recognize that, as a matter of policy, the Federal Government has made awards in excess of just compensation in other cases involving Indian lands. If the Congress determines that it wishes to provide for an extra payment in this case, it should not be done under the claim that it is just compensation. The amount, the method of computing it, and the equitable justification for it should be clearly established on acceptable premises. Neither the resolution nor the legislative history does this.[56]

What position the Interior Department took on the resolution and on the veto is unclear. During hearings held after the veto, the following exchange took place between Senator James E. Murray and Assistant Secretary Fred G. Aandahl:

> THE CHAIRMAN: I would like to inquire if the Interior Department had recommended to the President the signing of this bill.
>
> MR. AANDAHL: I wonder if that should not be considered an executive exchange, Senator. I would prefer to handle it in that manner.[57]

From such an exchange and Interior's prior behavior concerning Yellowtail, one is led to assume that the department opposed the resolution giving the Crows the $5 million assessor Dibble believed was just compensation. If that is the case, it appears that the Bureau of Reclamation once again triumphed against Indian interests within the department.

This, then, was the situation in mid-1956. Direct negotiations between the Crows and the government were stalemated. Condemnation procedures were progressing slowly; the Indians were in the midst of protesting the government's legal right to begin them at all. And Congress was trying to work out a way to avoid another presidential veto.

On January 11, 1957, Judge Charles Pray, of the Federal District Court in Montana, denied the Crows' motion to dismiss the government's condemnation proceedings.[58] In February, Senators Murray of Montana, Barrett and O'Mahoney of Wyoming, Malone of Nevada, and Anderson of New Mexico cosponsored Senate Joint Resolution 12. This resolution gave to the Crows $5 million in exchange for the lands needed for the dam and reservoir; to meet the President's objections, however, the resolution stated:

> Said sum includes both just compensation . . . and a share of the special value to the United States of said lands for utilization in connection with its authorized Missouri River Basin Project, in addition to other justifiable considerations. Nothing contained herein shall be taken as an admission by the United States that it is under any legal obligation to pay more than just compensation to said Crow Tribe.[59]

Furthermore, the resolution authorized court action by the Crows if they thought the $5 million settlement was unsatisfactory. However, even these safeguards did not make the Department of Interior happy. They had just won their court case, and sensed final victory if their condemnation proceedings were allowed to be completed. Consequently, on April 2, 1957, the department announced in a press release that:

> Assistant Secretary of the Interior has advised the Congress that the Administration could not recommend legislation that would pay the Crow Indians in Wyoming and Montana $5,000,000 for land needed to construct the Yellowtail Dam and Reservoir. . . . The Department of the Interior, while recommending compensation of $1,500,000 for the lands, said it would not object to the enactment of legislation establishing compensation if the figure of $5,000,000 was reduced to $2,500,000 or less.[60]

The Bureau of Reclamation had won another victory in the intradepartment political battle.

The resolution was passed intact by the Senate. However, the department brought its influence to bear when the resolution went to conference to be reconciled with a House version calling for $1.5 million. The conference hammered out a figure of $2.5 million but still allowed the Crows to go to court to get more if they wished.

The Crows, of course, so wished. And back into the courts went the dispute. It is in the preparations for the court case that the failure of the federal government to fulfill its trusteeship role became most apparent. To begin with, the Crows had to hire private counsel, for the government claimed that to have provided lawyers would have constituted conflict of interest.

Not only did the government fail to represent the Indians in the case, but they also planned on using misrepresentation and secrecy in order to win. For example, one of the Crows' arguments was that the proposed power plant would be too small to provide maximum benefits to the Indians and the other customers. A government memorandum, however, states:

> It was the opinion of the attorneys that if Mr. Tower [a consultant from the Federal Power Commission doing some investigative work for the case] finds that a greater power plant capacity is desirable, that evidence of this matter might be detrimental to our case. If the larger power plant is feasible, additional meetings should be held to fully review this problem and to be prepared to justify the proposed smaller installation at Yellowtail.[61]

In other words, the government apparently had never considered the possibility of a larger power plant, and wished to deny that one might be feasible—even if its own studies showed otherwise.

Another conflict with the government's trustee status arose over the question of which data was to be released to the Crows, and which was to be kept secret. A letter from the Bureau of Reclamation's field office in Billings stated:

> Mr. Bielefeld [the Regional Solicitor] advises that the United States Attorneys and the Field Solicitor participate closely with the judge in determining what data might be made available to counsel for the Crow Indians, that the material

or documents involved are such as they felt could properly be furnished.[62]

Not only did the Crows have to find their own legal staff, but they were also refused certain technical data which might be necessary for their case—data which would be very difficult and expensive to attain.

Eventually, however, the Crows won their case against the government. On October 1, 1963—nineteen years after the Yellowtail Dam was authorized by Congress—the dispute over the value of the Indian land came to an end. United States District Court Judge W. J. Jameson granted the Crows an additional $2 million, plus interest.[63] In all, the Crows received approximately $5 million (the interest was close to $500,000) for their property—a figure demanded years before and rejected by the government as "extravagant" and more than just compensation. Unable to receive justice from the executive branch of the federal government, the Crows obtained through the courts what they had sought. In the process, they learned that the government's trusteeship status is a sham when opposed by the Bureau of Reclamation.

CURRENT PROBLEMS AT YELLOWTAIL

The Bureau of Reclamation's outrageous treatment of the Crow Indians did not end with the construction of the Yellowtail Dam. Having tried to take the Crows' land without just compensation, the Bureau is now ignoring the Indians' water rights and depriving them of their fair share of the water from Bighorn Lake, the reservoir behind Yellowtail Dam.

The manner in which the Bureau of Reclamation has been selling water from Bighorn Lake for industrial use has generated much bitter criticism from the Indian tribes affected by the Bureau's policies. The Bureau has contracted with numerous large corporations, including Humble Oil and Refining Company, Shell Oil Company, Kerr-McGee Corporation, Sun Oil Company, and Peabody Coal Company, providing Bighorn River water for industrial use. In October,

1968, the Bureau's regional director in Billings, Montana, reported that—

> at Yellowtail, option contracts have been completed for 168,000 acre-feet per year, and an additional 110,000 acre-feet per year have been reserved for development of coal lands of the Indian tribes. The Bureau of Reclamation has applications on file for an additional 225,000 acre-feet per year. These sales, reservations, and applications total 503,000 acre-feet per year. If all develop, there will only be 137,000 acre-feet per year available for additional sales.[64]

It is clear from this summary that all available water from Yellowtail will be sold for industrial use, with proceeds going to the federal government. Water is being sold both above and below the dam at a price of $11 and $9 per acre-foot, respectively.

This policy of selling Bighorn water for industrial use is of dubious legality. The United States District Court in Montana has ruled that the federal right of "dominant control" does not apply to the case of Yellowtail Dam:

> On the basis of the treaties between the United States and the Crow Tribe of Indians, the provisions of the Crow Allotment Act of 1920, and the foregoing cases, I am compelled to reject plaintiff's [the United States'] theory of dominant control.[65]

Therefore, the United States, and its agent, the Bureau of Reclamation, cannot rely on any constitutional or inherent right to determine the use of water from Yellowtail Dam.

Instead, the government must rely solely on the purposes for which the U.S. District Court allowed the condemnation of the Bighorn River. Only if the Crows' rights to the river's water were condemned for the specific purpose of industrial sale can the Bureau of Reclamation use the water in that way. It seems clear, however, that this was not the case. The dam was presented by the government as being constructed primarily for the purpose of power generation. In considering the values for which just compensation must be paid to the Crows, Judge Jameson wrote in his opinion:

> In awarding just compensation, values which arise from the use and availability of the Yellowtail site for irrigation and recreation, as well as power production, may be considered to the extent that they could be realized by any private developer of the site.[66]

According to William Veeder, the water conservation and utilization specialist of the Bureau of Indian Affairs:

> In the entire Court's analysis—most comprehensive—there is not a single reference that the United States was condemning rights to the use of water for "sale" for industrial purposes.[67]

Consequently, Veeder concludes, that sale of water for industrial purposes by the Bureau of Reclamation is illegal and void.

On November 29, 1967, representatives of the Crow tribe met with the Commisisoner of Reclamation, and asked him to set aside 250,000 acre-feet per year from Yellowtail Reservoir for use in the development of Indian coal resources. The Bureau of Indian Affairs and the assistant secretaries of water and power development and public land management supported the tribe's request. The Bureau of Reclamation determined, however, that only 110,000 acre-feet of the 640,000 acre-feet of water available for immediate sale for industrial purposes could be reserved for the Indians' development of coal lands. The BIA then agreed to this figure, and it was adopted.

In October, 1968, however, only ten months after this agreement was made, Reclamation Regional Director Aldrich reported:

> Although not part of the original authorization for construction, recent computations indicate that Bighorn River can produce 775,000 acre-feet of water per year that can be used for industrial water purposes.[68]

It was never suggested, however, that the figure of 110,000 acre-feet of water reserved for the Crows might be revised as a result of this increased capacity. The Indians, of course, come last in any determination of water allocation made by the Bureau of Reclamation.

The dispute over the sale of water from Yellowtail Reservoir also involved the Wind River Indian Reservation in Wyoming. The Wind River reservation, the home of the Shoshone and Arapaho Indians, is upstream from Yellowtail (the Bighorn River flows northeast). Any water appropriated by other users, upstream or downstream, decreases the amount of water available to them.

The Bureau of Reclamation made the water sales from Yellowtail Reservoir without the knowledge or consent of the Wind River Indians. In April, 1968, the Shoshones' legal counsel, Marvin J. Sonosky, wrote Interior Secretary Stewart Udall:

> The purported sales include waters belonging to the Wind River Tribes. The Tribes were not a party to the negotiations, have never been consulted and have never consented to the attempt to dispose of their property rights. It is the position of the Tribes that the contracts are void since (a) there is no authority for the Secretary to sell the property of the Tribes; (b) the contracts impose a servitude on the treaty rights to the water and thus arbitrarily limit the use of the Reservation. . . .
>
> Even if your office were vested with authority to sell the water, the contracts of sale would constitute takings under the Fifth Amendment and no provision has been made for just compensation.[69]

On the same day, Sonosky wrote letters to each of the large corporate contractors for the Yellowtail water, which read in part:

> This is to put you on notice that the purported contracts of sale include waters belonging to the Wind River Tribes. . . . Unless a settlement can be reached, we are under instruction from our tribal clients to take the appropriate action to seek judicial relief to establish that the contracts are invalid, as an unauthorized disposition of tribal property.[70]

The Department of the Interior then began a process of evasion and delay. On April 25, 1968, Udall wrote Sonosky, confirming a promise made by the department's solicitor to hold a meeting to discuss with Sonosky the position of the tribes. In late October, however, Sonosky was forced to write the following letter to Secretary Udall:

> We wrote a letter dated April 10, 1968, to you asking for a meeting concerning the action of your Department in undertaking to sell water in which the Wind River Tribes have property rights.
>
> Your Solicitor promised a meeting at which the views of the Tribes would be heard. . . . Nothing has happened. No meeting has been set.
>
> It has become rather plain to us that in this conflict of interest situation between the Bureau of Reclamation and the Tribes, the Tribes are being relegated to their usual secondary position. The Tribes' rights have been violated. Their property has been taken. And they have not been afforded the courtesy of a hearing either before or after the action of your Department.[71]

Udall's delaying tactics continued, however, and no meeting materialized until President Nixon was elected and Walter Hickel became Secretary of the Interior.

On April 8, 1970—two years after the initial request—representatives and attorneys for the Wind River tribes held a meeting with Hickel to discuss the tribes' water rights. At that meeting, the tribes made two requests: (1) that the Bureau of Reclamation make no further commitments of water until the tribes' water rights had been adjudicated, and (2) that the Department allot approximately $60,000 to measure and determine the volume of water which the tribes needed. Hickel agreed to both requests.[72]

Again, however, the department reneged on its promises. On May 12, 1970, the tribal counsels received a letter from Harrison Loesch, Assistant Secretary of the Interior, reading in part:

> It is my understanding that the tribes were to present a request to the Secretary that a specific amount of water be set aside from disposal from Reclamation reservoirs for a specific period of time pending completion of a water need inventory. . . . It is our understanding that you were also to

provide us with an estimate of the amount of funds that you hoped the Bureau of Indian Affairs might be able to find for doing an inventory of the water needs of the tribes.[73]

It is clear that, however subtly, the department was beginning to back away from the reasonable position Hickel had taken on April 8. The department was not going to freeze water sales, but rather would just set aside a particular volume of water. Under the new policy, how could the tribes ask for a specific amount to be set aside unless they first knew what their water needs were? No longer was the department going to use $60,000 of its own funds for the water need inventory; the request had to be channeled through the BIA, which had no money to spare anyway.

At the time of this writing, no progress has been made in the tribes' negotiations with the department, although the tribes have begun the preliminary stages of inventorying their water needs. Worse yet, the Department of the Interior is making new contracts with industrial water users without consulting with the Indians about their water needs.[74]

RECOMMENDATIONS

Citizens and legislators must not continue to ignore the bad faith dealings that the Bureau of Reclamation is conducting with both the Crow tribe and the Wind River tribes in allocating the water from the Bighorn Lake. The Indians have been unable to persuade Secretary Rogers Morton to meet with them and discuss their water claims. Moreover, the Department of the Interior is making new contracts with industrial water users without consulting the Indians. We recommend that Congress and public groups as well as individuals urge the Secretary of the Interior to give the Indians their necessary and just share of this water. To determine this share, Congress should first appropriate enough funds for the Indians to obtain an accurate inventory of their present and future water needs.

e. Navajo Indian Irrigation Project:
A Wait of Many Moons

On June 13, 1962, Congress authorized the San Juan-Chama and the Navajo Indian irrigation projects in New Mexico. The San Juan-Chama project, of which only the initial stage has received authorization, will divert up to 270,000 acre-feet annually from the San Juan River in northern New Mexico to the Rio Grande Basin and the Albuquerque area. The water will be used to irrigate 120,900 acres of farmland, and for municipal and industrial purposes in Albuquerque and other municipal centers. The Navajo Indian irrigation project, which was authorized in its entirety, will divert 508,000 acre-feet from the Navajo Dam on the San Juan River to irrigate 110,630 acres of land—most of which is on the Navajo Reservation.

The projects were authorized only after several years of conflict over the terms under which the Navajos would receive a major irrigation project. The authorization bill for the two projects always fared well in the Senate, but repeatedly met insurmountable opposition in the House, particularly within the House Committee on Interior and Insular Affairs.

Regional politics explains the House Interior Committee's opposition. The San Juan River originates in and, for a significant portion of its length, flows through southwestern Colorado. Colorado has always opposed extensive development of the river in New Mexico, for it has felt that it would lose the future use of whatever water New Mexico appropriated for its own projects. Although the water does not belong to Colorado, and never has—the San Juan being a navigable stream under the jurisdiction of the federal government—Colorado has never been convinced of this fact.

Furthermore, the chairman of the House Interior Committee, Colorado's Representative Wayne Aspinall, wields very tight control of his committee. Consequently, he is able to quash Reclamation projects that do not meet with his approval. Unfortunately, the Navajo Indian irrigation project was such a project. Aspinall apparently feared that, given a large irrigation project, the Navajos would claim an indefinite amount of water by invoking the *Winters* doctrine. If this were to happen, little of the San Juan River would be available for use in Colorado. Consequently, Aspinall held up congressional approval of the Navajo project until the Navajos agreed to the following provisions of the authorization act:

> Section 11. (a) . . . Contracts, which, in the case of water for Indian uses, shall be executed with the Navajo Tribe, shall make provision, in any year in which the Secretary [of the Interior] anticipates a shortage, taking into account both prospective runoff originating above Navajo Reservoir and the available water in storage in Navajo Reservoir, for a sharing of the available water in the following manner: the prospective runoff shall be apportioned between the contractors diverting above and those diverting at or below Navajo Reservoir in the proportion that the total normal diversion requirement of each group bears to the total of all normal diversion requirements. . . .
>
> Section 12. (a) None of the project works or structures authorized by this Act shall be so operated as to create, implement, or satisfy any preferential right in the United States of any Indian tribe to the waters impounded, diverted, or used by means of such project works or structures.[75]

Section 11 (a) provided that shortages were to be shared by all contractors for the water, including the Navajos; therefore, the Navajos would not have first rights to the available water, as the *Winters* doctrine stipulates. Section 12 (a) further provided that the Navajos were to relinquish any "preferential right" to water made available by the building of the project works. That is, the Navajos had to give up their *Winters* doctrine water rights if they wished to receive any water for irrigation on their reservation.

Edward Weinberg, former solicitor of the Department of the Interior, insists that the Navajos "voluntarily gave up" these *Winters* doctrine rights.[76] He claims that they were the original proponents of such a trade, for they wanted the Navajo project and the indirect industrial benefits that the San Juan-Chama project might bring to the reservation.

The preponderance of evidence, however, contradicts

Weinberg's view. A letter to Aspinall from J. Maurice Mc-
Cabe, executive director of the Navajo tribe, states in part:

> This concession was only agreed to by the tribe in considera-
> tion of getting the Navajo Irrigation Project established in
> New Mexico as provided in the above bills.[77]

Furthermore, Steve Reynolds, state engineer of New Mexico,
observed during the 1961 Senate hearings on the authorization bill:

> The changes which we have discussed were agreed upon by
> the States of Colorado and New Mexico after intensive
> negotiations extending from early February through May 19,
> 1960. Representatives of the Navajo Tribe participated in
> these negotiations and the Indians have made no objection
> to these changes.[78]

It seems clear that the Navajos were not, as Weinberg insists,
the originators of such an arrangement. On the contrary, the
deal apparently was Aspinall's (and Colorado's) price for
allowing the Navajos to use San Juan River water.

It would be, perhaps, naïve to castigate Aspinall's political deal too strongly—assuming, of course, that the government's side of the bargain had been kept. The federal
government, however, has let the Navajo project fall decades
behind schedule. In 1969, Senator Joseph Montoya of New
Mexico declared:

> One can only pause in disbelief at the tremendously slow
> rate of progress which this project has been making. One
> would think that with all that we stand to gain from comple-
> tion of the project that every effort would be made to seek
> completion of the project at an early date. However, the
> very opposite has been true. The project has been proceed-
> ing at an unbelievably slow pace.
>
> For example, through fiscal year 1969, a total of
> $75,800,000 has been programmed for this project. Of
> this, however, only a total of $28,300,000 has been requested
> by the Bureau of the Budget and appropriated by the
> Congress. Although the project was scheduled to be com-
> pleted by 1979, 15 years from the beginning of construction,

it will now take 45 years or more to complete at the present rate of progress.[79]

At the present rate of progress, the Navajo project will not be completed until 2009—at the earliest. Meanwhile, the San Juan-Chama project is proceeding right on schedule, and will deliver water to the non-Indian farmers, industry and citizens of Albuquerque in the next few years.

The reasons for the discrepancy are not obscure. For one thing, the methods of funding the two projects are intentionally different. Although the Bureau of Reclamation actually builds the Navajo project, Congress decided to toss the burden of getting funds for the project into the lap of the Bureau of Indian Affairs. The BIA would request the necessary appropriations in its budget, and then transfer those funds to Reclamation to finance the actual construction. The San Juan-Chama project, on the other hand, is being funded directly through the Bureau of Reclamation. This funding arrangement was another brainchild of the ever-active mind of Wayne Aspinall. He refused to allow the projects to go through unless the BIA was assigned responsibility for the Navajo project funding.[80] Aspinall insisted on the unusual procedure because the Bureau of Indian Affairs has considerably less influence in Congress than does the Bureau of Reclamation. By assigning the problem of appropriations to the BIA, Aspinall has slowed construction of the Navajo project to almost a standstill. The figures on the following page illustrate BIA's inability to get the necessary funding for the Navajo project.

As Floyd Dominy, former Commissioner of Reclamation, wrote during 1969, "Only 16 percent of the total construction on the Navajo project has been accomplished, while the San Juan-Chama project is over 65 percent complete."[81]

Who has bottlenecked the appropriations for the Navajo project? Everyone pushes the blame onto another agency or office. According to Assistant Reclamation Commissioner Gilbert Stamm, the project has a low priority within the BIA; when the Department of the Interior limits the budgetary requests of the BIA, the Navajo project is one of the first to

Fiscal Year	Appropriations Requested by BIA	Appropriations Made by Congress
1964	$ 4,950,000	$ 1,800,000
1965	9,000,000	4,700,000
1966	13,500,000	6,500,000
1967	12,500,000	6,500,000
1968	15,000,000	5,300,000
1969	15,000,000	3,500,000
1970	15,000,000	3,500,000
1971	15,000,000	4,000,000
Total	99,950,000	35,800,000

go by the boards.[82] Frank Wiles, acting budget director of the Department of the Interior, agrees: given a limited budget and a choice between education and irrigation projects, "public works projects are the first to get cut back."[83] Former Reclamation Commissioner Floyd Dominy and former BIA Commissioner Robert Bennett attribute the Navajo project's plight to the costs of the Vietnam War.[84] The Navajo tribal council's explanation, however, seems closer to the mark:

> It appears that there is a deliberate and intentional effort to choke off the project in question.[85]

Henry Taliaferro—former assistant solicitor for Indian affairs in the Department of the Interior—insists that "the place to look is right square at Wayne Aspinall, and nobody else."[86] According to Taliaferro, the Bureau of Reclamation certainly wouldn't try to stop the Navajo project. "They [Reclamation] don't care if it's in Dupont Circle [a park in the middle of Washington, D.C.] as long as they can pour their concrete."[87]

Other insiders claim that the blame for the Navajo project's low priority lies with the Office of Management and Budget. Daniel A. Dreyfus, a staff member of the Senate Interior Committee and former Reclamation planner, terms the Navajo project a "project that hasn't got any sympathy on the part of the economists" within the Bureau of the Budget [now OMB].[88] BIA's budget office spokesman says that BIA pushes the project as hard as it can, but the economists within the Department of the Interior and in the OMB, who work solely on the basis of benefit-cost analysis, oppose its construction.[89]

Former Interior Secretary Stewart Udall maintains that the Navajo project, in effect, has been given a priority lower than comparable non-Indian Reclamation efforts:

> There are other projects just like it—non-Indian projects being built right now. . . . This Indian project, as compared with any non-Indian project, has been neglected and slow.[90]

Why do people throughout government ask searching questions about Indian projects that are not asked about non-Indian projects? A central problem of the Navajo Project, and with Indian Reclamation projects in general, is that the Bureau of Reclamation considers the Navajo project a marginal one. The land is 6,000 feet above sea level, the growing season is short, and the soil is not particularly rich. Since benefit estimates on marginally productive cropland are necessarily low, the benefit-cost ratios of irrigation projects to supply water to such land are also low. It should be remembered that the federal government placed the Navajos and other Indians on the worst land in the nation, where project benefit-cost ratios are bound to be low. As of March 1, 1971, the unemployment rate among the Navajos in Arizona was 57.5 percent.[91]

As long as economic efficiency is the root of priority setting, the Indians will remain impoverished. The federal government has a social and moral as well as legal obligation to construct the Navajo project, despite its marginal status. If the trustee status of the federal government has any meaning at all, the government should alleviate this situation immediately by building the Navajo irrigation project as fast as possible. If the federal government would give proper consideration to distributional impacts of Reclamation projects (as discussed in Chapter 4), then the Navajo irrigation project would pass any reasonable test of economic desirability.

Congress should appropriate the necessary funds immediately. At the very minimum these funds should equal BIA's annual appropriations request for the project. Such a recommendation will not be implemented easily, especially if congressmen like Wayne Aspinall use their power to prevent the Congress from acting to correct its breach of trust and from carrying out its original bargain with the Navajos concerning their rights to this water. Fairness and justice, however, demand no less.

f. A Proposal on Water Rights

Although each of the preceding case studies reveals a separate injustice, some general conclusions and recommendations can be drawn from them. The federal government's infringement of Indian water rights breaks down into two rough categories: (1) cases where the injustices are the result of the disparity in political power between the Indian and non-Indian parties, in which the government's use of its power is nakedly arbitrary—the result of an easily traced decision within the Interior Department; (2) cases where the blame is more subtle, in which the injustices are the result of the institutionalized inequities attributable to supposedly neutral procedures.

The cases in the first category—which might be called "intentional," as opposed to "institutional" injustices—are easier to expose and explain. These decisions are the outcome of clear political and economic conflicts. Many such cases are characterized by bureaucratic in-fighting between the Bureau of Indian Affairs (BIA) and the Bureau of Reclamation, where the Secretary of the Interior makes the final decisions. Sometimes, as we have seen, BIA refuses to press for the Indians' interests, thus leaving the Bureau of Reclamation's decision unchallenged. In every case cited in this report, and many others, where Indian interests conflicted with non-Indian interests, the Bureau of Reclamation ruled against the Indians.

While the Bureau of Reclamation cannot easily deny its intentional, conscious indifference or even belligerence toward the Indians, it does try to cover up its institutional biases by claiming that its procedures and policies are neutral. Procedures, however, are not value-free, and it is naïve, even unjust, to pretend that they are. It is analogous to the old French saying that the law prohibited both the rich and the poor from sleeping beneath the bridges of Paris; what seems fair on the surface may in reality be an instrument of discrimination.

Consider, for example, the use of benefit-cost analysis as a primary tool of decisionmaking. The Bureau's benefit-cost analyses tend to deny projects to Indians because the Indians have been placed by the federal government on the worst land in the West, thus lowering the benefit-cost ratio. We recommend that benefit-cost estimates take account of the federal government's legal and moral responsibility to the Indians as suggested in the last section of Chapter 4. Policymakers can then take relevant distributional impacts into account.

Distributional biases favoring Reclamation projects benefiting Indians with low incomes are essential, since all the water rights in the world are totally useless if there is no way to get water from the rivers and streams to the fields where it is needed. Failure to help the Indians make productive use of their water is perhaps a greater injustice than the theft of the water, for without active federal aid in improving the Indians' economic welfare, the government's trusteeship status remains a sham, and the Indians remain at the very bottom of the nation's economic ladder.

There is yet another institutional bias. The water rights of the Indians is a federal matter; the states have absolutely no jurisdiction. Indian water rights are protected by federal, not state, law. By filing their claims under state laws, therefore, the Bureau of Reclamation does nothing to protect Indian water rights.

There is a related problem which further complicates the situation. The state laws, which rely on the doctrine of prior appropriation, quantify all recorded water rights. Ranch A, for example, is entitled by law to y acre-feet a year. By adding up all the quantified rights, the Bureau of Reclamation and the state governments can calculate approximately how much water will be available for future Reclamation projects. *Winters* doctrine rights, however, are not quantified. The *Winters* doctrine does not assign a particular amount of water to the different Indian tribes; it allows them first claim to water for any "beneficial use." Neither the Bureau nor the states can conclusively plan water resource development without knowing the amount of water the Indians will use annually, now and in the future.

Consequently, the Bureau or other users can steal Indian water without really intending to. If water is scarce, the other users can take the amount of water to which they are entitled under state law, leave the Indians with little or none, and thus preclude future use by Indians attempting to improve their lot by irrigation or industrial development. Attempts to plan intelligently for the distribution of available water are made more complicated if the user with first right cannot or does not claim a specific amount. That user is very often bypassed, for all intents and purposes, when the available supply of water is claimed—especially when that user is politically and economically weak, and operates under different laws than everyone else.

The first attempt to quantify *Winters* doctrine rights was made in the Supreme Court in the 1963 case of *Arizona* v. *California*. As part of the Court's effort to clarify the water situation along the Colorado River, it quantified the water rights of many of the tribes in that area. This has not, however, been tried on any widespread scale. It should be. A comprehensive inventory of all Indians' present and future water should be conducted. Perhaps a procedure such as the following might be used to accomplish this end:

1. Establish a special Indian Water Rights Quantification Commission, with Indian representatives, a qualified staff of hydrological experts, and attorneys familiar with water law. The job of this commission would be to determine administratively the present and future water needs of every Indian tribe.

2. If any Indian tribe were to dispute the commission's determination, there must be procedures established to grant that tribe the right to a prompt appeal through the courts.

The solicitor's office of the Department of the Interior, or any attorney chosen by the tribe and paid by the department, should try these appeals on the Indians' behalf: in either case all court and litigation expenses should be assumed by the federal government.

3. Because of the changing nature of water needs, any tribe should be able, at any time, to have its water claim adjusted to allow for increased water use. This adjustment should be considered either by the Quantifications Commission, if it were to be permanent, or by the courts. If done by the commission, there would, of course, be a right of appeal. Again, all expenses in this procedure should be borne by the federal government.

Probably the most significant institutional barrier blocking the fulfillment of Indian water rights concerns the structure of the Department of the Interior. The Bureau of Reclamation and the Bureau of Indian Affairs are both within the department, so any conflicts between the two are resolved in behind-the-scenes political bargaining. The compromise solutions depend, not upon the legal or moral merits of the case, but upon the relative levels of political power of the disputants inside the bureaucracy. Such a situation, of course, works against the interests of the Indians.

Part of the problem is the structure of legal representation within the Department of the Interior. There is one solicitor's office which takes care of the legal work for every bureau and agency within the department. The solicitor's office is broken down into smaller offices, one for each of the major bureaus and agencies. There is an office for Indian affairs, and one for reclamation, each performing the legal work for its particular division of the department. However, what happens if there is a legal dispute between these two offices? Unfortunately, as in the department as a whole, there is no adversary system established within the solicitor's office to assure a fair hearing to both parties and a fair decision based on the merits of the case. These legal disputes are all too often decided on political grounds within the solicitor's office or within the office of the Secretary. The result of this situation is that the Indians have no independent legal advocate anywhere within the government. If the Indians are in legal battle with another agency within the department, such as the Bureau of Reclamation, the solution is reached administratively; and the department as a whole, in its relations with other parts of the federal government, tends to represent the agencies within it with the greatest amount of political clout. In short, the department has a severe conflict of interests, being forced to represent both sides of an issue.

This conflict of interests exists in other areas and levels of the federal government which are responsible for determining the Indians' legal rights. Much of the department's legal work is done in the field, in regional solicitor's offices in cities around the nation. In these regional offices, the duties are not divided as they are in Washington; there is no separate personnel working on behalf of the Indians or on behalf of Reclamation. The various offices merely have of a pool of attorneys; one man might represent the Indians in one case and Reclamation in the next. One man may develop an informal specialization, and thus may tend to represent Indians more often, but such a division of labor is casual at best. As a former assistant solicitor has said, the Indian, in hoping for fair legal representation at the regional level, "is at the mercy of accidents of personnel."[92] Some regional offices, such as those in Los Angeles and Sacramento (which has handled much of the Pyramid Lake controversy), are noted as being generally pro-Reclamation. Others, such as the one in Minneapolis, are more pro-Indian. This kind of reliance on "accidents of personnel" certainly does not help the Indian to find independent legal advocacy anywhere within the department's legal structure.

The situation is no better within the Justice Department, which, because its workload is high, must decide which of thousands of possible cases to prosecute. This decision is inevitably political. And again, the Indians tend to lose out. If the Indians are in conflict with the Bureau of Reclamation, the Justice Department usually fails to represent the Indians adequately in any legal proceedings. This is what has happened in the Pyramid Lake case. The government has refused to pursue the cause of the Indians, although it purports to be their trustee; instead it has taken up the banner of Reclamation and its Western clients. The Northern Paiutes, therefore, have been forced to sue the government; that is, the ward has sued the trustee for its legal rights.

Furthermore, the Indians are restricted in hiring their own independent counsel. Under the present regulations, the federal government must approve all contracts Indian tribes make with lawyers and fix the fees. That is, the government must approve the appointment of an attorney who might proceed against it. In one case, a tribe had legal work done by a legal aid organization known as California Indian Legal Services. The government, however, refused to approve the situation. The tribe and the attorneys circumvented the government's veto only by arranging to have the legal work done without charge.

Another legal hurdle for the Indians is the extremely high cost of court litigation. Assuming that the department approves the tribe's choice of independent counsel, a counsel that does not have to be responsible to Rogers Morton or Richard Kleindienst, then the money must be found to finance the long legal battle ahead. And, unfortunately, water rights cases are particularly expensive, as they require engineering reports, hydrological reports, etc. But where is the money to be found? The Indians, of all the groups in this nation, are perhaps the least able to raise the necessary funds.

A way must be found to eliminate the conflict of interest which presently exists within the Department of the Interior and especially within its solicitor's office. In his message to Congress on Indian affairs on July 8, 1970, President Nixon proposed the following:

> I am calling on the Congress to establish an Indian trust counsel authority to assure independent legal representation for the Indians' natural resource rights. This authority would be governed by a three-man board of directors, appointed by the President with the advice and consent of the Senate. At least two of the board members would be Indian. The chief legal officer of the authority would be designated as the Indian trust counsel.

The Indian trust counsel authority would be independent of the Departments of Interior and Justice and would be expressly empowered to bring suit in the name of the United States in its trustee capacity. The United States would waive its sovereign immunity from suit in connection with litigation involving the authority.[93]

The President's proposal should be approved by Congress as quickly as possible. The administration should actively work for its speedy enactment. Such a change would, it seems, go very far in solving the problems of the Indians' lack of independent legal advocacy.

Part 3 | Challenging Bureau Policies

But if you are trying to tell us that municipal water is going to be put out of existence or push into the background our irrigation projects and our power projects, . . . then I think I am about ready to kiss reclamation good-bye.

—Congressman Wayne Aspinall in Hearings before the Subcommittee on Irrigation and Reclamation, Ninety-second Congress, First Session, March 23 and 24, 1971

8

Plans and Proposals

For years, policymakers as well as outside critics have recognized that the Bureau's evaluation methods are deceptive, antiquated, and often harmful. In 1962 President Kennedy approved an interim attempt to update planning procedures with Senate Document No. 97. The preceding chapters showed how this revision failed to solve any of the evaluation problems and even made some considerations, such as regional and secondary benefits, more dubious. Responding to the criticism leveled at SD 97, Congress passed the 1965 Water Resources Planning Act.[1] This act directed the Water Resources Council (an executive agency responsible for coordinating federal water resource efforts) to develop principles, standards, and procedures to be used in the evaluation of water resource projects. In 1969, the Water Resources Council (WRC) Special Task Force issued a report on *Procedures for Evaluation of Water and Related Land Resource Projects*, nicknamed the "Blue Book."[2]

While this report was only a preliminary document, it still received bitter criticism. One member of the original WRC Task Force, who asked to remain anonymous, gave perhaps the most accurate statement of the reason for the Blue Book's defects:

> At least in the early period, the Corps of Engineers was far too strong. This was a function of two things. The Corps of Engineers is powerful, and Bob Gidez [the Corps's representative] is powerful. Gidez is a persuasive debater. . . . He just overwhelmed everyone else. . . . He is really terrible on paper though. He wrote the Task Force's Blue Book almost single-handedly, and you know how bad that report is.[3]

Although the general public didn't know the reasons underlying the mediocrity of the Blue Book, it was aware of the report's dismal quality. An eight-inch thick compilation of public hearings testifies to the public's dissatisfaction with the preliminary report.

After the Blue Book debacle, the WRC Task Force went back to work in 1969 to draft a new document called the *Principles for Planning Water and Land Resources*, which has not yet been finally approved by the President.* The interagency group which actually drafted this new report consisted of—

> Water Resources Council (WRC)
> > Harry A. Steele, Chairman
> > John B. Roose
> > Gary D. Cobb
>
> Interior (DI)
> > Dr. James J. Flannery (DI)
> > Dick L. Porter (BuRec)
>
> Army Corps of Engineers (CE)
> > Robert M. Gidez
> > William J. Donovan
>
> Agriculture (USDA)
> > R. Neil Lane (SCS)
> > Richard D. Parker (ERS)
> > Roger W. Strobehn (ERS)
>
> Federal Power Commission (FPC)
> > George G. Adkins
>
> Tennessee Valley Authority (TVA)
> > W. Glenn O'Neal

* The WRC Task Force also worked on *The Standards for Planning Water and Land Resources*, which gives an elaboration on the *Principles*.

A member of the Nader Study Group spent several weeks talking with these men, sitting in on their meetings, and reading through hundreds of pages of their documents. He concluded that the WRC Task Force members all sincerely wanted to do a good job; yet, apparently, many of them were able to bring little more to bear on the *Principles* than their sincerity and good-natured cooperation.

While WRC reports are now published with orange instead of blue covers, little has changed in either the quality of WRC recommendations or in the pervasive influence of the Corps of Engineers. The *Principles* actually intensifies and expands the weaknesses of Reclamation's benefit-cost framework.

A CRITIQUE OF THE WRC PRINCIPLES

The *Principles* would abolish the traditional single benefit-cost ratio, and replace it with four separate accounts listing four different groups of benefits and costs.[4] The accounts are (1) the national economic development account, (2) the social well-being account, (3) the environmental account, and (4) the regional development account. Since these revisions are potentially quite significant, we believe it is necessary to raise major objections to WRC's recommendations *now*, before the Administration finally approves them.

First, the economic development account erroneously ignores equity considerations.[5] This is neither good economics nor good public policy. Economists as well as the American public realize that recognition of the distribution of projects effects by income class of the beneficiaries is vital to determining the economic desirability of projects. These equity considerations should be integrated into economic analyses as suggested in Chapter 4 of this report—instead of being separated from "economic" criteria as advocated by the WRC Task Force.

Second, WRC's national economic development account excludes most environmental considerations. The WRC set up a separate environmental quality account that fails to provide dollar values for environmental impacts.[6] The WRC apparently does not consider these impacts significant enough to warrant inclusion of them in the national economic development account. However, water quality deterioration, for example, is a very tangible cost; and failure to give it dollar values is a distortion of economic rationality. Although there is not yet a price tag for many environmental damages, these effects should not be ignored or relegated to an account that does not reflect dollar impacts. We believe that appropriate dollar values, even estimated ones, should be given to ecological effects, as suggested in Chapter 3 of this report, and included in a single account of all benefits and costs.

A third problem with the four-account system is that some benefits will be double counted horizontally; that is, the same benefits will be considered in more than one account. The *Principles* states that "the multiobjectives are not mutually exclusive with respect to benefits and costs."[7] The use of unemployed resources, for example, is treated as a benefit in three different accounts (the national economic development, regional economic development, and social well-being accounts), and thus is triple counted.[8] Other examples of double and triple counting across the accounts are plentiful. Such duplications would make meaningful decisionmaking difficult, if not impossible. The bulk of all project costs, on the other hand, appear only once—in the national economic development account.

Fourth, the national economic development account overstates the economic efficiency benefits. By counting the value to users of increased output, the value of output created by external economies, and the value of output using unemployed or underemployed resources, the WRC guaranteed the vertical double counting of each economic effect and made possible the counting of some economic effects three times.[9] For example, counting both the value of increased crop production and the value of increased farm income is double counting since production and income are opposite sides of the same coin. Although such blatant double counting will please Reclamation and Army Corps of Engineers officials by making large project benefit estimates possible, it will also provide misleading information that can only deceive the inquiring congressman or citizen.

A fifth limitation of the *Principles* is vertical duplications in the regional development account. In an amazing display of ingenuity, the WRC Task Force managed to find six different ways to count the same regional impact: (1) the value to the users of increased outputs, (2) the value of output due to external economies, (3) the value of output created using unemployed or underemployed resources, (4) the net income accruing to the region, (5) the increased number and types of jobs, and (6) improvements in the region's economic base.[10] The rampant degree of overlap between these categories makes any display of such regional impacts worthless as a guide to policymaking.

Sixth, the *Principles* document specifies no method of reconciling crucial tradeoffs among policy goals. For example, the environmental objective calls for the preservation and enhancement of wild rivers and lakes.[11] These objectives almost invariably compete both with each other and with other, quantified objectives in the planning of Reclamation projects. Failure to specify methods for handling such conflicts will promote Bureau planners' continued disregard for environmental impacts.

A seventh objection is that the *Principles* requires planners to specify project effects on only those income and racial "groups defined as being relevant to evaluation of a plan."[12] Thus, the Bureau can omit from its economic analysis a project's unfavorable distributional effects by failing to define adversely affected groups as relevant. Such discretionary authority should not be placed in the hands of the Bureau of Reclamation. Instead, as suggested in Chapter 4 of this report, the Office of Management and Budget should set up predetermined distributional categories for which a breakdown of project effects is required.

Eighth, there is no justification for a regional development account. To say that one region should get a project rather than some other region—on other than economic grounds which include equity considerations—is equivalent to saying that it is more deserving to live in Colorado than Louisiana. Such a concept is indefensible. The regional account is only a porkbarrel account and should be recognized as such.

Ninth, WRC's statement concerning the discount rate is vague. Although suggesting no method for settling the discount rate dispute, the WRC asserts that the discount rate should "reflect the relative values placed by society on benefits and costs toward the multi-objectives."[13] What this means is unclear, to say the least. The only economic concept that the WRC discount rate resembles even remotely is Professor Marglin's social rate of discount, which holds that the discount rate merely reflects society's intertemporal preferences toward aggregate consumption. But does the WRC believe that society's preferences for attainment of the multi-objectives in various time periods differ from society's relative preferences toward aggregate consumption in the same periods? And are society's intertemporal preferences the same for each of the multi-objectives? What working principle does the WRC intend to use in setting the discount rate? These and many similar unanswered questions lead us to conclude that the WRC discount rate concept has no practical significance and is intentionally vague.

A tenth objection to the *Principles* is that they give no way to determine net project benefits. Benefit-cost analysis becomes useless as a project evaluation tool because the sum of a project's benefits cannot be determined using the *Principles*. It is not even possible to weight the different benefit accounts and then add them together, as the chairman of the WRC Task Force suggested.[14] This could only be done if the accounts were mutually exclusive with respect to benefits and costs; and they are not. Congressmen may see a regional benefit of $1 million for a project without being able to tell how much of that benefit has already been treated in other accounts. Hence, it is highly doubtful that congressmen will be able to determine a project's desirability under this system.

The flaws in the *Principles* document certainly do not end here. The rigid, narrow perspective of the WRC Task Force, for instance, not only biased its recommendations in the *Principles* but also led it to reject the well-founded suggestions of its own consultants. The WRC Task Force rejected all ten revisions offered by Professor Jack Knetsch,[15] seventeen of the eighteen changes suggested by Professor Charles Howe,[16] and all but two of the twenty-one revisions suggested by Professor Robert Haveman.[17]

THE POLITICKING BEHIND THE WRC PRINCIPLES

In a memo to assistant secretary of the interior for water and power development, former Reclamation Commissioner Floyd E. Dominy set the ground rules the WRC Task Force followed in preparing the shoddy report:

> We believe that we have been extremely conservative in the past in evaluating water resources projects and that if any change is to be made it should be in the direction of liberalizing our analyses. . . .
>
> The major factor in our conservative benefit estimates, however, is our inability to place a dollar value on the intangible effects of our projects. Many facets of resource development considered intangible include stabilization of income, creation of job opportunities, provision of economic flexibility, redistribution of income, dispersal of population, resource preservation, and the general economic and social well-being of people. These are all positive, important benefits that, not being readily susceptible to dollar evaluation, are largely ignored in decision-making although regularly accorded lip service. . . .
>
> On the other hand, the adverse intangible effects of projects that involve minor infringements of wilderness areas or national parks consistently become of over-riding significance and have controlling effect in decision-making. It has been our experience that only when intangible benefits are adverse do they enter into the decision-making process. . . .
>
> If the intangible benefits of water resources development projects are adequately recognized, we are confident that water programs will survive competition with other national programs. If they are not, it will indeed be ironic that such programs of proven worth are scuttled by a weapon of their own making and used only in their own demise—the benefit-cost ratio.

> I recommend strongly that Interior representatives in Water Resources Council activities present and support these views and that Secretary Udall, as chairman of the Council, be fully informed as to them.[18]

In the WRC documents, benefit-cost evaluation procedures were liberalized, as Dominy suggested. Moreover, the *Principles* included both the social well-being and regional development accounts that Dominy mentioned in the second paragraph. The WRC document also included an environmental account which Dominy advocated in the third paragraph. In short, Dominy and the Bureau could not have been more pleased with the WRC Task Force's recommendations.

Robert Gidez, the representative for the Army Corps of Engineers, was all too happy to expedite Dominy's ideas. What was good for Reclamation was good for the Corps of Engineers. Gidez subsequently dominated the WRC Task Force.

He was able to do so, USDA economist William Green noted, because "the Task Force just didn't have the kind of highly qualified people I would like to have seen. Intellectually, Gidez was more up to date."[19] Neil Lane, the chief USDA representative, echoed and amplified Mr. Green's statement:

> The WRC activities were a little deep for me. I'm the designated member, but Roger Strobehn helped out a lot. The Task Force activities were technical in scope, but my training wasn't in economics. I think the Corps of Engineers had considerable influence.[20]

George Adkins, the FPC representative, also bemoaned:

> I'm not an economist. Neither is Neil Lane. My training is in engineering. I wasn't up on all of the new methods as some of the others.[21]

A member of the Nader Study Group attended several WRC Task Force sessions and verified these observations. With the exception of Dr. James J. Flannery, of the Department of the Interior, Roger Strobehn of USDA's Economic Research Service, and Harry Steele, the Task Force chairman, nobody on the Task Force felt qualified to dispute Gidez's views. Unfortunately, Dr. Flannery was not a full-time member of the Task Force. Though Flannery (a former HEW economist and a participant in drafting SD97) was instrumental in developing the concept of a social well-being account and its recognition of equity considerations, he was only an occasional participant in more recent WRC activities. Dick Porter, of the Bureau of Reclamations, bore the brunt of the work for Interior. Strobehn's incisive objections at Task Force meetings were frequently swamped by Gidez's analysis and the rhetoric of assistant Corps representative Bill Donovan. And while Harry Steele moderated and organized the meetings, he did not appear to be strong enough to oppose the Corps faction unilaterally. That wasn't his function, anyway; if the report was to be made acceptable to the affected agencies, he couldn't override the consensus of the rest of the members. Consequently, when it came time for a section to be rewritten, chairman Steele invariably called upon Gidez to compose the final version.

One reason for the Corps's influence was the organizational backup it had. For example, the Corps's Appalachian study provided virtually all the information at the Task Force's disposal concerning regional benefits.

The power of Gidez's personality was another reason for his dominating influence. Gidez himself asserts that he dominated the Task Force. "I was probably the major author of the *Principles* document."[22] Gidez's influence, however, has not extended beyond the WRC Task Force. At the time of this writing, the *Principles* remains in limbo. After over a year of review, the Office of Management and Budget remains reluctant to approve it for agency use.

Even after all behind-the-scenes negotiations are completed, the *Principles* will not go into effect immediately. The scenario has included a series of public hearings held in March, 1972, on the revised *Principles*. After dutifully listening to this public discussion, the WRC will presumably then make whatever revisions it sees fit before seeking final executive authorization for implementing its report. A recent revision of the *Principles* has been issued for public comment in the *Federal Register*. (See Appendix for the testimony presented by W. Kip Viscusi at the hearings.)

RECOMMENDATIONS

We believe that the *Principles* is so misguided that it is beyond repair. The current members of the WRC Task Force have demonstrated an inability to make the kind of unbiased revisions needed to secure the rational allocation of the nation's resources. The thousands of dollars of taxpayers' money needed to fund the WRC activities could be spent better elsewhere. Moreover, millions of dollars will be ill-spent for every week that passes without appropriate alteration of Reclamation activities.

Indeed the Bureau of Reclamation itself has outlasted its chief purpose. No longer is there a need for more and bigger dams and irrigation canals to reclaim the arid lands of the West. Yet the Bureau doggedly pursues this counterproductive goal that benefits politicians, bureaucrats, and a few profiteering irrigators but not the nation as a whole.

The Bureau manipulates its economic analyses to justify unneeded projects, not to evaluate them—much like a drunk who uses a lamppost for support instead of illumination. If the Bureau can show that a project has a benefit-cost ratio greater than 1.0, then the project passes the test required for congressional and Office of Management and Budget approval. From that point on, project critics can do little to stop or alter a project's construction.

To get benefit-cost ratios over 1.0, the Bureau persists in claiming enormous benefits from continued irrigation of the West. As we saw in Chapter 2, the Bureau's routine irrigation benefit calculations are a sham. The country needs no more farm land. Reclamation irrigation facilities not only cost billions of dollars to build and operate, but also drive thousands of non-Reclamation farmers out of their jobs, and increase the amount of money that the U.S. Department of Agriculture must spend to curtail surplus crop production and to support agricultural prices. Thus, taxpayers are hit twice. Irrigators are recipients of huge subsidies because they have persuaded the Bureau and Congress that they pay for their water. We recommended that irrigation be counted as at most a zero benefit. All backlogged and future Bureau efforts should be evaluated giving no benefit to irrigation. If this recommendation is implemented, then almost all currently planned projects will either fail the economic test or will pass only after considerable changes in project goals.

Although the Bureau of Reclamation should cease its irrigation activities, there is no reason why it should cease to exist. It must still operate and maintain its existing dams and other facilities. More important, the Bureau should apply its seasoned expertise in a saner way to the West's modern water resource needs.

The first place to start is with the Bureau's environmental impacts. To date, Reclamation dams and levees have ravaged a good deal of the West's natural resources. In typical subservience to the wishes of irrigation, the Bureau has harnessed the free-flowing Snake River to the point where millions of fish have been killed and Northwest residents have been forced to abandon the Snake as a source of water and recreation. The Colorado River, as well, has suffered from the severe salinity and sedimentation problems occasioned by the Bureau's myopic concern with irrigation.

The American taxpayers have to pay for the Bureau of Reclamation's plunder of the West's natural environment. If anything, the Bureau should be paying the taxpayer for flooding out scenic areas, damming up wild-running streams, and engaging in ecologically dangerous weather modification efforts, as well as threatening unique species of Western fish and wildlife. The Bureau of Reclamation even tried to dam up America's greatest natural wonder—the Grand Canyon. Such activity is hardly a bargain—at any price. Again, these atrocities are attributable to the Bureau's faulty economic practices. By failing to give appropriate dollar values to environmental impacts, Bureau officials remain oblivious to such consequences.

We believe that if the Bureau of Reclamation applies consistent and meaningful dollar values to both environmental improvements and damages, then its projects will begin to develop the water resources of the West for the benefit of all citizens—not just for the irrigators. In addition, we recommend that Reclamation funds and water be allocated to water quality improvement as a major objective of project design and operations.

In Chapter 4 we analyzed more technical economic criteria. We found that the Bureau of Reclamation's 200 percent cost overruns gave its projects a place high on the list of tax-supported government boondoggles. The Bureau's use of an unjustifiably low discount rate also hurt the American taxpayer by making him pay for Reclamation dams that benefit primarily a few heavily subsidized irrigators. Private businessmen and American consumers also suffer from the Bureau of Reclamation's overestimated power and municipal and industrial water "benefits" that displace more desirable private alternatives. Finally, the Bureau's current practice of hiding the distribution of project benefits and costs should stop. To alleviate these technical problems, we recommend that the Office of Management and Budget and the General Accounting Office increase their supervision over the Bureau of Reclamation's economic evaluations and adopt the many specific suggestions made in Chapters 2, 3, and 4. The President, Congress, and the American people should know who really benefits and who really suffers from Bureau of Reclamation projects.

In Chapter 5, we found that the Central Arizona project, like so many other Reclamation projects, would benefit primarily a few irrigators, politicians, and bureaucrats at the expense of the city dwellers in Arizona and the American taxpayers. CAP would supply central Arizona municipal and industrial water users with water they do not need, at prices they cannot afford. Moreover, CAP will probably require a huge interbasin rescue operation, since there will not even be enough water in the Colorado Basin to fill CAP goals. We therefore strongly recommend that this $1.4 billion pork-barrel blunder be scrapped now.

CAP is not the only Reclamation project that benefits only a special few. Chapter 6 details how the Bureau hides its enormous subsidies—especially those given to irrigators. The direct subsidy with each acre-foot of water combines with the

Bureau's lax enforcement of excess land laws, to bestow million-dollar windfalls on select profiteers.

In recent years, the policies of the Bureau of Reclamation have come under increasing attack, as concern for the environment and for the civil rights of Indians has mounted. The Bureau, like the Corps of Engineers and other water manipulators, has made some attempt to respond to the criticism. But the Bureau's response has been made from a position of arrogance: piecemeal, narrow interpretations of the *Winters* doctrine and discount rate recommendations. While the Bureau's press releases have undergone a shift in tone and emphasis, agency activities have remained unchanged. Reclamation is still building its projects to provide primarily unneeded irrigation for the benefit of profiteers. The only difference is that now these senseless activities are touted as ecological improvements. To stress the recreational and the fish-and-wildlife activities of its reports, the Department of the Interior has even made publicity films that are seen on TV in such unlikely places as Boston—about 2,000 miles from Reclamation country.

The Bureau of Reclamation naturally has a vested interest in its own continued existence, but it is both unfortunate and disrespectful to the public that the Bureau has responded to well-taken criticism haughtily, if at all. It appears that Reclamation will change only if compelled by other parts of the executive branch and by Congress.

We believe that the recommendations contained in this book are sufficient to end the Bureau of Reclamation's senseless damming of the West; we believe too, that there is a place for the Bureau of Reclamation, and that its currently operational projects should be continued as long as they provide legitimate benefits to the West. Until such time as the Bureau of Reclamation is ready to scrap or revamp its destructive new activities and concentrate on constructive ones, we call upon Congress and the President to freeze all Bureau of Reclamation construction.

Appendix

TABLE 1-A

General Reclamation Statistics

(as of June 30, 1970, unless specified)

Bureau established by Act of Congress, signed by President Theodore Roosevelt, June 17, 1902		
Current staff, June 30, 1970	9,424	
Job Corps	226	
Serves 17 Western states and Hawaii		
17 Western states, total area in square miles	1,832,000	
17 Western states, total population—1970	52,510,000	
Projects authorized to January 2, 1971		153
Range in size from Intake project, a canal and pumping plant costing $88,000, to Missouri River Basin in ten states, and Central Valley ultimately costing $2.5 billion.		
Total estimated cost when completed (excludes Missouri River Basin units requiring reauthorization)		$11,476,000,000
Actual cost to date		$6,156,000,000

Physical Features Constructed and Under Construction, June 30, 1970

Storage dams and dikes:		
Completed or rehabilitated (217 reservoirs)	276	
Under construction (5 reservoirs)	9	
Total (222 reservoirs)	285	
Total storage capacity in acre-feet		133,656,000
Total storage capacity in acre-feet		815,000
Total storage capacity in acre-feet		134,471,000
Diversion dams, completed or rehabilitated	132	
Under construction	5	
Total	137	
Canals		
Length in miles		356
Tunnels		6,935
Length in feet		178
Major pumping plants, over 1,000 horsepower	111	1,091,000
Horsepower	1,749,000	
Pipelines, length in miles		763

Summary of Operations

Irrigation Facilities in Operation, Crop Year 1969

Irrigated acres:
Full supply   4,070,000
Supplemental supply and temporary   4,506,000
Total irrigated acres   8,576,000

Irrigable acres for service:
Full supply   4,839,000
Supplemental supply and temporary   5,301,000
Subtotal   10,140,000

Irrigable acres not for service, under construction 4,978,000
Total irrigable acres   15,118,000

Crop value—crop year 1969 $1,885 million
—cumulative $30,484 million
Total acreage irrigated, 1964—17 states   33,208,318

Hydroelectric Power, Fiscal Year 1970

Projects, Bureau constructed and operated   22
Powerplants   49
Capacity installed, KW, ultimate   7,689,000
  actual   7,413,000
Capacity under construction by Bureau KW   4,339,000
Additional authorized powerplants, KW   315,000

Financial Summary

Investment in Facilities, through Fiscal Year 1970

Completed plant in service:
Irrigation $1,255 million
Power, electric   1,232 million
Multipurpose and other   2,917 million
Total, in service   5,404 million
Cost of plant under construction   633 million
Total investments in facilities   6,037 million

Estimated Total Authorized Project Cost Allocations

Reimbursable:
Irrigation $5,844 million
Commercial power   2,833 million
Municipal and industrial water   1,105 million
State funds not allocated   183 million
Deferred allocations   115 million
Other purposes   76 million
Subtotal, reimbursable—88.5%   10,156 million

Nonreimbursable:
Flood control and navigation   658 million
Fish and wildlife conservation   322 million
Irrigation   103 million
Recreation, health, & safety   100 million

TABLE 1-A *continued*
General Reclamation Statistics
(as of June 30, 1970, unless specified)

Powerplants, Bureau marketing only	7
Capacity installed, KW	2,079,500
Transmission lines in circuit miles	16,000
Substations in operation	300
Gross generation—FY 1970, KWH	48 billion
—cumulative KWH	762 billion
Kilowatt hours sold, FY 1970 KWH	47 billion
Income—from sales, FY 1970	$139.2 million
other electric, FY 1970	$10.0 million
cumulative	$2.00 billion
Total U.S. generating capacity January 1, 1968, KW	288,000,000
Total world generating capacity January 1, 1968, KW	895,000,000
Municipal, Industrial, and Nonagricultural Water	
Deliveries 1969, gallons or acre-feet	646 billion 1,982,000
cumulative from 1956, gallons	6,014 billion
Population served	14.5 million
Income from operations, FY 1970	$1,923,000
cumulative	19,226,000
Other purposes	137 million
Subtotal, Nonreimbursable—10.5%	1,320 million
Total	11,476 million
Construction Costs Repaid June 30, 1970	
Repayment contracts	$253 million
Power revenues	635 million
Service contracts, contributions	248 million
Total	1,136 million
Repayment Contracts	
In effect June 30, 1970	$1,603 million
Pending	483 million
Total ultimate	2,086 million
Bureau Income from Operations, Fiscal Year 1970	
Irrigation water rentals and assessments	$17,971,000
Municipal and industrial water sales	1,923,000
Electric power revenues	155,423,000
Total operating income	175,317,000
Net income after expenses and other deductions	43,201,000

Recreation

Recreation areas on projects	237
Visitor days, 1969	34.5 million
cumulative from 1958	421.5 million
Shorelines, miles	11,600
Water area, acres available	1.7 million
Land area, acres available	3.8 million

Total Federal Funds Available
Through FY '71 to date

Investigations	$364 million
Advance planning	80 million
Construction	6,028 million
Rehabilitation and betterment	62 million
Operation and maintenance	959 million
Administration	207 million
Loan program	157 million
Permanent operating authorizations	212 million
Emergency fund	8 million
Total	8,077 million

SOURCE: Summary Report of the Commissioner of Reclamation, 1970 Statistical and Financial Appendix.

TABLE 1–B
Programming and Financing
1971 and 1972
Summary of Appropriations

Fiscal Year 1971 Appropriation	Appropriation Amount	Prior Year Funds Applied	Contribution and Other	Revenues Applied	Pay Raise	Under-financing	Budgetary Reserve	Total Program
General investigation	$19,065,000	$ 380,871	$ 77,316	$ —	$ 721,000	$424,000	$ —	$ 20,668,187
General administrative expenses	13,652,000	—			708,000	—	—	14,360,000
Operation and maintenance	57,800,000	—	10,879,749[a]	1,685,000	1,049,000	—	—	71,413,749
Loan program	8,550,000	818,553				—	− 4,350,000	5,018,553
Construction and rehabilitation—total	186,793,000	20,834,769	2,238,114				− 18,579,000	191,286,883
Reclamation	(183,713,000)	(20,641,511)	(2,238,114)				(− 18,579,000)	(188,013,625)
MRB—other agencies	(3,080,000)	(193,258)					—	(3,273,258)
Upper Colorado River storage project Reclamation (Sec. 5)	22,375,000	4,003,085	179,500	315,000			− 3,733,000	23,139,583
Reclamation (Sec. 5)	(21,230,000)	(2,208,930)	(179,500)	(315,000)			(− 3,393,000)	(20,540,430)
Recreation, fish & wildlife (Sec. 8)	(1,145,000)	(1,794,155)					(− 340,000)	(2,599,155)
Upper Colorado River storage project, operation and maintenance	—	—		9,225,000			—	9,225,000
Colorado River Basin project	7,698,000	6,767,629	685,000		44,000		− 1,200,000	13,994,629
Emergency funds	—	1,560,065	10,000				—	1,570,065
Permanent appropriation	3,600,000	—	—				—	3,600,000
Trust funds	(4,500,000)[c]	(467,684)	—				—	(4,967,684)
Total	319,533,000[d]	34,364,972	14,069,679	11,225,000	2,522,000	424,000	−27,862,000	$354,276,651
Navajo Indian irrigation project	3,822,000	3,424,683	—				—	7,246,683

SOURCE: Bureau of Reclamation, FY 1972 Justifications, Jan. 29, 1971.
a Water Users, $5,836,400; Other $5,043,349.
b Water Users, $6,028,950; Other $6,011,775.
c Non-appropriation trust funds included in other programs.
d Includes $37,200 GSA transfer.

Fiscal Year 1972 Appropriation	Appropriation Estimate	Prior Year Funds Applied	Contribution and Other	Revenues Applied	Underfinancing	Carried Over to F.Y. 1973	Total Program
General investigation	$ 21,335,000	$ —	$ —	$ —	$ 569,000	$ —	$ 21,904,000
General administrative expenses	14,725,000	—	—	—	—	—	14,725,000
Operation and maintenance	68,200,000	—	12,129,725 b	2,014,000	—	—	82,343,725
Loan program	9,975,000	4,350,000	—	—	457,000	—	14,782,000
Construction and rehabilitation—total	190,500,000	18,579,000	2,035,000	—	17,160,000	− 350,000	227,924,000
Reclamation	(190,500,000)	(18,579,000)	(2,035,000)	—	(17,160,000)	(− 350,000)	(227,924,000)
MRB—other agencies	—	—	—	—	—	—	—
Upper Colorado River storage project Reclamation (Section 5)	19,256,000	3,733,000	65,000	50,000	1,700,000	− 250,000	24,554,000
Reclamation (Section 5)	(18,651,000)	(3,393,000)	(65,000)	(50,000)	(1,700,000)	(− 250,000)	(23,609,000)
Recreation, fish & wildlife (Sec. 8)	(605,000)	(340,000)	—	—	—	—	(945,000)
Upper Colorado River storage project, operation and maintenance	—	—	—	9,501,000	—	—	9,501,000
Colorado River Basin project	33,000,000	1,200,000	—	—	—	−1,200,000	33,000,000
Emergency funds	1,000,000	—	—	—	—	—	1,000,000
Permanent appropriation	3,600,000	—	—	—	—	—	3,600,000
Trust funds	(3,900,000)e	—	—	—	—	—	(3,900,000)
Total	361,591,000	27,862,000	14,229,725	11,565,000	19,886,000	−1,800,000	$433,333,725
Navajo Indian irrigation project	9,000,000	—	—	—	—	—	—

368,900,000
31,500,000 Navajo Power
337,400,000 (Includes 2.3 million for new starts.)

219

TABLE 1–C

Benefit-Cost Ratios of Projects for which Funds
Were Requested for the 1970 Fiscal Year

Project	Total Cost (thousands of $)	Benefit– Cost Ratio
Chief Joseph Dam, Manson unit, Washington	13,935	4.8
Tualatin Project, Oreg.	21,055	2.06
Mountain Park, Okla.	20,740	1.9
Colorado River Front Work and Levee System, Ariz.–Calif.	37,822	—[a]
Pacific N.W.–Pacific S.W. Intertie, Ariz.–Calif.–Nev.	169,606	2.5
Parker-Davis Project, Ariz.–Calif.–Nev.	151,061	—[b]
San Luis Unit, Central Valley, Calif.	686,918	6.15
Auburn-Folsom South Unit, Calif.	494,762	3.56
San Felipe Division, Calif.	131,086	2.76
Washoe, Nev.–Calif.	61,289	1.8
Fryingpan, Ark.–Colo.	241,727	1.74
Teton Basin, Lower Teton Division, Idaho	52,034	2.23
Southern Nevada Water Project, Nev.	83,462	1.3
Pecos River Basin Water Salvage, N. Mex.–Texas	2,520	—[c]
Whitestone Coulee Unit, Wash.	6,476	4.6
Columbia Basin, Wash.	1,851,215	3.5
Third Powerplant, Grand Coulee, Wash.	417,681	3.2
Garrison Diversion Unit, N. Dak.–S. Dak.	285,607	2.06
Glen Elder, Kans.	62,639	1.53
Missouri River Basin Transmission Division	366,026	—[d]
Yellowtail Unit, Mont.–Wyo.	97,018	3.28
Nebraska Mid-state Division, Neb.	106,232	1.25
Oahe Unit, S. Dak.	237,798	2.5
Jensen Unit, Utah	11,618	1.7
Upalco Unit, Utah	18,408	1.6
Fruitland Mesa, Colo.	34,189	1.52
Savery–Pot Hook, Colo.–Wyo.	15,526	2.40
Curecanti Unit, Colo.	129,840	1.10
Transmission Division, Ariz.–Colo.–N. Mex.–Utah–Wyo.	159,830	—[d]
Bostwick Park, Colo.	6,500	2.0
Bonneville Unit, Utah	340,478	1.8
Lyman Participating Project, Utah–Wyo.	13,795	1.00
San Juan–Chama, Colo.–N. Mex.	79,624	1.2
Central Arizona, Ariz.–N. Mex.	851,712	2.2
Dixie, Utah	60,237	1.1

SOURCE: Hearings on AEC and Public Works Appropriations before the Senate Committee on Appropriations, 1969.

[a] No benefit-cost ratio was required.

[b] Project was authorized in 1935, before B-C ratios were required.

[c] Benefits (elimination of phreatophyte infestation) cannot be accurately quantified.

[d] Project costs were included in the generating units' B-C ratios.

TABLE 1–D
Distribution of Benefit-Cost Ratios of Projects for
which Funds Were Requested for the 1970 Fiscal Year

B–C Range	Number of Projects	Total Cost (thousands of $)
0. —0.99	0	0
1.0—1.19	3	203,872
1.2—1.39	3	269,118
1.4—1.59	2	96,828
1.6—1.79	3	271,753
1.8—1.99	3	422,507
2.0—2.49	6	1,232,434
2.5—2.99	3	538,490
3.0—3.49	2	514,699
3.5—4.99	4	2,366,388
5.0 and above	1	686,918
No B–C ratio given	5	717,259

SOURCE: Hearings on AEC and Public Works Appropriations before the
Senate Committee on Appropriations, 1969.

TABLE 2–A

Acreage, Production, and Gross Crop Value
by Crops and Types of Crops, 1968

| Crops | Irrigated Lands | | Tonnage | | Gross Crop Value | |
	Total Acres	Percent of Total Percent	Total Tons	Percent of Total Percent	Total Dollars	Percent of Total[a] Percent
Cereals:						
Barley	639,282	7.62	1,029,416	2.153	45,211,800	2.45
Corn	431,070	5.14	1,108,045	2.317	43,710,956	2.38
Oats	115,513	1.38	120,642	.252	5,802,737	.32
Rice	208,882	2.49	555,034	1.161	54,064,464	2.94
Rye	2,522	.03	2,602	.005	118,421	.01
Sorghums (sorgo, kaffir, etc.)	219,823	2.62	360,220	.753	16,638,458	.90
Wheat	435,516	5.19	836,043	1.748	33,696,973	1.83
Other cereals	118,272	1.41	192,530	.403	7,279,346	.40
Total—cereals	2,170,880	25.88	4,204,532	8.792	206,523,155	11.23
Forage:						
Alfalfa hay	1,794,762	21.40	7,958,905	16.642	183,446,226	9.97
Other hay	180,539	2.15	384,195	.803	7,883,567	.43
Irrigated pasture	1,042,432	12.43	2,855,184	5.971	36,696,464	1.99
Corn fodder	1,972	.02	23,433	.049	148,626	.01
Silage or ensilage	330,121	3.94	5,741,249	12.006	38,611,650	2.10
Crop residue: beet tops	—	—	3,251,332	6.799	3,903,641	.21
stubble, stalks, etc.	—	—	262,304	.549	2,622,881	.14
straw (all kinds)	—	—	149,647	.313	1,245,382	.07
Root crops (carrots, etc.)	—	—	—	—	—	—

Other forage	52,718	.63	144,760	.303	2,077,380	.11
Total—Forage	3,402,544	40.57	20,771,009	43.435	276,635,817	15.03
Miscellaneous field crops:						
Beans, castor	281	—	171	.001	22,120	.01
Beans, dry and edible	325,550	3.88	288,422	.603	44,582,852	2.42
Broomcorn	242	—	36	—	14,400	—
Cotton, lint (Upland)	488,348	5.82	241,208	.504	113,601,605	6.17
Cotton, seed (Upland)	—	—	385,337	.806	19,929,756	1.08
Cotton, lint (Am. Egypt.)	42,446	.51	10,992	.023	7,674,918	.42
Cotton, seed (Am. Egypt.)	—	—	17,444	.036	961,720	.05
Hops	21,766	.26	18,447	.039	17,064,000	.93
Peppermint	39,031	.47	1,200	.003	10,559,564	.57
Spearmint	11,981	.14	418	.001	4,091,667	.22
Sugar Beets	517,301	6.17	9,849,331	20.596	131,588,653	7.15
Other miscellaneous field crops	15,905	.19	37,888	.079	1,956,309	.11
Total—Miscellaneous field crops	1,462,851	17.44	10,850,894	22.691	352,047,564	19.13
Vegetables:						
Asparagus	18,452	.24	32,485	.069	11,282,761	.61
Beans (processing)	26,890	.32	49,446	.103	7,433,870	.40
Beans (fresh market)	1,990	.02	7,288	.015	2,324,403	.13
Broccoli	2,864	.03	13,842	.029	2,003,681	.11
Cabbage	7,055	.08	94,734	.198	5,827,092	.32
Carrots	23,931	.29	262,215	.548	19,278,091	1.05
Cauliflower	1,779	.02	12,683	.027	2,144,086	.12
Celery	2,404	.03	66,464	.139	6,126,351	.33
Corn, sweet (processing)	56,631	.68	354,406	.741	9,633,203	.52
Corn, sweet (fresh market)	7,714	.09	36,390	.076	4,303,272	.23
Cucumbers	2,695	.03	23,115	.048	2,477,680	.13
Greens (kale, etc.)	1,101	.01	6,585	.014	301,074	.02

TABLE 2-A—(continued)
Acreage, Production, and Gross Crop Value
by Crops and Types of Crops, 1968

Crops	Irrigated Lands		Tonnage		Gross Crop Value	
	Total Acres	Percent of Total Percent	Total Tons	Percent of Total Percent	Total Dollars	Percent of Total[a] Percent
Lettuce	83,932	1.00	846,688	1.771	76,183,768	4.14
Melons: Cantaloupes, etc.	50,606	.60	357,215	.747	40,604,886	2.21
Honey ball, honeydew, etc.	2,899	.03	34,510	.072	2,769,503	.15
Watermelons	8,425	.10	63,384	.133	3,361,188	.18
Onions, dry	31,824	.38	593,727	1.242	28,916,606	1.57
Onions, green	3,190	.04	70,829	.148	5,398,243	.29
Peas, green (processing)	15,372	.18	27,710	.058	2,498,570	.14
Peas, green (fresh market)	1,595	.02	1,551	.003	460,833	.03
Peppers	5,886	.07	28,866	.060	6,449,662	.35
Potatoes, early	72,666	.87	1,157,270	2.420	49,608,929	2.70
Potatoes, late	239,488	2.86	2,761,069	5.774	87,409,889	4.75
Squash	2,281	.03	13,137	.027	1,167,914	.06
Sweet potatoes	818	.01	4,960	.010	753,789	.04
Tomatoes (canning)	60,619	.72	1,294,374	2.707	46,948,832	2.55
Tomatoes (fresh market)	11,070	.13	103,887	.217	24,021,376	1.31
Other vegetables	22,859	.27	241,887	.506	45,622,661	2.48
Total—Vegetables	767,036	9.15	8,560,717	17.902	495,312,213	26.92
Total nursery	6,572	.08	—	—	17,863,534	.97
Seeds:						
Alfalfa	78,933	.92	21,133	.045	14,242,161	.77

Clover (all kinds)	11,386	.14	2,398	.005	1,803,691	.10
Corn	10,551	.13	10,279	.021	2,278,963	.12
Flaxseed	2,455	.03	2,390	.005	289,028	.02
Grass (all kinds)	29,278	.35	10,477	.022	5,421,665	.29
Lettuce	590	.01	142	—	190,121	.01
Onion	3,058	.04	1,345	.003	1,200,277	.07
Pea	33,169	.40	38,391	.080	3,517,064	.19
Potato (all kinds)	1,690	.02	15,367	.032	1,053,476	.06
Sugar beet	4,427	.05	5,795	.012	2,057,928	.11
Other seed	63,586	.76	51,567	.108	12,623,141	.69
Total—Seeds	239,123	2.85	159,284	.333	44,677,515	2.43
Fruits:						
Apples	59,749	.70	337,522	.705	50,007,045	2.71
Apricots	16,781	.20	65,479	.137	10,981,879	.60
Berries (all kinds)	1,455	.02	10,998	.023	4,346,572	.24
Cherries	11,353	.14	20,837	.044	9,658,152	.52
Citrus: Grapefruit	16,101	.19	195,336	.408	13,994,466	.76
Lemons and limes	13,507	.16	194,614	.407	14,236,748	.77
Oranges and tangerines	91,470	1.09	428,345	.896	39,121,496	2.13
Dates	4,029	.05	17,613	.037	7,191,915	.39
Grapes, table	68,534	.82	391,354	.818	33,740,649	1.83
Grapes, other	115,880	1.38	1,057,176	2.211	58,625,757	3.19
Olives	13,064	.16	43,452	.091	16,315,767	.89
Peaches	24,288	.29	165,047	.345	17,186,951	.93
Pears	27,682	.33	167,266	.350	20,918,100	1.14
Prunes and plums	28,443	.34	111,459	.233	18,351,352	1.00
Other fruits	15,317	.18	31,068	.065	7,198,855	.39
Total—Fruits	507,653	6.05	3,237,566	6.770	321,875,704	17.49
Nuts:						

TABLE 2-A—(continued)
Acreage, Production, and Gross Crop Value
by Crops and Types of Crops, 1968

Crops	Irrigated Lands		Tonnage		Gross Crop Value	
	Total Acres	Percent of Total Percent	Total Tons	Percent of Total Percent	Total Dollars	Percent of Total[a] Percent
Almonds	32,216	.38	20,040	.041	11,842,133	.64
Pecans	5,700	.07	5,617	.012	4,946,728	.27
Walnuts	17,190	.20	10,790	.023	6,564,291	.36
Other nuts	604	.01	533	.001	90,885	—
Total—Nuts	55,710	.66	36,980	.077	23,444,037	1.27
Family gardens and orchards	19,839	.24	—	—	5,430,274	.30
Total—All crops	8,632,208	102.92	47,820,982	100.000	1,743,809,813	94.77
less multiple cropped	454,491	5.42				
Total harvested cropland and pasture	8,177,717	97.50				
Cropland not harvested	150,834	1.80				
Soil building	58,487	.70				
Acres irrigated	8,387,038	100.00				
Additional revenues[b]					96,271,858	5.23
Total gross crop value					1,840,081,671	100.00
Full irrigation service	3,940,055	46.97			813,041,747	44.19
Supplemental irrigation service	4,381,914	52.25			1,004,947,287	54.61
Temporary irrigation service	65,069	.78			22,092,637	1.20

SOURCE: United States Department of the Interior, Bureau of Reclamation.
[a] Additional revenues are included in computing percentages.
[b] Includes payments received from federal and commercial agencies.

TABLE 2–B
Backlogged Projects with No Construction Begun as of 1971

Project Name	Cost Allocated to Irrigation (in millions)	Total Cost (in millions)	Percentage Irrigation (irrigation cost ÷ total cost)	Benefit–Cost Ratio	Balance to Complete (in millions)	Amount of Irrigable Land Full (in acres)	Amount of Irrigable Land Supplemental (in acres)
San Felipe div.—CVP	$ 67.2	$ 133.6	50	2.76	91.9	14,700	31,159
Palmetto Bend proj.	0	38.0	0	1.9	36.5	0	0
Mountain Park proj.	0	20.7	0	1.9	18.7	0	0
Tualatin proj.	15.5	21.1	74	2.06	18.5	13,060	3,040
Manson unit, Chief Joseph Dam	16.6	16.6	100	4.3	14.1	1,935	3,995
Nebraska Mid-state div.—MRBP	105.6	106.0	100	1.25	105.1	0	140,000
Oahe unit—MRBP	205.8	237.8	87	2.5	189.3	190,000	0
Animas–La Plata proj.—UCRSP	84.0	118.0	74	1.59	114.1	46,520	25,600
Dallas Creek proj.—UCRSP	30.7	42.7	72	1.65	40.0	14,900	8,720
Dolores proj.—UCRSP	48.2	54.5	88	1.67	52.0	32,340	28,660
Fruitland Mesa proj.—UCRSP	33.3	36.1	92	1.39	34.6	15,870	7,010
Savery–Pot Hook proj.—UCRSP	15.3	15.5	99	2.40	14.4	21,920	13,345
Jensen unit–Central Utah proj.—UCRSP	2.6	11.4	23	1.9	9.7	440	3,640
Central Arizona proj.—LCRB	358.2	886.6	40	2.2	849.1	0	1,202,000
Dixie proj.—LCRB	48.5	60.2	81	1.1	57.6	6,900	9,650
Merlin div.—Rogue River proj.	22.0	28.8	76	1.3	28.8	9,000	260
Touchet div.—Walla Walla proj.	5.3	15.7	34	1.72	15.7	3,520	6,440
Kennewick div.—Yakima proj.	6.6	6.7	98	2.8	6.7	6,300	—
East Greenacres unit—Rothdrum Prairie proj.	4.8	5.3	91	1.55	5.3	3,500	1,770
Narrows unit—MRBP	21.1	68.1	31	1.89	68.1	—	166,370
Minot extension unit—MRBP	0	18.2	0	1.93	12.3	0	0
San Miguel proj.—UCRSP	56.0	74.0	76	1.34	71.0	26,420	12,530
Upalco unit—Central Utah proj.	16.1	22.5	72	1.6	22.5	0	42,610
West Divide proj.	74.3	108.8	68	1.98	108.8	18,890	21,030
Riverton extension unit—Riverton proj.	41.0	43.1	93	1.78	43.1	drainage for old irrigation	
Totals	1,191.4	2,190.0	55		2,027.9	426,305	1,727,829

SOURCE: Figures compiled from 1971 Senate Appropriation Hearings and supplemental information supplied by the Bureau of Reclamation.

TABLE 2-C

Backlogged Major Projects with Partial Construction as of 1971

	Percent Complete	Cost Allocated to Irrigation (in $ millions)	Total cost (in $ millions)	Percent Irrigation	Benefit-Cost Ratio	Balance to Complete (in $ millions)	Amount of Full (in acres)	Irrigable Land Supplemental (in acres)
Teton Basin project	3	48.4	64.3	7	1.6	59.0	37,000	111,120
Garrison diversion unit—MRBP	5	239.7	299.3	80	2.06	227.7	1,000,000	0
Bonneville unit, Central Utah project	11	203.2	380.5	53	1.7	301.7	43,740	112,790
Fryingpan-Arkansas project	31	99.0	249.3	40	1.7	143.0	0	280,600
Columbia Basin project, including East High Canal irrigation unit	37 (5)	1,202.0 (495.1)	1,904.0 (495.1)	63 (100)	3.3 (none)	1,073.0 (491.4)	1,095,000 (unknown)	0 (unknown)
Pacific Northwest–Southwest intertie	47	0	0	0	2.5	81.0	0	0
Central Valley project, Calif., including Auburn Folsom south unit	55	1,389.2	2,572.9	54	varies for each unit	905.0	273,074	2,194,041
Miscellaneous smaller projects	(5) various but above 50	(166.5) various	(529.9) various	32 various	(3.56) various	(435.8) 724.7	(29,340) various	(300,000) various
Totals		3181.5	5470.3	58		3,442.2	2,448,814 +	2,698,641 +

SOURCE: Figures compiled from FY '71 Senate Appropriation Hearings and supplemental information supplied by the Bureau of Reclamation.

TABLE 3–A
Recreation Benefit Data for the
Mountain Park Project

Activity	Activity Days	Value per Day	Benefit
Total annual visitation:	133,000		
General use:	133,000	$.52	$ 69,160
Boating, water skiing:	55,160	.55	30,338
Camping:	33,000	.50	16,500
Total recreation benefits			$116,000*

SOURCE: House Document No. 438, *Mountain Park Project*, 89th Congress, 2d Session (1966).
* Figure was rounded off from $115,998.

TABLE 4–A
Discount Rates Used in
Reclamation Feasibility Studies

Fiscal Year	Discount Rate
1959	2.5
1960	2.5
1961	2.5
1962	2⅝
1963	2⅞
1964	3
1965	3⅛
1966	3⅛
1967	3⅛
1968	3¼
1969	3¼
	4⅝*
1970	4⅞
1971	5⅛

* This increase was due to the Water Resources Council's issuing of new procedures for setting discount rates.

TABLE 4–B
Benefit-Cost Evaluations at 4⅞% Discount Rate

NOTE: This hypothetical example has been provided to display the effect of the discount rate upon a project's benefits and costs. All project costs are incurred during the first ten years of operation. Net project benefits of $10 per year are assumed to occur from the eleventh till the fiftieth year of operation. No project benefits after fifty years are considered.

Year of Operation	Expected Yearly Cost	Expected Yearly Benefit	Discount Factor for 4⅞%	Present Value Cost (Col. 2 × Col. 4)	Present Value Benefit (Col. 3 × Col. 4)
Col. 1	Col. 2	Col. 3	Col. 4	Col. 5	Col. 6
1	$10	$ 0	.954	$ 9.5	$0
2	15	0	.909	13.6	0
3	20	0	.867	17.4	0
4	10	0	.827	8.3	0
5	10	0	.788	7.9	0
6	10	0	.752	7.5	0
7	5	0	.717	3.6	0
8	5	0	.683	3.4	0
8	5	0	.467	3.3	0
10	5	0	.621	3.1	0
11	0	10	.592	0	5.9
12	0	10	.565	0	5.7
13	0	10	.539	0	5.4
14	0	10	.514	0	5.1
15	0	10	.490	0	4.9
16	0	10	.467	0	4.7
17	0	10	.445	0	4.5
:	:	:	:	:	:
50	0	10	.093	0	.9

Present value benefit (the sum of column six): $108.5
Present value cost (the sum of column five): $77.6
The hypothetical project's B–C ratio is given by the present value benefit divided by the present value cost.

$$\text{B–C ratio} = \frac{\$108.5}{\$\ 77.6} = 1.39$$

TABLE 4–C
Benefit-Cost Evaluations at 10% Discount Rate

Year of Operation	Expected Cost Yearly	Expected Yearly Benefit	Discount Factor for 10%	Present Value Cost (Col. 2 × Col. 4)	Present Value Benefit (Col. 3 × Col. 4)
Col. 1	Col. 2	Col. 3	Col. 4	Col. 5	Col. 6
1	$10	$ 0	.909	$ 9.1	$0
2	15	0	.826	12.5	0
3	20	0	.751	15.0	0
4	10	0	.683	6.8	0
5	10	0	.621	6.2	0
6	10	0	.564	5.6	0
7	5	0	.513	2.6	0
9	5	0	.652	2.3	0
9	5	0	.424	2.1	0
10	5	0	.386	1.9	0
11	0	10	.350	0	3.5
12	0	10	.319	0	3.2
13	0	10	.290	0	2.9
14	0	10	.263	0	2.6
15	0	10	.239	0	2.4
16	0	10	.218	0	2.2
17	0	10	.198	0	2.0
18	0	10	.180	0	1.8
19	0	10	.164	0	1.6
:	:	:	:	:	:
50	0	10	.009	0	.1

Present value benefit (the sum of column six): $37.7
Present value cost (the sum of column five): $65.1
The hypothetical project's B–C ratio is given by the present value benefit divided by the present value cost.

$$\text{B–C ratio} = \frac{\$37.7}{\$65.1} = .58$$

TABLE 6–A

Statistics on Irrigation Investment on Projects in Fiscal Year 1972 Budget

Appropriation and Project	Total Estimated Cost for Allocation	Appropriations to June 30, 1971	Allocation to Irrigation	Repayment of Irrigation Allocation		
				Water Users	Power	Others
CONSTRUCTION AND REHABILITATION						
Central Valley project, California, San Felipe division (acres served: full, 14,700; supplemental, 31,159):						
Dollars	117,156,000	404,956	58,894,000	26,328,000		32,566,000 [a]
Per acre			1,284	574		710
Chief Joseph Dam project, Manson unit, Washington (acres served: full, 1,935; supplemental, 3,995):						
Dollars	16,624,000	1,551,938	16,624,000	3,781,000	12,843,000	
Per acre			2,803	637	2,166	
Columbia Basin project, Washington (acres served: full, 1,095,000; supplemental, 0):						
Dollars	1,903,949,000	774,820,450	1,201,940,000	144,602,000	1,045,838,000	11,500,000 [b]
Per acre			1,098	132	955	11

Pick-Sloan Missouri River Basin program, North and South Dakota, Garrison diversion unit (acres served: full, supplemental, 250,000; 0):

Dollars	327,200,000	28,144,421	262,698,000	19,296,000	243,402,000
Per acre			1,051	77	974

Oahe unit (acres served: full, supplemental, 190,000; 0):

Dollars	237,798,000	1,748,664	205,790,000	33,440,000	172,350,000
Per acre			1,083	176	907

Tualatin project, Oregon (acres served: full, supplemental, 10,700; 6,300):

Dollars	32,064,000	2,339,096	17,763,000	5,501,000	12,262,000
Per acre			1,045	324	721

UPPER COLORADO RIVER STORAGE PROJECT

Animas–La Plata participating project, Colorado–New Mexico (acres served: full 46,250; supplemental 25,600):

233

TABLE 6-A—*continued*

Satistics on Irrigation Investment on Projects in Fiscal Year 1972 Budget

Appropriation and Project	Total Estimated Cost for Allocation	Appropriations to June, 30 1971	Allocation to Irrigation	Repayment of Irrigation Allocation		
				Water Users	Power	Others
Central Utah participating project, Bonneville unit, Utah (acres served: full, 43,740; supplemental, 112,790):						
Dollars	117,955,000	225,000	84,030,000	11,240,000	0	72,790,000 [c]
Per acre			1,165	156	0	1,009
Dallas Creek participating project, Colorado (acres served: 14,900; supplemental, 8,720):						
Dollars	413,250,800	48,228,398	220,409,000	16,400,000	55,248,000	148,761,000 [d]
Per acre			1,408	105	353	950
San Miguel participating project, Colorado (acres served: full, 26,420; supplemental, 12,530):						
Dollars	42,655,000	230,000	30,677,000	2,805,000	0	27,872,000 [e]
Per acre			1,299	119	0	1,180
Dollars	74,031,700	50,000	56,022,000	5,155,000	0	50,867,000 [f]
Per acre			1,438	132	0	1,306

SOURCE: Hearings before the Senate Committee on Appropriations: Public Works for Water and Power Development and Atomic Energy Commission Appropriations, Fiscal Year 1972, Part 2, pp. 11–12.

[a] Represents the amount of irrigation allocation to be repaid by power and municipal and industrial water revenues derived from the Central Valley project.

[b] Represents receipts from sale and lease of government-owned project lands which partially offset costs allocated to irrigation.

[c] Includes $64,382,000 of the irrigation allocation to be repaid from power and other revenues accumulated to the Upper Colorado River Basin Fund. Also includes $7,737,000 from ad valorem taxes and $671,000 for investigations costs funded from the Colorado River Development Fund and from contributions.

[d] Includes $110,025,000 of the irrigation allocation to be repaid from power and other revenues accumulated to the Upper Colorado River Basin Fund. Also includes $38,037,000 from ad valorem taxes and $699,000 for investigations costs funded from the Colorado River Development Fund and from contributions.

[e] Includes $25,094,000 of the irrigation allocation to be repaid from power and other revenues accumulated to the Upper Colorado River Basin Fund. Also includes $2,496,000 from ad valorem taxes and $282,000 for investigations costs funded from the Colorado River Development Fund.

[f] Includes $49,958,000 of the irrigation allocation to be repaid from power and other revenues accumulated to the Upper Colorado River Basin Fund. Also includes $587,000 for ad valorem taxes and $322,000 for investigations costs funded from the Colorado River Development Fund and contributions.

235

TABLE 6–B

Excess-land Ownership in Westlands Water District of CVP

I.   Total number of landowners = 2,516
II. Total acreage = 566,670 including:
     a. 136,632 non-excess
     b. 430,098 excess
III. Total under recordable contract = 145,443 including:
     a. 3,359 sold
     b. 142,084 balance
IV. Total District's land value increase = 556,760 × $300 per acre = $167,028,000
V.   Total number of excess-landowners = 236
     a. Number holding less than 641 acres = 140
     b. Number holding 641–5,121 acres = 96 (including several members of Giffen, O'Neils, Hoyt, Vernon Thomas, Pilibos, Matheson, and Harris families)
     c. Number holding more than 5,121 acres = 16. The figures for those sixteen are shown in the table.

	Non-Excess	Excess	Total Acreage	Under Recordable Contract	Direct Annual Subsidy to Acres Receiving Water[a]	Total Subsidy for Total Acreage in Area[b]	Potential Capitalized Unearned Increment[c]
Airway Farms, Inc.	160	6,221	6,781		$ 13,440	$ 5,743,507	$ 2,034,300
Anderson Clayton & Co.	160	30,568	30,728	25,782	2,179,128	26,026,616	9,218,400
Boston Ranch Co.	160	22,221	22,381		13,440	18,956,707	6,714,300
Cort Ranch, Inc.	160	6,107	6,267	6,101	525,924	5,308,149	1,880,100
Deal & Co., W. J. Inc.	160	9,756	9,916	5,394	466,536	8,398,852	2,974,800
Diener, Frank C.	3,815	2,902	6,717		320,460	5,689,299	2,015,100

Giffen, Inc.	2	39,505	39,507	20,609	1,731,324	33,462,429	11,852,100
Giffen, Russell & Ruth P.	315	5,121	5,436	1,431	146,664	4,604,292	1,630,800
Reece, H. C. & Irene	320	5,003	5,323		26,880	4,508,581	1,596,900
South Lake Farms, Inc.	160	10,126	10,286	7,201	618,324	8,712,242	3,085,800
Southern Pacific Co.	160	78,763	78,923	28,975	2,447,340	66,847,781	23,676,900
Southern Pacific Land Co.		30,056	30,056			25,457,432	9,916,800
Standard Oil Co. of California	160	10,281	10,441		13,440	8,843,527	3,132,300
Thomas, Raymond Inc.	160	9,679	9,839	4,513	392,532	8,333,633	2,951,700
Thomas, Raymond—Murieta Farms	5,026	3,508	8,570	590	555,744	7,258,790	2,571,000
Westhaven Farming Co.	160	10,118	10,278		13,440	8,705,466	3,083,400

SOURCE: Bureau of Reclamation summary sheets dated 12/31/70 and authors' computations.

[a] Using $84 per acre per year times number of acres receiving water (i.e., non-excess and those under recordable contract).

[b] Using $847 per acre total Reclamation subsidy times total acreage, since even acres not receiving water get potential unearned increment by increase in water table and free option to sign recordable contract.

[c] Based on known $300 appreciation per acre and assumed average for land in Westlands times total acres owned.

STATEMENT BY W. KIP VISCUSI BEFORE
THE WATER RESOURCES COUNCIL,
March 21, 1972

I would like to thank the members of the Water Resources Council (WRC) for giving me this opportunity to present my views at this public hearing. While serving as editor and co-author of the Nader task force report on the Bureau of Reclamation, I have followed the various stages of the WRC's efforts with great care.

The most recent version of the *Principles and Standards*, published in the *Federal Register**, is a mammoth document. Unfortunately, length is seldom an indicator of quality, and the *Principles and Standards* document is no exception.

I would like to begin by expressing general disagreement with the three-objective system advocated by the WRC. Although I am an advocate of multi-objective planning, I can only express dismay at the scheme recommended. First, the objectives of regional development, national economic development, and environmental quality are defined at such an aggregative level as to undermine the spirit of multi-objective planning. A second drawback is that a well-formulated objective is supposed to describe magnitudes of which society always prefers more. This is not the case for the WRC framework. For example, one component of the WRC's regional development objective is the "diversification of the regional economic base" (p. 24162). This apparent mandate in the direction of regional self-sufficiency is misguided, at best. A region should concentrate in producing those products in which it possesses a comparative advantage. The necessity for avoiding the economic isolationism that would be promoted by the WRC document is especially apparent when one realizes that there are 173 regional accounting areas recommended for use in project planning.

A third limitation of the WRC objective format is that there is considerable overlap in the evaluation of project effects. For example, a direct increase in farmers' income from irrigation water could appear as a national economic benefit of increased output and as a regional economic benefit consisting of the value of the output to the region, the increased number of jobs in the region, the additional net income to the region, and the improve-

* Water Resources Council, "Proposed Principles and Standards for Planning Water and Related Land Resources," *Federal Register*, vol. 36, no. 245, Part II, pp. 24144–24194.

ment in the regional economic base. Such duplication makes it impossible for congressmen or other policymakers to determine the net desirability of a project.

At one point, the *Standards* asserts that if explicit weights existed for the multi-objectives, the net desirability of a project could be readily determined. This is just not true. The rampant overlap among and within the accounts precludes any possibility of systematic assessment of a proposal's desirability.

Let us now turn to the accounts used for each of the three objectives. National economic development impacts make up the first account. Unfortunately, this objective is both ill-conceived and misdefined. Many crucial components have been omitted. For example, environmental quality impacts are vital economic effects on society's scarce resources even though no market prices exist for many of these effects. The WRC's separation of such environmental effects from the national economic development objective is not good economics. Nor is it good public policy.

Similarly, the WRC displayed its myopia in divorcing equity considerations from the economic development objective. The distributional consequences of all project effects should be a mandatory part of any analysis of benefits and costs. The WRC should specify a mutually exclusive and collectively exhaustive set of income group breakdowns for displays of project consequences. To place all projects on a comparable basis, the WRC should require a distributional breakdown of all projects' benefits and costs to be presented for these prespecified income categories.

The flaws in the national economic development account go far beyond the slighting of environmental and equity considerations. Virtually the entire discussion of the economic magnitudes to be measured consists of nonoperational economic platitudes that seem somewhat inappropriate for a document that is supposed to guide water and land resource planning. In the rare moments when the discussion begins to get specific, what is said is either wrong or will lead to bad consequences.

A case in point concerns irrigation benefit measurement. In several places, the WRC discusses the methods for measuring positive irrigation benefits. Nowhere does the WRC recognize that the overall impact of additional irrigation is deleterious. An overwhelming amount of evidence indicates that irrigation results in the displacement of thousands of farmers as well as millions of dollars in administrative costs for the price support program.

While the WRC pays lip service to the general advisability of measuring such external effects, it admits that quantification of these impacts is difficult. The lesson from past Reclamation practices in the area of irrigation is that only positive impacts will be quantified. Due to the preponderance of evidence against the advisability of more irrigation, we urge that no positive irrigation benefits be attributed to any irrigation until there is precise quantification of the pervasive externalities.

Turning now to the recreation benefit question, we find that current practices will be made worse. The problems begin with the conceptually fallacious recommendation of a travel cost method of approximating recreation benefit values. It does not require too much analytic sophistication to realize that costs incurred for travel to a recreation area may have little or no relation to actual benefits of recreation to society. This conceptual error snowballs as the WRC's specification of unit day values for recreation use have been so broadened that the recreation benefit values assigned could fluctuate by factors of two or more depending on the whims of the project planners. For example, specialized activities can take on values from $3 to $9 per day. This wide range is so dependent on subjective assessments of planners that it is unlikely to yield comparable benefit evaluations for different projects of various agencies.

In addition, even if the unit values could be defined for narrower categories, there appears to be a distributional bias in the values. The activities receiving the highest value under the WRC scheme are principally those that "often may involve a large personal expense by the user" (p. 24157). However, there is no valid theoretical rationale for assigning a higher value to activities which may involve equipment or travel costs that prohibit participation of lower income groups. We would urge that the WRC not introduce any new unit value ranges until they evaluate the theoretically correct economic magnitudes in a meaningful way.

Let us now turn to the alternative cost principle, which will be used for evaluating benefits such as the provision of electric power and the provision of municipal water supplies. The provision of such quantities often cannot be evaluated directly, so as a surrogate for measuring such benefits analysts use the cost of an alternative source of supply. It should be noted that any such alternative cost measure really is not an accurate estimator of benefits. Implicit in the technique is an assumed existence of a demand for the output. Combining this presumption with the traditional organizational bias of the evaluation agencies results in a significant upward bias in benefit estimates.

The question remains as to what measure of alternative cost is appropriate in this world of biased project evaluation. A more theoretically appealing measure is the expected cost to society as determined through the use of Bayesian decision analysis. Since this procedure has not found favor with water and land resource agencies, a convenient surrogate has to be used. The *Principles and Standards* calls for the use of the cost of the "most likely" alternative as a benefit measure. The cost of the "most likely" alternative, however, has no theoretical justification. In addition, from a practical standpoint, it only serves to exacerbate the already significant upward bias in benefit estimation.

Consequently, we recommend the use of the "least cost" alternative in benefit estimation. In cases where the least cost alternative is not built by private enterprise or the government, the reason may well be that the assumed demand upon which the alternative cost principle relies was overestimated. Thus, the least cost principle would provide a check on the abuse of the alternative cost technique. In addition, in cases where projects are mutually exclusive, use of the cost of the most likely alternative could lead to inefficiencies through the displacement of less costly alternatives that were not judged to be the most likely.

In summary, for economic as well as organizational reasons, we urge that the alternative cost used be that of the least cost alternative, not that of the most likely alternative.

A final point on the national economic development account concerns the WRC's apparent failure to value a very scarce resource—water. We would urge that all water used by a project be treated as an opportunity cost of the project. The expected value of the alternative use of this water should be quantified and treated as a real dollar cost of all water resource projects.

Let us now turn to the second account—the environmental objective. While the WRC is apparently going to provide for extensive nonmonetary quantification of environmental effects, many problems remain. As already mentioned, there is no reasonable justification for making a distinction between environmental impacts and economic impacts. Environmental consequences merit dollar values even though usually no convenient market indicators of environmental benefits exist. A crucial unanswered question is how environmental tradeoffs will be incorporated into the planning process.

The WRC has correctly observed that there are many varied perceptions as to whether a particular environmental impact is an improvement or not. For example, it often happens that the dam-building agencies' views are at odds with the views of well-known environmental groups. Because of this lack of consensus, it is especially important that a method for determining the environmental tradeoffs be formulated explicitly to serve as a guideline for the planning and design of projects.

The importance of a systematic tradeoff system in project evaluation and selection also cannot be overstressed. Congressmen and other concerned individuals are unlikely to comprehend the overall significance of reams of sterile environmental statistics given in terms of parts per million of salt concentration or acres of flat water created. Swamping public officials with relatively meaningless statistics is not the path to optimal policymaking.

Environmental impacts will remain neglected impacts until they are quantified in dollar terms. The WRC should direct the EPA, in conjunction with private economists, to formulate unit value ranges for various classes of environmental effects. Critics of such quantification traditionally argue that monetary values on environmental effects might tend to be inaccurate due to the paucity of meaningful market prices. However, I would caution against such seeking of refuge in complexity. An economic analyst is deluding himself if he thinks that the dollar values placed on environmental effects would be less accurate than the other quantified benefits. For example, the use of recreation unit day values or the alternative cost principle, at best, serves as a crude substitute for direct benefit estimation.

In essence, monetary quantification of environmental effects is perhaps the only way to integrate crucial environmental tradeoffs into project design, planning, and evaluation.

Let us now turn to the regional development objective. The regional development account apparently is going to be optional, presumably at the discretion of Congress. Unfortunately, the fact that the regional account is optional doesn't improve its quality. All relevant efficiency and equity magnitudes can be measured within a national economic development framework. It is indefensible to claim regional benefits that are not net national benefits. To do so would be tantamount to claiming that a person is more deserving because he lives in Colorado than Louisiana.

A typical instance in which it might be thought that a regional objective is justified is when a project is being targeted at an impoverished area. One such area is the Appalachian region in my home state of Kentucky. However, the justification for showing a special preference toward Appalachia stems not from the fact that Appalachia is a region per se, but because it is a poor region. Thus, the justification stems from equity considerations which will already be adequately recognized through the distributional breakdown of project effects that we have suggested.

But even if there existed a rationale for a regional development account, the WRC's formulation would merit criticism. The main reason for this criticism is that the magnitudes measured within the regional development account overlap considerably. It is well known that income and output are opposite sides of the same coin. For example, gross national product and gross national income are equivalent due to an accounting identity.

Rampant multiple counting of regional effects would accrue from the measurement of the quantities specified by the WRC. They have recommended the evaluation of the value of increased output to the users, the value of output due to external economies, the value of output due to the use of unemployed or underemployed resources, the income induced by project construction and associated activities, and the amount of increased regional employment. Thus, the WRC has virtually guaranteed the multiple counting of regional impacts.

What we see then is that the regional development objective is merely an ill-conceived porkbarrel account and should be recognized as such. We urge that the regional objective be eliminated from the *Standards*.

The WRC's *Standards* also calls for measurement of impacts on social factors even though this treatment is not formalized as an objective. Equity considerations constitute one part of this social factors appendage. As I have already indicated, equity considerations should be considered as a crucial part of the national economic development account and should not be just one of many miscellaneous social factors.

There is one portion of the social factors appendage which should not be included at all. This extraneous portion is that relating to emergency preparedness benefits. As an example of such emergency preparedness benefits, the WRC cites the provision of a "reserve food production potential" (p. 24165). But the United States already has one-third of its cropland lying idle which could be used in such an emergency. Moreover, how much is it worth to society to have a few thousand more tons of surplus grain rotting in government warehouses? The WRC's makeshift provisions for possible calamities are likely to result in project overdevelopment and the display of an inordinate degree of risk aversion.

Until risk and uncertainty are incorporated explicitly into the analysis of all project effects through the use of Bayesian decision theory, all efforts such as the provision for possible emergency preparedness benefits are likely to be excessive. We urge that consideration of what the WRC calls emergency preparedness impacts be eliminated from the *Principles and Standards*.

A perennial issue is that of the determination of the discount rate. The controversy stems from the fact that economists have no easy or specific answers to the discount rate question. What we do know is that the discount rate is supposed to reflect the intertemporal preferences of society toward aggregate consumption. Moreover, the discount rate ought to be the same for all federal agencies.

The WRC's endorsement of the opportunity cost of capital concept is not the solution. As economists have long recognized, a variety of market imperfections make market interest rates and private rates of return inappropriate indicators of the proper discount rate. For example, the absence of perfect insurance markets makes market interest rates too low since savings are supraoptimal.

While the economics behind the WRC's opportunity cost principle is highly questionable, the opportunity cost figure of 10 percent discussed by the WRC seems to be an appropriate discount rate. What is indefensible is that after the WRC stated that the correct discount rate is 10 percent, it then urged that a 7 percent discount rate be used. The justification for this inconsistency derives from the WRC's claim that "the revealed preferences of the Federal political process clearly indicate a desire to transfer income to people in specific regions by subsidizing water-resource projects" (p. 24167).

Although this argument may serve to mystify many readers, it is certainly not good economics. If we could rely on an omniscient federal political process to maximize social welfare, we wouldn't be here. Proper evaluation of the distributional and efficiency economic impacts of projects includes all relevant magnitudes. If discounting these magnitudes at a proper discount rate of 10 percent results in the rejection of certain projects, then so be it. A 7 percent rate cannot be tolerated on the basis of the specious reasoning presented in the *Standards*. We urge that the discount rate be raised to 10 percent.

Another analytic question raised by the *Standards* concerns the proper period of analysis. The WRC urges that the analysis be cut off at that year when the design of the project would not be altered by consideration of benefits and costs in subsequent years. A problem with that recommendation is that the cutoff might result in the exclusion of benefits and costs that would affect project evaluation and selection. For example, what about the future costs of dead, sediment-filled dams. These costs should not merely be blithely forgotten. The discount rate is sufficient to express society's intertemporal preferences. If, for the sake of convenience, a cutoff date for the analysis has to be employed, that cutoff date should be required not to eliminate any project impacts relevant for project design, selection, or evaluation.

Another consideration that is crucial for planning purposes centers on the selection of the recommended plan and its alternatives. The *Standards* provides for the selection of a recommended plan and some alternatives by the planning agency. However, it is highly likely that stating a couple of alternatives will distort effective decisionmaking since the recommended plan typically will be framed with obviously inferior alternatives.

This problem can be remedied. All that need be done is for the planning agency to make the policymakers aware of the continuum of project options and their characteristics. The consideration of discrete projects from the menu could be used to determine which portion of the continuum should be focused upon for the final selection of the actual project.

In addition to the planning and economic evaluation aspects of projects which we have discussed so far, there is also the financial aspect. Many goods provided by public works projects, such as electric power or irrigation water, are privately consumed. A crucial question is what should the repayment obligation be for these privately distributed goods? The *Standards* correctly recognizes that the separable costs-remaining benefits method is the best existing method for cost allocation. Some of the complications necessitated by the three-account system can be eliminated by returning to a one-account format in the manner I have discussed.

However, the question remains as to what the appropriate interest rate should be for repayment obligations. Since the *Standards* is somewhat ambiguous on this point, I would like to suggest the following clarification. The interest rate applied to repayment obligations should be no less than the discount rate being used for project evaluation. Any lower repayment rate merely subsidizes the porkbarreling profiteers at the expense of the general public.

A final point concerns the applicability of the final version of the *Principles and Standards*. As now written, the WRC provisions would not affect projects already authorized or submitted for authorization. This loophole would leave billions of dollars of backlogged projects to keep the construction agencies occupied for at least the next decade. The Bureau of Reclamation alone has a $5.5 billion backlog of authorized but unfinished projects. We urge that the final version of the *Principles and Standards* at the minimum should affect all projects not yet under construction.

On balance, we see that the *Principles and Standards* might worsen the current problem by swamping policymakers with reams of misleading and irrelevant data. Provisions for environmental quality and equity considerations are steps in the right direction, but inadequate. The increase in the discount rate too is a step in the right direction, but falls far short of a more appropriate 10 percent level. There are many problems with the three-objective format recommended by the WRC. The greatest of these drawbacks is the entire concept of a regional development account, which should be discarded altogether.

In my past contact with the individuals who formulated the *Principles and Standards*, I found them to be well-intentioned, sincere public officials. Hopefully, they will make the revisions needed to rectify the many limitations of the *Principles and Standards*. Only with such changes will there be an end to the economic myopia that threatens to burden the nation with countless counterproductive water resource projects.

Notes

Chapter 1

1. Reclamation Law 32 Stat. 388 (1902), 43 USC 391.
2. Hearings before a Subcommittee of the Senate Committee on Appropriations, *AEC and Public Works Appropriations, FY 1971*, Part 2, 91st Congress, 2nd Session, p. 278.
3. Interview by Daniel Barney with Congressman Morris K. Udall (D-Ariz.), July 16, 1971.
4. Senate Appropriations Hearings, *op. cit.* Also see Bureau of Reclamation, "Bureau of Reclamation Planning Activities," December 1968.
5. Interview by W. Kip Viscusi with Daniel Dreyfus, Senate Interior and Insular Affairs Committee staff, June 22, 1970.
6. Interview by W. Kip Viscusi with David Flipse, chief of the Bureau of Reclamation Economics Branch, June 24, 1970.

Chapter 2

1. Reclamation Law, 32 Stat. 388 (1902), 43 USC 391.
2. Bureau of Reclamation, *Reclamation Instruction* Series 110, Part 116.4.12.A (1959).
3. Senate Document 97, *Policies, Standards and Procedures in the Formulation, Evaluation, and Review of Plans for Use and Development of Water and Related Land Resources*, 87th Congress, 2nd Session, p. 9 (1962).
4. Marion Clawson, *A New Policy Direction for American Agriculture*, Resources for the Future Reprint No. 82, p. 5, (1970).
5. USDA Agricultural Stabilization and Conservation Service, *Surplus Cropland*, pp. 1–2 (1965).
6. Bureau of Reclamation, *The West—A Potential Future Food Deficit Area* (April 4, 1963).
7. *Ibid.*, Chart II.
8. Report of the National Advisory Commission on Food and Fiber, *Food and Fiber for the Future*, p. 14 (1967).
9. USDA Agricultural Stabilization and Conservation Service, *op. cit.*
10. National Advisory Commission on Food and Fiber, *Food Needs and U.S. Agriculture in 1980*, Technical papers, Vol. I, p. 1 (1967).
11. Interview by W. Kip Viscusi with Roger Strobehn, USDA Economics Research Service, August 7, 1970.
12. Marion Clawson, *op. cit.*
13. Charles W. Howe and K. William Easter, *Interbasin Transfers of Water* (Baltimore: Johns Hopkins Press, 1971), pp. 163–164.
14. *Ibid.*, pp. 144–145.
15. *Ibid.*, p. 139. For Howe and Easter's study, the West consisted of 11 Reclamation states; the South included two Reclamation states (Texas, Okla.) and 14 non-Reclamation states; the North

included four Reclamation states (N.Dak., S.Dak., Nebr., and Kans.) and 17 non-Reclamation states.

16. *Ibid.*, pp. 144–145.
17. *Ibid.*, pp. 152–153.
18. *Ibid.*, p. 151.
19. *Ibid.*, p. 139.
20. *Ibid.*, p. 144.
21. Bureau of Reclamation, *Reclamation and the Crop Surplus Problem*, p. 6 (1961).
22. Charles Howe and William Easter, *op. cit.*, p. 160.
23. Interview by W. Kip Viscusi with Marion Clawson, economist with Resources for the Future, July 24, 1970.
24. Charles Howe and William Easter, *op. cit.*, p. 139.
25. *Ibid.*, pp. 142, 154.
26. G. S. Tolley, "Reclamation's Influence on the Rest of Agriculture," *Land Economics*, Vol. XXV, Number 2, May 1969, pp. 176–180.
27. Charles Howe and William Easter, *op. cit.*, p. 140.
28. *Ibid.*, p. 143.
29. Hearings of the House Subcommittee of the Committee on Appropriations, *Public Works for Water and Power Development and Atomic Energy Commission Appropriation Bill, FY 1972*, 92nd Congress, 1st Session, Part 3, p. 39.
30. Otto Eckstein, *Water-Resource Development* (Cambridge: Harvard University Press, 1958), p. 201.
31. House Subcommittee Hearings, *op. cit.*
32. Phone interview by Richard Berkman with Wayne C. Palmer, Environmental Data Service, July 22, 1971.
33. Phone interview by Richard Berkman with Don Durost, USDA, July 22, 1971.
34. Hearings of the Senate Committee on Appropriations, *Public Works for Water, Pollution Control, and Power Development and Atomic Energy Commission Appropriations, FY 1971*, 91st Congress, Second Session, Part 2. p. 278.

Chapter 3

1. Remarks by Ellis L. Armstrong, Commissioner-designate of the Bureau of Reclamation, before the National Reclamation Association, Spokane, Washington, October 24, 1969.
2. Interview by W. Kip Viscusi with R. L. Coughlin, Federal Water Quality Administration, July 17, 1970.
3. Bureau of Reclamation, *Active: Names of Bureau Projects and Major Structures*, Active Names—Region 1 (Nov. 1969).
4. Federal Water Pollution Control Administration (now part of the U.S. Environmental Protection Agency), *Water Quality Control and Management: The Snake River Basin*, p. 51, (1968).
5. *Ibid.*, p. 24.
6. *Ibid.*, p. 22.
7. *Ibid.*, p. 34.
8. *Ibid.*, p. 69.

9. *Ibid.*, p. 37.

10. *Ibid.*, p. 32.

11. *Ibid.*, p. 32.

12. *Ibid.*, p. 38.

13. *Ibid.*, p. 55.

14. Lester R. Brown, "Human Food Production in the Biosphere," *Scientific American*, September 1970, p. 166.

15. Bureau of Reclamation, *Colorado River Water Quality Improvement Program* (February 1972), p. 2.

16. *Ibid.*, p. 1.

17. U.S. Environmental Protection Agency, *The Mineral Quality Problem in the Colorado River Basin* (1971), "Appendix A—Natural and Man-Made Conditions Affecting Mineral Quality," p. 149.

18. Bureau of Reclamation, *Colorado River Water Quality Improvement Program, op. cit.*, p. 11.

19. *Ibid.*, p. 9.

20. U.S. Environmental Protection Agency, Regions VIII and IX, *The Mineral Quality Problem in the Colorado River Basin—Summary Report* (1971), p. 32.

21. U.S. Environmental Protection Agency, *op. cit.*, "Summary Report," p. 28.

22. Colorado River Storage Project Act, 70 Stat. 105 (1956); Navajo Indian Irrigation Project Act, 76 Stat. 96 (1962); and Fryingpan-Arkansas Project Act, 76 Stat. 102 (1962).

23. Bureau of Reclamation, *Quality of Water, Colorado River Basin—Report No. 4*, p. 87 (January 1969).

24. Bureau of Reclamation, *Quality of Water in Colorado River Basin—Progress Report No. 5* (January 1971), p. 83.

25. U.S. Environmental Protection Agency, *op. cit.*, "Summary Report," p. 1.

26. See Bureau of Reclamation, "Cooperative Salinity Control Reconnaissance Study, Colorado River Basin," 1970.

27. U.S. Environmental Protection Agency, *op. cit.*, p. 39.

28. Hearings before the Senate Committee on Appropriations, *Public Works for Water and Power Development and Atomic Energy Commission Appropriations for FY 1972*, 92nd Congress, 1st Session, Part 2, p. 345.

29. U.S. Environmental Protection Agency, *op. cit.*, Appendix A, p. 149.

30. See the document by the U.S. Environmental Protection Agency, "Summary of Conference, Seventh Session, Pollution of the Interstate Waters of the Colorado River and its Tributaries," February 15–17 and April 26–27, 1972.

31. Bureau of Reclamation, *Colorado River Water Quality Improvement Program, op. cit.*

32. *Ibid.*, pp. 36, 77ff.

33. *Ibid.*, p. xv.

34. *Ibid.*, p. 45.

35. *Ibid.*, pp. 31, 34.

36. *Ibid.*, pp. 37–39.

37. U.S. Environmental Protection Agency, "Summary of Conference," *op. cit.*, p. 5.
38. *Ibid.*, p. 5.
39. U.S.–Mexican Water Treaty, 59 Stat. 1219; TS 994; 3 UNTS 313.
40. Interview by Jamie O. Harris with T. R. Martin, special assistant, Office of Mexican Affairs, Department of State, July 22, 1970.
41. Telephone interview by Daniel R. Barney with T. R. Martin, August 26, 1971.
42. Memorandum from former Acting Commissioner of Reclamation Bennett to former Secretary of the Interior Stewart Udall, July 5, 1968.
43. Testimony of E. J. Struzeski, Field Investigations Unit, Third Session (May 1962) of the Conference on Pollution of the Interstate Waters of the Colorado River and Its Tributaries, *Transcript of Conference*, Public Health Service, Department of Health, Education, and Welfare, 1962, p. 20.
44. Norris Hundley, Jr., "The Colorado River Dispute," *Foreign Affairs*, April 1964, p. 499.
45. Interview by entire Study Group with Stewart Udall, July 8, 1970.
46. Interview by Jamie O. Harris with T. R. Martin, July 22, 1970.
47. Hundley, *op. cit.*, p. 497.
48. "Table 15—Projected Water Quality, Phase 1," in Bureau of Reclamation, *Special Studies—Delivery of Water to Mexico,* February 1963, p. 88.
49. Minute 218, TIAS 6988 Pursuant to P.L. 89–497, July 8, 1966; 80 Stat. 271; 1 USC 113.
50. Interview by Daniel R. Barney with T. R. Martin, August 23, 1971.
51. Confidential interview by Richard L. Berkman, August, 1971.
52. Interview by Jamie O. Harris with T. R. Martin, July 22, 1970.
53. Interview by Daniel R. Barney with Maurice N. Langley, Chief, Division of Water and Land, Bureau of Reclamation, August 23, 1971.
54. U.S. Environmental Protection Agency, *op. cit.*, p. 24.
55. Thomas H. Means, "Damage to Properties of Needles, California, by Floods in the Colorado River," April 12, 1947, p. 1.
56. Commissioner Dominy's Commemoration Speech for the 25th Anniversary of Hoover Dam as reported in Department of Interior Information Service, Jan. 31, 1960, p. 4.
57. Means, *op. cit.*
58. *Ibid.*, p. 4.
59. "Mr. Workman's Notes on the Factual Situation, City of Needles, April 22, 1947," part of a letter from the assistant chief counsel of the Bureau of Reclamation to the Commissioner of Reclamation.
60. Bureau of Reclamation, "River Control Work and Investigations, Lower Colorado River Basin," 11th Annual Report, 1945.
61. Letter from Commissioner of Reclamation to former Senator William Knowland of California, June 2, 1947.
62. Acting Regional Director of Boulder City Office of Bureau of Reclamation, "Report to the Commissioner of Reclamation," September 6, 1945.

63. Hearings before a subcommittee of the House Committee on Appropriations, *Public Works Appropriations for FY 1966*, 89th Congress, 1st Session.

64. Bureau of Reclamation, *Summary Report* of the Commissioner, Statistical Appendix, Part IV, p. 61 (1970).

65. Phone interview by Jamie O. Harris, with Thomas Maddock, U.S. Geological Survey, Phoenix, Arizona, August 10, 1970.

66. Department of Transportation, Bureau of Public Roads, Notes on Sedimentation Activities, Calendar Year 1968, p. 25.

67. Report to the assistant commissioner and chief engineer on the "Middle Rio Grande Project Operation and Maintenance," January 12, 1949.

68. Interview by W. Kip Viscusi with Carl Stutzman, Bureau of Sport Fisheries and Wildlife (BSFW), Department of Interior, July 14, 1970.

69. Letter from T. L. Kimball, secretary of the Arizona Game and Fish Commission, to Reclamation Commissioner Straus, January 19, 1949.

70. Estimates by Arizona Fish and Game Commission quoted in the *Arizona Republic*, Phoenix, Arizona, October 29, 1950.

71. As quoted by J. C. Fraser, Chief, Water Projects Branch, Department of Fish and Game, State of California, in an address "Fish and Wildlife Resources in Relation to Lower Colorado River Channelization and Vegetation Control Programs," at a meeting of the Inland Council of Conservation Clubs in Needles, California, March 13, 1965 (footnote 17), p. 3.

72. Interview by Jamie Harris with Earl Walker, River Basin Studies Office, BSFW, July 7, 1970.

73. Fraser, *op. cit.*, pp. 3–4.

74. Aldo Leopold, *A Sand County Almanac and Sketches Here and There* (Oxford: Oxford University Press, 1968), pp. 141–143.

75. Fraser, *op. cit.*, p. 1.

76. Interview by W. Kip Viscusi and Jamie Harris with Bill Lawson, Bureau of Outdoor Recreation, Department of Interior, July 16, 1970.

77. Otto Eckstein, *Water-Resource Development* (Cambridge: Harvard University Press, 1958), pp. 41–42.

78. President's Ad Hoc Water Resources Council, *Evaluation Standards for Primary Outdoor Recreation Benefits*, Supplement No. 1 to Sen. Doc. No. 97, pp. 4–5 (June 4, 1964).

79. *Ibid.*, p. 3.

80. *Mountain Park Project*, House Document 438, 89th Congress, 2d Session, p. 102 (1966).

81. Bureau of Outdoor Recreation, *Recreation Aspects of the Sun-Teton Unit* (Feasibility Report), p. 14 (1967).

82. Interview by W. Kip Viscusi with Carl Stutzman, BSFW, July 14, 1970.

83. Comptroller General of the United States, *Costs Incurred to Preserve the Columbia River Basin as a Source of Salmon and Steelhead Trout*, B-157612, p. 10 (1969).

84. Federal Water Project Recreation Act, 79 Stat. 213 (1965),

Section 1; Fish and Wildlife Coordination Act, 72 Stat. 563 (1958), as amended by 79 Stat. 213 (1965), Section 2b.

85. Interview by W. Kip Viscusi with Carl Stutzman, BSFW, July 14, 1970.

86. State of Washington Department of Fisheries and State of Oregon Fish Commission in cooperation with U.S. Fish and Wildlife Service, *A Program of Rehabilitation of the Columbia River Fisheries*, p. 5 (1947).

87. Interview by W. Kip Viscusi with Carl Stutzman, BSFW, July 14, 1970.

88. Letter from Frank H. Dunkle, Montana Fish and Game Director, to Mr. Cecil Gubser, BSFW Supervisor of Missouri River Basin Studies, March 10, 1965.

89. Bureau of Reclamation, *Project Skywater: Annual Report*, p. 3 (1968).

90. Interview with Floyd Dominy, at his Virginia farm, August 11, 1970.

91. Interview by Jamie O. Harris with James Kerr, Washington Coordinator of Weather Modification Research, Project Skywater, Bureau of Reclamation, July 15, 1970.

92. Bureau of Reclamation, "Plan to Develop Technology for Increasing Water Yield from Atmospheric Sources: An Atmospheric Water Resources Program," November, 1966 (hereafter referred to as "Plan").

93. Hearings before the Subcommittee on Irrigation and Reclamation of the Senate Committee on Interior and Insular Affairs, "A Program for Increasing Precipitation on the Colorado River Basin," 88th Congress, 2nd Session, p. 22 (1964).

94. James D. McDonald (Institute of Atmospheric Physics, University of Arizona), "Evaluation of Weather Modification Field Tests," in *Weather Modification and Public Policy*, Robert G. Fleagle, ed., (Seattle: University of Washington Press, 1968).

95. Interview with Floyd Dominy, Aug. 11, 1970.

96. Presidential Advisory Committee on Weather Control, *Final Report*, Vol. I, as quoted in Paul E. Waggoner's "Weather Modification and the Living Environment," in Darling and Milton's *Future Environments of North America* (Garden City: Natural History Press, 1966), pp. 88–89.

97. National Academy of Sciences–National Research Council, *Scientific Problems of Weather Modification* (1964), as quoted in *Future Environments of North America, op. cit.*, p. 88.

98. National Academy of Sciences, *Weather and Climate Modification: Problems and Prospects* (Washington, D.C.: National Academy of Sciences, 1966), Part I, p. 13.

99. National Science Foundation, Weather Modification Research Program, *6th Annual Report*, 1964, p. 6. (Initiated by PL 85-518, 85th Congress, 1958, directing the NSF to conduct a program of basic research in weather and weather modification with annual reports to the president and Congress, the program has continued to the present day with emphasis on basic as opposed to operational research.)

100. Senate Hearings, "A Program for Increasing Participation on the Colorado River Basin," *op. cit.*, p. 20.
101. Interview by Jamie O. Harris with Elwood Seaman, Assistant to the Commissioner for Ecology, Bureau of Reclamation, July 21, 1970.
102. Letter from Myron Tribus to Office of Science and Technology, Executive Office of the President, June 5, 1969.
103. Interview with Floyd Dominy, August 11, 1970.
104. Interview by Jamie O. Harris with Luna B. Leopold, research hydrologist, former chief hydrologist, U.S. Geological Survey, July 6, 1970.
105. Hearings before a subcommittee of the Committee on Appropriations, U.S. House of Representatives, *AEC and Public Works Appropriations for FY 1971*, 91st Congress, 2nd Session, Part 3, pp. 382–390.
106. Bureau of Reclamation, "Plan" *op. cit.*, p. 19.
107. National Science Foundation, *Weather and Climate Modification*, Report of the Special Commission on Weather Modification, NSF Report No. 66–3, 1966, p. 18 *et seq.*
108. W. T. Edmonson (Professor of Zoology, University of Washington), "Ecology and Weather Modification," in Fleagle, *op. cit.*, p. 91.
109. *Ibid.*, p. 66.
110. Charles F. Cooper and William C. Jolly (University of Michigan), "Ecological Effects of Weather Modification: A Problem Analysis," Bureau of Reclamation, May 1969.
111. *Ibid.*, p. 8.
112. *Ibid.*, p. 7.
113. National Science Foundation, Weather Modification Program, *7th Annual Report*, p. 57 (1965); Bureau of Reclamation, *Project Skywater Annual Report, 1969*; Interview by Jamie O. Harris with James Kerr, Bureau of Reclamation Washington Coordinator of Project Skywater, July 15, 1970.
114. Interview by Jamie O. Harris with James Kerr, July 15, 1970.
115. Interview by Jamie O. Harris with Charles Cooper, National Science Foundation, August 5, 1970.
116. Interview by Jamie O. Harris with James Kerr, July 15, 1970.
117. Interview with Floyd Dominy, August 11, 1970.
118. *Project Skywater, Annual Report, 1968, op. cit.*
119. Statement by Commissioner Ellis A. Armstrong, Hearings before a House subcommittee of the Committee on Appropriations, *Public Works for Water and Power Development and Atomic Energy Commission Appropriations Bill, 1972*, 92nd Congress, 1st Session, Part 3, p. 29.
120. Interview by W. Kip Viscusi and Jamie O. Harris with Edwin Johnson, Federal Water Quality Administration, August 4, 1970.
121. National Environmental Policy Act of 1969 (PL 91-190, 91st Congress, 1969).
122. Letter from Edward Berlin, Counsel, Environmental Defense Fund, Washington, D.C., to Rogers Morton, Secretary of the Interior, April 14, 1971.

123. See Alan P. Carlin, *Rand Report No. P-3505-1* (1967); Alan P. Carlin and William E. Hoehn, *Rand Report No. P-3546* (1967).

Chapter 4

1. Commission on Organization of the Executive Branch of the Government, *Water Resources and Power*, A Report to the Congress, Vol. I, pp. 47–48 (1955).
2. Bureau of Reclamation, *Summary Report of the Commissioner, 1969*, Part IV of Statistical Appendix.
3. Hearings before the Senate Subcommittee on Appropriations, *Public Works for Water, Pollution Control, and Power Development and Atomic Energy Commission Appropriations, FY 1971*, 91st Congress, 2nd Session, Part 2, p. 494.
4. Comptroller General of the United States, *Questionable Aspects Concerning Information Presented to the Congress on Construction and Operation of the San Luis Unit, Central Valley Projects*, Report No. B-125045, p. 2 (1970).
5. Comptroller General of the United States, *Need to Improve Policies and Procedures for Relocating Railroad Facilities at Federal Water Resource Projects*, Report No. B-114885, pp. 1–2 (1968).
6. Interview by W. Kip Viscusi with Neil Lane, Water Resources Council Representative from the Soil Conservation Service, August 10, 1970.
7. Interview by W. Kip Viscusi with William A. Green, Deputy Director, Natural Resource Economics Division, Economics Research Service, U.S. Department of Agriculture, August 6, 1970.
8. Charles Howe and K. William Easter, *Interbasin Transfers of Water* (Baltimore: Johns Hopkins Press, 1971).
9. Interview by W. Kip Viscusi with Aldon Nielsen, chief of the Bureau of Reclamation's Economics and Statistics Branch, July 30, 1970.
10. Irving Fisher, *The Theory of Interest: As Determined by Impatience to Spend Income and Opportunity to Invest It*, originally published in 1930 (republished New York: Augustus M. Kelly, 1961).
11. Bureau of Reclamation, *Reclamation Instructions*, Series 110, Part 116, Section 4.9 (1959).
12. Senate Document 97, *Policies, Standards and Procedures in the Formulation, Evaluation, and Review of Plans for Use and Development of Water and Related Land Resources*, 87th Congress, 2nd Session, p. 12 (1962).
13. Speedletter from Assistant Commissioner William Palmer, June 1, 1962.
14. Memorandum from Commissioner Floyd E. Dominy to the Assistant Secretary for Water and Power Development, March 15, 1968.
15. Interview by W. Kip Viscusi with David Flipse, chief of the Bureau of Reclamation Economics Branch, June 24, 1970.
16. *Federal Register*, Vol. 33, No. 249, Part 704.39 (Dec. 24, 1968).

17. Bureau of the Budget, *Circular No. A-94*, Section 6-b (June 26, 1969).
18. Report of the Subcommittee on Economy in Government of the Joint Economic Committee, *Economic Analysis of Public Investment Decisions: Interest Rate Policy and Discounting Analysis*, 90th Congress, 2d Session, p. 10 (1968).
19. *Ibid.*, p. 1.
20. Stephen Marglin, "Intertemporal Choice: The Social Value of Investment," in *Manual on Formulation of Industrial Projects* (New York: United Nations Industrial Development Organization, 1968).
21. Memorandum from Office of Management and Budget to W. Don Maughan, executive director, Water Resources Council, Dec. 2, 1970.
22. *Ibid.*
23. Report of the Comptroller General to the Joint Economic Committee, *Survey of Use by Federal Agencies of the Discounting Technique in Evaluating Future Programs*, p. 22 (Jan. 29, 1968).
24. National Waterways Conference, *Criteria News*, Issue No. 40, Dec. 11, 1970, p. 1.
25. Water Resources Council, *The Nation's Water Resources*, pp. 4–1–3, 4–2–5 (1968).
26. The President's Water Resources Council, Senate Document, *op. cit.*, p. 10 (1962).
27. *Ibid.*
28. Alan P. Carlin and William E. Hoehn, "The Grand Canyon Controversy—1967: Further Economic Comparisons of Nuclear Alternatives," RAND Report, P-3546 (1967).
29. Alan Carlin, "The Grand Canyon Controversy: Lessons for Federal Cost-Benefit Practices," RAND Report, P-3505-1, pp. 5–6 (1967).
30. Interview by W. Kip Viscusi with Daniel McCarthy, chief of Bureau of Reclamation planning, July 29, 1970.
31. Interview by W. Kip Viscusi with David Flipse, chief of the Bureau of Reclamation Economics Branch, July 5, 1970.
32. Bureau of Reclamation, *Reclamation Instruction* Series 110, Part 116.3.176 (1959).
33. Interview by W. Kip Viscusi with Daniel McCarthy, chief of Bureau of Reclamation planning, July 29, 1970.
34. Federal Power Commission, *National Power Survey*, Part I, pp. 131–136 (1964).
35. Federal Power Commission, *The 1970 National Power Survey*, Part III, p. III-1-28 (1970).
36. Otto Eckstein, *op. cit.*, p. 248.
37. *The 1970 National Power Survey, op. cit.*, p. III-3-9 (1970).
38. *Reclamation Instructions, op. cit.*, Series 110, Part 116.4.12B (1959).
39. Bureau of Reclamation, *Reclamation Manual*, Vol. XIII, Chapter 2.2.7 (1951).
40. Department of the Interior, *Report of the Panel of Consultants on Secondary or Indirect Benefits of Water-Use Projects* to Michael Straus, Commissioner of Reclamation, pp. 13, 19–21, 42 (June 26, 1952).

41. Otto Eckstein, *Water Resource Development* (Cambridge: Harvard University Press, 1958), p. 211.

42. *Reclamation Instructions, op. cit.*, Series 110, Part 116.4.12 (1959).

43. Otto Eckstein, *op. cit.*, p. 215.

44. *Reclamation Instructions, op. cit.*, Series 110, Part 116.4.12.C.2 (1959).

45. Dr. Ellis Armstrong, Commissioner of Reclamation, *The Bureau of Reclamation's Role in America's Growth*, Interior-Reclamation B.C., BuRec file # Nev. 11-70.

46. T. W. Roesler, F. C. Lamphear, and M. David Beveridge, *The Economic Impact of Irrigated Agriculture on the Economy of Nebraska* (Lincoln: Bureau of Business Research, Sept. 1968), p. 1.

47. *Ibid.*

48. Charles W. Howe, *Water Resources and Regional Economic Growth in the United States, 1950–1960*, Resources for the Future Reprint Number 73 (1968).

49. *Ibid.*, p. 488.

50. Robert H. Haveman and John V. Krutilla, *Unemployment, Idle Capacity, and the Evaluation of Public Expenditures* (Baltimore: Johns Hopkins Press, 1968).

51. *Ibid.*, p. 63.

52. For a more detailed discussion of this technique, see Stephen Marglin, "National Parameters: Meaning, Significance and Derivation," in *Manual on Formulation of Industrial Projects* (New York: United Nations Industrial Development Organization, 1968), or Burton Weisbrod's paper in *Problems in Public Expenditure Analysis*, ed. by Samuel B. Chase (Washington: Brookings Institution, 1968).

Chapter 5

1. Interview with former Commissioner of Reclamation Floyd Dominy, August 11, 1970.

2. Bureau of Reclamation, "Central Arizona Project" (U.S. Government Printing Office, 1970).

3. Phone interview by Daniel R. Barney with Walter W. Meek, reporter for the Arizona *Republic*, Phoenix, July 16, 1971.

4. Interview by Daniel R. Barney with Edward Weinberg, solicitor of the Department of the Interior (1967–68), July 12, 1971.

5. Interview by Daniel R. Barney with Daniel V. McCarthy, chief of Bureau of Reclamation planning, July 21, 1971.

6. See Colorado River Compact Act: 42 Stat. 171 (1921) and 70 Cong. Rec. 324 (1924).

7. Boulder Canyon Project Act: 45 Stat. 1057 (1928), 43 USC 617.

8. U.S. Senate, *Central Arizona Project*, Report No. 408, 90th Congress, 1st Session, July 26, 1967, p. 18.

9. A historical summary of the Central Arizona Project, by the Central Arizona Project Association, Phoenix (undated), asserts: "The Salt River Project almost ran out of water in 1929 and 1930, and again in 1940, the reservoirs were substantially dry. The San Carlos Project, too, had been disappointed by the construction of

Coolidge Dam, which has never filled, and were disappointed in their expectations of a much larger project when the water supply proved to be inadequate. These two major irrigation units could have generated sufficient interest in the supplemental water from the Colorado River, and this is probably where serious interest initially began," as quoted in a letter from Walter W. Meek to Daniel R. Barney, July 16, 1971.

10. U.S. House of Representatives, *Colorado River Basin Project*, Report No. 1312, 90th Congress, 2d Session, 1968, p. 27.

11. Interview by Daniel R. Barney with Daniel V. McCarthy, July 20, 1971.

12. Bureau of Reclamation, *Report on Central Arizona Project*, Project Planning Report No. 3-8b.4-2, December 1947, in *Central Arizona Project*, House Document No. 136, 81st Congress, 1st Session, 1949, p. 131ff.

13. House Document No. 136, *op. cit.*, pp. 144–149.

14. *Ibid.*, pp. 103–105.

15. *Ibid.*, p. 108.

16. *Ibid.*, pp. 95–99.

17. *Ibid.*, pp. 13–94.

18. See the Bureau's revision of its original plan in an appraisal report, dated January 1962, prepared for and financed by the State of Arizona. Also see the supplemental information report on CAP, January 1964, a supplement to the Pacific Southwest Water Plan, released by the Secretary of the Interior also in January 1964, and the "Summary Report—Central Arizona Project with Federal Prepayment Power Arrangements, February 1967."

19. Interview by Daniel R. Barney with Daniel V. McCarthy, July 21, 1971.

20. *Arizona* v. *California*, opinion, 373 U.S. 546 (1963); decree, 376 U.S. 340 (1964).

21. "Central Arizona Project Association Board of Directors, 1971," supplied by Morley Fox, Washington representative of CAPA, Hotel Congressional, Washington, D.C., July 13, 1971.

22. According to former Interior Department Solicitor Edward Weinberg, Secretary Udall "jeopardized his own political future in Arizona by taking a broader view of water resource development in the Southwest." Udall insisted upon playing a leading role in the CAP fight and in gaining authorization of the project only in the context of regional project development, and, says Weinberg, "he was pilloried for it in Arizona." Interview by Daniel R. Barney with Edward Weinberg, July 30, 1971.

23. Interview with Stewart Udall, Secretary of the Interior (1961–1968), July 8, 1970.

24. Interview with Floyd Dominy, August 11, 1970.

25. Interview by Daniel R. Barney with Daniel A. Dreyfus, Senate Interior and Insular Affairs Committee staff, former employee in the Planning Division of the Bureau of Reclamation, July 13, 1971.

26. Interview by Andrew Gelman with Edward Weinberg, August 5, 1970.

27. Interview by Andrew Gelman with Daniel A. Dreyfus, August 27, 1970.

28. Interview by Daniel R. Barney with Edward Weinberg, July 12, 1971.
29. Interview by Andrew Gelman with Daniel A. Dreyfus, July 17, 1970.
30. Interview with Floyd Dominy, August 11, 1970.
31. Congressman Aspinall represents Colorado's 4th Congressional District, which comprises most of the western half of the state. The five Reclamation projects will be located in the southwestern corner of the state. See Bureau of Reclamation, *Colorado River Basin Project Reference Maps*, March 1966, and *Congressional Directory*, 92nd Congress, 1st Session, 1971, p. 889.
32. Bureau of Reclamation, *Cumulative Supplement to the 1957 Edition of Bureau of Reclamation Project Feasibilities and Authorizations*, 1968; Letter from the Bureau of the Budget to the Secretary of the Interior, April 30, 1966, pp. 250–253.
33. Interview by Daniel R. Barney with Daniel A. Dreyfus, July 13, 1971.
34. Interview by Daniel R. Barney with Edward Weinberg, July 12, 1971.
35. Interview by Daniel R. Barney with Daniel V. McCarthy, July 8, 1971.
36. U.S. Bureau of Reclamation, *Summary Report—Central Arizona Project with Federal Prepayment Power Arrangements*, February 1967.
37. Interview by Daniel R. Barney with Daniel V. McCarthy, July 30, 1971.
38. Hearings before the House Subcommittee on Irrigation and Reclamation of the Committee on Interior and Insular Affairs, *Colorado River Basin Project*, 90th Congress, 2nd Session, Part II, p. 720.
39. *Ibid.*
40. Letter from James R. Smith, Assistant Secretary of the Interior for Water and Power, to George P. Schultz, Director, Office of Management and Budget, March 17, 1971.
41. Walter W. Meek, "Water Report Brings Second Glance at CAP," Arizona *Republic*, July 1, 1970.
42. Interview with Stewart Udall, *op. cit.*
43. For additional details, see J. W. Harshbarger, *et al.*, *Arizona Water*, U.S. Geological Survey Water Supply Paper 1648 (1966).
44. Walter W. Meek, "Water Report Brings Second Glance at C.A.P.," *op. cit.*
45. *Jarvis* v. *State Land Development, et al.*, 104 Ariz. 527, 456 P.2d 385 (1969).
46. Letter to Daniel R. Barney from Walter W. Meek, reporter for the Arizona *Republic*, Phoenix, Arizona, August 5, 1971.
47. The report found that in the early 1960s the annual storage depletion in the Tucson Basin groundwater supply was 80,200 acre-feet ("Water Budget Table," p. 213), and that "the volume of potable and recoverable groundwater in storage to a depth of 500 feet below the 1966 water table was about 30.5 million acre-feet" (p. 217). The report also said that "the recoverable volume of water in storage to a depth of 1,000 feet below the 1966 water

table was about 52 million acre-feet," but noted that further study would have to be devoted to the quality of this extremely deep water. Edward S. Davidson, *Geohydrology and Water Resources of the Tucson Basin*, Preliminary Report, Open File Repository, U.S. Geological Survey, February 1970.

48. Interview by Daniel R. Barney with Walter W. Meek, July 16, 1971.
49. Interview by Daniel R. Barney with Edward Weinberg, July 12, 1971.
50. Interview by Daniel R. Barney with Daniel V. McCarthy, July 8, 1971.
51. House Document No. 136, *op. cit.*, p. 191.
52. Interview by Daniel R. Barney with Daniel V. McCarthy, July 21, 1971.
53. A September 24, 1965, memorandum from Maurice N. Langley, then Acting Assistant Commissioner of Reclamation, to Kenneth Holum, Assistant Secretary of the Interior, included the following table:

Central Arizona Unit
Projected Irrigated Acres

Year	Without Colorado River Water	With Colorado River Water [With CAP]
1960	930,000	—
1970	830,000	—
1975	790,000	790,000
1980	740,000	760,000
1990	590,000	710,000
2000	380,000	620,000
2010	200,000	470,000
2020	70,000	260,000
2030	0	100,000

It seems probable from the Bureau's table that even with CAP water central Arizona irrigated agriculture will virtually die soon after the year 2030.

54. Economic Research Department, Valley National Bank, *Arizona Statistical Review* (Phoenix: September 1970), p. 3.
55. In 1969, Arizona agricultural production yielded $662,004,000 in personal income, out of a total of $5,709,000,000 for all sectors of the state's economy, *ibid.*, p. 2.
56. "Cropland irrigation accounts for over 90 per cent of the water consumed each year in Arizona. All uses other than crop irrigation —manufacturing, thermal generation of electricity, mining and smelting, livestock watering, timber products, recreation, municipal and household uses—together take only one-half million acre-feet of the six and one-half million used." Robert A. Young, William E. Martin, "The Economics of Arizona's Water Problem," *The Arizona Review*, March 1967, Vol. 16, No. 3, pp. 9–10.
57. Hearings before the Subcommittee on Irrigation and Reclamation of the Senate Committee on Interior and Insular Affairs, *Central*

Arizona Project, 88th Congress, 1st and 2nd Sessions, 1963–64, p. 33.

58. Committee on Water of the National Research Council, Gilbert F. White, Chairman, *Water and Choice in the Colorado Basin* (Washington: National Academy of Sciences, 1968), p. 64.

59. Interview by Daniel R. Barney with Daniel A. Dreyfus, July 13, 1971.

60. *Ibid.*

61. Interview by Daniel R. Barney with Congressman John J. Rhodes (R-Ariz.), ranking minority member of the Public Works Subcommittee of the House Committee on Appropriations, July 16, 1971.

62. We computed the average cost of CAP water by dividing the amount of water the Bureau of Reclamation claims CAP will deliver during its fifty-year anticipated repayment period (1979–2030)—450,000 acre-feet $\times$ 50 years—by the total CAP construction costs the Bureau has assigned to Arizona water users for repayment— $780,208,000. House Hearings, *op. cit.*, p. 720 and the "CAP Project Data Sheet" in Hearings before the Subcommittee of the Committee on Appropriations, *Public Works for Water, Pollution Control, and Power Development and Atomic Energy Commission Appropriations*, 91st Congress, 2nd Session, Part 2, p. 853.

63. Bureau of Reclamation, *Summary Report—Central Arizona Project with Federal Prepayment Power Arrangements, op. cit.,* pp. 31–32.

64. See the Bureau's discussion of the relative advantages and disadvantages of four CAP financing plans other than the original proposal involving construction of the Hualapai ("cash register") Dam, in the January 26, 1967, memorandum from Kenneth Holum, Assistant Secretary of the Interior for Water and Power Development, to the Secretary of the Interior.

65. An Arizona act putting OMB's suggestion into effect noted that "the Office of Management and Budget and the Secretary of the Interior of the United States request that an organization having power to levy ad valorem taxes be formed within the State prior to commencement of such construction." Arizona House of Representatives, 30th Legislature, 1st Regular Session, House Bill 333, April 1971, p. 2.

66. *Ibid.*

67. Ben Avery, "Nine of Fifteen Posts Filled on CAP District Board," Arizona *Republic*, July 8, 1971.

Chapter 6

1. Interview by W. Kip Viscusi with Loren Holt, Bureau of Reclamation, July 2, 1970.

2. 105 Cong. Rec. 6738 (daily ed. May 5, 1959).

3. Bureau of Reclamation, *Summary Report* of the Commissioner, Statistical Appendix, Parts I, II, III, p. ix (1969).

4. *Reclamation Instruction* Series 110, Part 116.5.19, (1959).

5. Reclamation Act of 1902 (32 Stat. 388, 43 USC 391).

6. Reclamation Extension Act of 1914 (38 Stat. 686).
7. Fact Finders' Act of 1924 (43 Stat. 672).
8. Omnibus Adjustments Act of 1926 (44 Stat. 636).
9. Reclamation Project Act of 1939 (53 Stat. 1187, 43 USC 485).
10. *Reclamation Instruction* Series 110, Part 116.6.2 (1959).
11. Hearings before a House subcommittee of the Committee on Appropriations, *Public Works for Water and Power Development and Atomic Energy Commission Appropriation Bill, 1972*, 92nd Congress, 1st Session, Part 3, p. 379 (1971).
12. Bureau of Reclamation, *Power Systems: Average Rate and Repayment Studies FY 1969*, Schedule 1.
13. Hearings before the Senate Committee on Interior and Insular Affairs, *Columbia River Basin Account*, p. 19 (1965).
14. *Ibid.*, p. 11.
15. Hearings before a House Appropriations subcommittee, *op. cit.*, p. 33.
16. Charles Howe and K. Williams Easter, *Interbasin Transfers of Water*, (Baltimore: Johns Hopkins Press, 1971), p. 136.
17. Comptroller General of the United States, *Change Proposed in Interest Rate Criteria for Determining Financing Costs of Federal Programs*, B-167712, p. 2 (1970).
18. *Ibid.*, p. 2.
19. *Ibid.*, p. 7.
20. *Ibid.*
21. Former Senator Claire Engle, as quoted in an unpublished address by Dr. Paul Taylor to the American Association for the Advancement of Science, July 1970, p. 9.
22. 32 Stat. 389 (1902); 43 USC 431.
23. 38 Stat. 689 (1914); 43 USC 418.
24. 44 Stat. 649 (1926); 43 USC 423 (e).
25. Memo to Richard Berkman from Al Burrows, compliance and settlement officer for the Bureau of Reclamation, August 3, 1971.
26. *Ibid.*
27. *Ivanhoe Irrigation District* v. *McCracken*, 357 U.S., 275, 297 (1958).
28. Memo to Regional Solicitor in Sacramento from J. Lane Morthland, Department of Interior Associate Solicitor for Reclamation and Power, March 31, 1971, p. 2.
29. *Ibid.*
30. *Ibid.*
31. Michael Kinsley, "Ben Yellen's Fine Madness," *Washington Monthly*, January 1971, Vol. II, No. 11, p. 45.
32. Bureau of Reclamation, "Exemptions, Modifications Waivers, and Special Provisions Applicable to Land Limitations Provisions of Federal Reclamation Laws," unpublished report, Feb. 1, 1971.
33. Memo from Al Burrows, *op. cit.*
34. Paul S. Taylor, "Excess Land Law: Secretary's Decision? A Study in Administration of Federal-State Relations," *UCLA Law Review*, Vol. 9:1, 1962, p. 4. See also "Acreage Limitation Policy," June 1964.
35. Small Projects Reclamation Act, 70 Stat 1044 (1956), 43 USC 422a.

36. Taylor, *op. cit.*, p. 5.
37. Hearings before Senate Committee on Interior and Insular Affairs, *Proposed Contract Between the Secretary of the Interior and Westlands Water District . . . in the San Luis Unit, Central Valley Project, California*, 88th Cong, 2nd sess. (July 8, 1964), p. 34.
38. Memo from Al Burrows, *op. cit.*
39. "List of Excess Landowners Owning Land in More than One District," supplied by Bureau of Reclamation, July 22, 1971.
40. Letter to Senator Jackson from former Commissioner Dominy cited at 110 Cong. Rec. 17497 (daily ed. Aug. 5, 1964).
41. Subcommittee on Irrigation and Reclamation, *Acreage Limitation Review*, 85 Cong., 2nd Session, pp. 87–88 (1958).
42. The Nader Task Force Report, *Power and Land in California*, Robert C. Fellmeth, Editor, 1971, Chapter 3.
43. Hearings before the Senate Committee on Appropriations, *Public Works for Water, Pollution Control and Power Development and Atomic Energy Commission Appropriations*, 91st Congress, 2d session, Part 2, Data Sheet, p. 464.
44. The Nader Task Force Report, *op. cit.*
45. Interview by Richard Berkman with Al Burrows, compliance and settlement officer for the Bureau of Reclamation, August 3, 1971.

Chapter 7

1. Joseph L. Sax, *Water Law, Planning and Policy* (Indianapolis: Bobbs-Merrill, 1968), p. 1.
2. Sax, *op. cit.*, pp. 2–3.
3. *Winters v. United States*, 207 U.S. 564, 575-577 (1907).
4. *Ibid.*, p. 577.
5. *Conrad Investment Company v. United States*, 161 Fed. 829 (CA9,1908).
6. *Arizona v. California*, 373 U.S. 546, 598-600 (1963); *see also, United States v. Walker River Irrigation District*, 104 F. 2d 334 (CA9, 1939); *United States v. Ahtanum Irrigation District*, 236 F. 2d 321 (CA9, 1956); Appellees' *cert. denied* 352 U.S. 988; 330 F. 2d 897 (CA9, 1964); 338 F. 2d (CA9, 1965), *cert. denied* 381 U.S. 924.
7. *United States v. District Court in and for the County of Eagle, et al.* (No. 87) and *United States v. District Court in and for Water Division No. 5, et al.* (No. 812), Supreme Court of the United States, decided March 24, 1971.
8. William Veeder, Bureau of Indian Affairs, *A Preface to Disaster for the American Indian People*, Appendix, p. 79, "Brief for the United States on Water Division 5," filed January 14, 1971, fn. 3.
9. *Ibid.*, Appendix, p. 20, "Brief for the United States in Eagle River Case," filed March 21, 1970, Argument paragraph 3.
10. *Albuquerque Journal*, July 1, 1971, p. E–2.
11. Interview by Burt Solomon with Edward Davis, assistant solicitor for Reclamation, July 15, 1970.
12. C. J. Kappler, *Indian Affairs: Laws and Treaties*, v. 2, p. 583.

13. Winters, *op. cit.*, p. 576.
14. Interview by Burt Solomon with Gilbert Stamm, Assistant Commissioner of Reclamation for Resource Management, July 15, 1970.
15. *Ibid.*
16. Interview by Burt Solomon with George Myron, former Associate Solicitor for Reclamation, July 27, 1970.
17. Alvin M. Josephy, Jr., "Here in Nevada A Terrible Crime . . . ," *Heritage* magazine, Vol. 21, June 1970, pp. 95–96. *See also* William H. Veeder, "Federal Encroachment on Indian Water Rights and the Impairment of Reservation Development" in *Toward Economic Development for Native American Communities*, Subcommittee on Economy in Government of the Joint Economic Committee, 91st Congress, 1st Sess (Comm. Print 1969).
18. *Ibid.*
19. *Ibid.*, p. 97.
20. *Ibid.*, p. 99.
21. *Ibid.*, p. 100; *See also* Walter J. Hickel, former Secretary of the Interior; Press Conference of July 7, 1969, in *Transcript of Proceedings* (Hoover Reporting Company, Inc., Washington, D.C.).
22. Memo from Regional Director H. J. Nelson, Boise Office, to G. G. Stamm and D. R. Burnett, Washington Office, May 26, 1961, Bureau of Reclamation files.
23. Letter from Marshall Shaw of Balcom & Moe, Inc., to Lloyd Miller of Sunnyside, Washington, March 31, 1961.
24. Hearings on S.742 before the Subcommittee on Water and Power Resources of the Senate Committee on Interior and Insular Affairs, 91st Cong., 1st Sess., March 4, 1969, p. 3.
25. *Kennewick Division Extension, Yakima Project, Washington,* House Document #296, 88th Congress, 2d Sess., p. 19.
26. Letter from Robert Jim, Tribal Council Chairman, to Senator Jackson, July 22, 1969.
27. *Ibid.*
28. Letter from Walter Hickel to Senator Jackson, August 12, 1969.
29. Bureau of Reclamation reply to memorandum of William Veeder, BIA, July 15, 1969.
30. Telegram from Tribal Chairman Robert Jim to President Nixon asking him to veto S.742, June 24, 1969.
31. Interview by Burt Solomon with Daniel Dreyfus, Senate Interior and Insular Affairs Committee staff, July 23, 1970.
32. *Ibid.*
33. Interview by Burt Solomon with Mr. Suller, in the Indian branch of the Interior Department's solicitor's office, July 28, 1970.
34. Interview with Dreyfus, *op. cit.*
35. Memo from BIA Commissioner to Reclamation Commissioner, September 17, 1962.
36. Flood Control Act, 58 Stat. 887, December 22, 1944.
37. Solicitor's Opinion M-35093 of March 28, 1949.
38. Solicitor's Opinion M-36015 of October 7, 1949.
39. Letter from Acting Commissioner of Reclamation S. W. Crosthwait to Senator Joseph C. O'Mahoney, September 29, 1955.

40. Memo from Field Solicitor A. D. Bielefeld to the regional director of the Bureau of Reclamation in Billings, Montana, October 16, 1957.

41. Judge W. J. Jameson Opinion, *The Crow Tribe of Indians of Montana v. U.S.*, Civil No. 214 (D. Montana, unreported October 1, 1963), fn. 30, p. 31. *See also* 104 Cong. Rec., p. 12980.

42. Solicitor's Opinion M-36148 of October 27, 1952.

43. 60 Stat. 333,336 (1946).

44. Opinion M-36148, *op. cit.*, p. 4.

45. Memo from regional director in Billings, Montana, to the Reclamation Commissioner, October 15, 1953.

46. Memo from regional director in Billings, Montana, to Reclamation Commissioner, December 31, 1953.

47. *Ibid.*

48. Solicitor's Opinion M-36148 (Supp.) of February 3, 1954.

49. Memo from Regional Director F. M. Clinton to Reclamation Commissioner, July 2, 1954.

50. Senate Appropriations Committee's "Report on the Public Works Appropriations Bill," 1956.

51. Letter from Henry S. Ruegamer, president of Big Horn County Chamber of Commerce, to Senator James Murray, July 30, 1955.

52. Letter from Reclamation Commissioner Dexheimer to Tribal Chairman Wall, December 12, 1955.

53. Telegram from Secretary of the Interior McKay to Tribal Chairman Wall, January 9, 1956.

54. Letter from Department of the Interior Solicitor Armstrong to the Attorney General, January 25, 1956.

55. Telegram from area director J. M. Cooper to BIA Commissioner, February 27, 1956.

56. Hearings on S. J. Res 12 before the Subcommittee on Irrigation and Reclamation of the Senate Committee on Interior and Insular Affairs, 85th Congress, 1st Session, February 6, 1957, p. 6.

57. *Ibid.*, p. 17.

58. *U.S. v. 5,677.94 Acres of Land, Etc.*, 152 F. Supp. 861 (D. Billings, Montana, 1957).

59. *Ibid.*, p. 2.

60. Department of Interior press release, April 2, 1957.

61. Memo to Files from Assistant Regional Director of the Bureau of Reclamation in Billings, Montana, January 26, 1960.

62. Letter from Les Bartsch to Dan McCarthy, assistant chief of planning in the Bureau of Reclamation, December 8, 1959.

63. Jameson Opinion, *op. cit.*, p. 39.

64. Telegram from H. E. Aldrich, regional director at Billings to Reclamation Commissioner, October 7, 1968.

65. *United States v. 5,677.94 Acres of Land*, 162 F. Supp. 108, 114 (D. Montana, 1958).

66. Jameson Opinion, *op. cit.*, p. 39.

67. William Veeder, "Memorandum Respecting Crow Indian Rights to the Use of Water in the Big Horn River and its Tributaries," August 12, 1969, p. 14.

68. Telegram from Aldrich to Reclamation Commissioner, *op. cit.*, p. 3.

69. Letter from Marvin J. Sonosky, counsel to the Shoshone Indians, to Secretary of the Interior Stewart Udall, April 10, 1968.

70. Letter from Marvin J. Sonosky to Humble Oil and Refinery Company, Shell Oil Company, Kerr-McGee Corporation, Sun Oil Company, and Peabody Coal Company, April 10, 1968.

71. Letter from Glen Wilkinson, attorney for the Arapahos, to Stewart Udall, October 24, 1968.

72. Phone interview by Richard Berkman with Martin Sonosky, legal counsel for the Shoshone Indians, August 4, 1971.

73. Letter from Harrison Loesch, Assistant Secretary of the Interior, to Marvin Sonosky, May 12, 1970.

74. Phone interview by Richard Berkman with Marvin Sonosky, August 4, 1971.

75. Navajo Indian Irrigation Project Act, 76 Stat 96 (1962), Public Law 87–483.

76. Interview by Burt Solomon with Edward Weinberg, former solicitor of the Department of the Interior, July 27, 1970.

77. Letter from Maurice McCabe, printed in Hearings before Subcommittee on Irrigation and Reclamation of House Interior and Insular Affairs Committee, April 24–26 and June 1, 1961.

78. Hearings before the Subcommittee on Irrigation and Reclamation of the Senate Committee on Interior and Insular Affairs, *Navajo Irrigation Project and San Juan-Chama Project*, 87th Cong., 1st Sess., March 15, 1961, p. 32.

79. Statement by Senator Montoya on hearings before the Subcommittee on Water and Power Resources of the Senate Committee on Interior and Insular Affairs, 88th Cong., 2d Sess., July 15, 1969, p. 6.

80. Interview by Burt Solomon with Claude Wood, administrative assistant to Senator Clinton Anderson of New Mexico, July 19, 1970.

81. Letter from Commissioner Dominy to Undersecretary of the Interior, September 16, 1969.

82. Interview with Stamm, *op. cit.*, July 15, 1970.

83. Interview by Burt Solomon with Frank Wiles, acting budget director of the Department of the Interior, July 23, 1970.

84. Letter from Reclamation Commissioner Floyd Dominy to Donald Pigford, president of the Farmington, N. Mex., Rotary Club, February 29, 1968; and letter from BIA Commissioner Robert Bennett to Congressman E. S. "Johnny" Walker, March 8, 1968, in Bureau of Reclamation and BIA files.

85. Navajo Tribal Council Resolution passed February 1968.

86. Interview by Burt Solomon with Henry Taliaferro, former assistant solicitor for Indian Affairs in the Department of the Interior, July 22, 1970.

87. *Ibid.*

88. Interview by Burt Solomon with Dan Dreyfus, *op. cit.*, July 21, 1970.

89. Interview by Burt Solomon with Mr. Sabers, Budget Office of BIA, July 23, 1970.

90. Interview with Stewart Udall, July 8, 1970.

91. Bureau of Indian Affairs, Statistics Division, *Indian Population,*

Labor Force, Unemployment and Underemployment by State and Reservations, March 1, 1971.

92. Interview by Burt Solomon with Taliaferro, *op. cit.*, July 22, 1970.
93. *New York Times*, July 9, 1970, p. 18.

Chapter 8

1. Water Resources Planning Act, PL 89-80 (1965).
2. Water Resources Council, *Procedures for Evaluation of Water and Related Land Resource Projects* (1965).
3. Confidential interview by W. Kip Viscusi with Water Resources Council Task Force member, August 1970.
4. Water Resources Council, *Principles for Planning Water and Related Land Resources*, pp. 2–3 (July 1970).
5. *Ibid.*, p. 4.
6. *Ibid.*
7. *Ibid.*
8. *Ibid.*, pp. 4–6.
9. *Ibid.*, p. 4.
10. *Ibid.*, p. 7.
11. *Ibid.*, p. 5.
12. *Ibid.*, p. 6.
13. *Ibid.*, p. 12.
14. Statement by Harry Steele, Task Force Chairman, at a Meeting of the WRC Council of Representatives, Aug. 12, 1970.
15. Letter from Jack Knetsch, Director and Professor of Economics, National Resources Policy Center, to Harry Steele, April 7, 1970.
16. Letter from Charles W. Howe, Director of the Water Resources Program, Resources for the Future, to Harry Steele, March 24, 1970.
17. Letter from Robert Haveman, Research Associate, Resources for the Future, to Harry Steele, March 30, 1970.
18. Memo from Floyd Dominy to the Assistant Secretary for Water and Power Development, Dept. of Interior, March 15, 1968.
19. Interview by W. Kip Viscusi with William A. Greene, USDA, Deputy Director of the Economics Research Service Resource Economics Division, Aug. 6, 1970.
20. Interview by W. Kip Viscusi with Neil Lane, USDA Soil Conservation Service, Aug. 10, 1970.
21. Interview by W. Kip Viscusi with George Adkins, Federal Power Commission, Division of River Basins, Aug. 10, 1970.
22. Interview by W. Kip Viscusi with Robert Gidez, Army Corps of Engineers economics division, Aug. 14, 1970.

Index